A CRITICAL STUDY IN METHOD

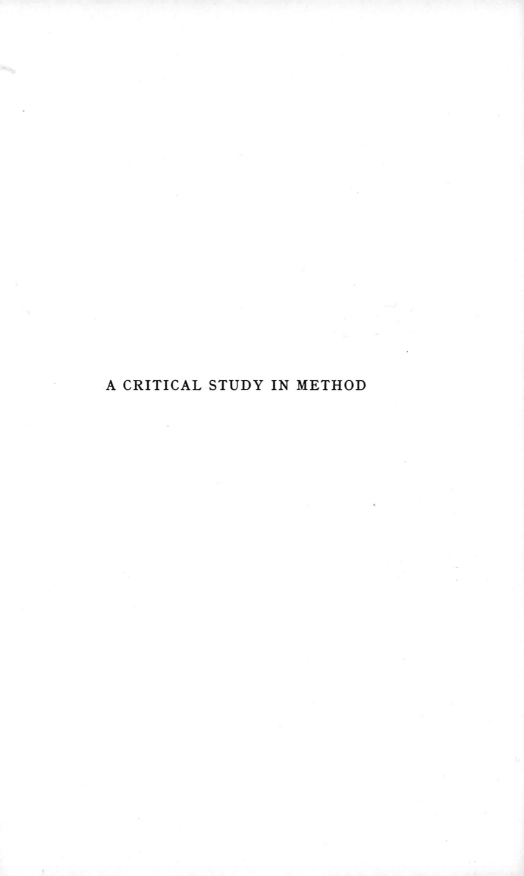

A CRITICAL STUDY IN METHOD

by

HAIG KHATCHADOURIAN, M.A., PH.D.

Associate Professor of Philosophy
American University of Beirut

MARTINUS NIJHOFF / THE HAGUE / 1967

PRINTED IN THE NETHERLANDS

to Father, Mother and Katch

INTRODUCTION

It is neither far-fetched nor over-modest to assume that some readers will feel that another book on philosophical analysis is superfluous, seeing that there are at present a number of fine books, essays or collections of essays on the subject. Part of the reason which makes me hope that the present book is not superfluous is that its aim is different from that of many of these books or essays. What I myself have attempted to do is to outline my own views regarding the nature and possible types and forms of philosophical analysis: the result of sustained reflection on the subject for the past few years. The methods of analysis that are here regarded as "proper," and in a greater or lesser degree philosophically useful methods are not, in their general features, really anything new. They are advocated or are actually being practised by different contemporary philosophers; and some of them have a long and hallowed history behind them. However, the present work attempts to present these methods in a form or manner which, it is hoped, will make them acceptable, or less inacceptable, to philosophers with widely-divergent attitudes or biases. An important feature of the book is that no *one* method or type of method is regarded as *the* proper method or type of method of philosophical analysis to the exclusion of others; in sharp contrast to the views or practice of a considerable number of contemporary philosophers. The methods presented and analysed are all regarded as proper, or possible methods; but each within some narrow or broad area of philosophical inquiry, in respect to certain objects of analysis, or in relation to certain philosophical queries. (Hence they differ – some quite appreciably – with respect to their usefulness as methods of analysis.) In that light, most or all of the various methods presented are seen to be complementary rather than mutually exclusive, incompatible.

The determination of the proper objects or areas of application of each of these methods, and the logical relations between these methods, constitutes a second major aim of the present work. Here, too, an attempt has been made to arive at a more catholic outlook than one encounters nowadays in many philosophical quarters.

One, to my mind quite important, aspect of the general catholicity of outlook which I have just mentioned is the "advocacy" of what I have called (following the suggestion of Professor Edmund Furlong) "extra-linguistic analysis," as a legitimate and useful method of philosophical analysis. The now rather unpopular view which it implies is that philosophy is not merely a "critique of language," is not concerned with semantic analysis alone, but is also concerned with the logical or conceptual analysis of empirical objects, and the empirical discoveries of modern science. The logical relation of this type of analysis to the other major, semantic type of analysis is also traced, showing how and to what extent the former rests on the latter, and how it carries philosophical inquiry one step beyond the semantic type of analysis.

The book consists of two Parts. Part One deals with a number of logical and semantic matters whose clarification is necessary for a proper understanding of philosophical analysis. It thus prepares the ground for Part Two, which critically analyses the major types and forms of philosophical analysis. However, the topics dealt with in Part One are important in their own right; and an attempt is made to deal with them on their own merit, in the space allotted to them.

Besides the detailed examination of the various methods of philosophical analysis, separate chapters or parts of chapters in Part Two are devoted to various important questions that arise from, or in relation to, analysis. Thus a long section is devoted to the question of the reconstruction of ordinary language; and separate chapters are devoted to the use of deductive inference in relation to analysis, and to the possible use of correct ordinary language as a criterion of truth.

The whole work should be regarded as only a first step toward the effecting of a harmonious synthesis of traditional and contemporary methods of philosophical analysis; and hence, by implication, of the traditional and contemporary views of the nature and major tasks of philosophy. The detailed execution of this program in the various areas or branches of philosophical inquiry is a long-range task, and must be left to future works.

The strong influence of various current philosophical writings on the present work is obvious and scarcely needs mentioning here. My indebtedness to the views of the Oxford School is particularly great and clear; though I do not, by any means, think that what I have maintained in the book as a whole or in individual sections of it will be accepted by all or even the majority of the School's members. Whether anything new has been contributed in specific parts or in the work as a whole is of course for the reader to judge.

Beirut, Lebanon
1960

HAIG KHATCHADOURIAN

ACKNOWLEDGMENTS

The following publishers have kindly allowed the use of quotations from the publications cited.

Appleton-Century-Crofts, Inc.: *Readings In Ethical Theory*, edited by Wilfrid Sellars and John Hospers. Basil Blackwell, Oxford: *Logic And Language*, Second Series, edited by Antony Flew; *Aesthetics And Language*, edited by William Elton; *Philosophy and Analysis*, edited by Margaret Macdonald; *Ethics*, by Patrick Nowell-Smith; *G. E. Moore*, by A. R. White; and *Philosophical Investigations*, by Ludwig Wittgenstein, translated by G. E. M. Anscombe. Casa Editrice G. C. Sansoni: *Proceedings of the XIIth International Congress of Philosophy*, vol. 1, 1958: quotation from one article. Victor Gollancz, Ltd.: *Language, Truth And Logic*, by A. J. Ayer. Holt, Rinehart and Winston, Inc.: *A Modern Book of Esthetics*, Revised Edition, edited by Melvin Rader. Hutchinson Publishing Group Ltd.: *The Philosophy Of Science*, by Stephen Toulmin. Macmillan & Co. Ltd.: *The Revolution In Philosophy*, by A. J. Ayer *et al.*, and *Essays In Conceptual Analysis*, edited by Antony Flew. Methuen & Co. Ltd.: *Introduction To Logical Theory* and *Individuals*, by P. F. Strawson. Oxford University Press: *English Philosophy Since 1900* (Home University Library), by G. J. Warnock. Prentice-Hall, Inc.: *Critical Thinking:* An Introduction to Logic and Scientific Method, Second Edition, by Max Black. The Clarendon Press, Oxford: *Philosophical Arguments*, by Gilbert Ryle. The Editors of *The Journal Of Philosophy:* Quotations from three articles. The Editor of *Mind:* Quotations from four articles. The Editor of *Philosophy And Phenomenological Research:* Quotation from one article. The Open Court Publishing Company: *The Philosophy of G. E. Moore*, edited by P. A. Schilpp. The University of Chicago Press: Selections: *From Descartes To Locke*, edited by T.V. Smith and Margorie Grene. The University of Illinois Press: *Semantics and the Philosophy of Language*, edited by Leonard Linsky. Yale University Press: *Semantics And Necessary Truth*, by Arthur Pap.

CONTENTS

PART ONE

CHAPTER ONE

PHILOSOPHICAL ANALYSIS: A GENERAL DISCUSSION

The terms 'analysis' and 'analyse' are used in all sorts of ways in ordinary discourse and in technical, specialized contexts. Thus we speak of analysis of the news, analysis of the present situation in this or that troubled area of the world, analysis of the ideas or views of an Albert Schweitzer, and of the story of the latest movie in town. In more specialized or technical discourse we speak of chemical analysis, mathematical analysis,[1] a critic's analysis of a poem or a painting, a student's grammatical analysis of a sentence, and a philosopher's analysis of a given proposition, concept or phenomenon.

We may state this in a different but related way by saying that the words 'analysis' and 'analyse' have different ordinary senses or meanings; and similarly with the more specialized uses of these terms.

Since we are concerned with the precise nature and the possible types and forms of philosophical analysis, we must consider the ordinary meanings of the terms 'analyse' and 'analysis' and must adapt them to (a) the nature of philosophy in general, and – in the light of past and present philosophical theory and practice – (b) to the general goals of philosophical analysis in particular. (a) and (b) are obviously related; a state of affairs can constitute a legitimate goal of philosophical analysis if and only if it is in conformity with the nature of philosophy. But any activity or procedure, and its results, to qualify as philosophical *analysis*, must in addition satisfy the aims generally regarded as the aims of such an activity or procedure. In this connection we must be careful to distinguish between what past and present *philosophers* have been doing in practising what we call philosophy – in elaborating that body of ideas we refer to as the history of philosophy – and what they have been aiming at in so doing. We should therefore also distinguish between the former and what philosophers have been *thinking* they are

[1] By this I do *not* mean the *philosophical* "analysis" of mathematical concepts and the like.

doing in "doing philosophy," whether or not this conforms to their actual practice. Similar distinctions must be made with regard to "analysis."

The major thesis that I wish to maintain and elaborate along general lines in the present chapter is this. First, that the overall aim of philosophical inquiry, negatively speaking, is the elimination of perplexity, confusion or error, in regard to phenomena generally regarded as objects of philosophical inquiry. The overall positive aim of philosophical inquiry, on the other hand, is the attainment of a certain kind of clarity and understanding generally regarded as philosophical, as against, say, scientific, clarity and understanding.

Second, the clarification or understanding of an object of philosophical inquiry will not be a form of *analysis* unless if it consists in the examination of the constitution or structure of its analysanda.[1]

Third, any given instance of analysis will be a *good* or *adequate* analysis if, *qua* analysis, it successfully clarifies the nature of the particular analysandum in hand. This will be possible only if the analysis is adapted to the specific character of the particular analysandum.

The foregoing conditions are necessary, but by no means sufficient, conditions of philosophical analysis. Indeed, the existence of conditions that are sufficient in respect to any and every type or form of philosophical analysis is quite doubtful. Moreover, the stipulation that a *good* or *adequate* analysis clarify its particular analysandum, introduces an element of relativity in the determination of an analysis' adequacy as analysis, and as a particular analysis with a particular analysandum. A given analysis may successfully clarify something for one person or group, but fail to clarify it for another or others. In this respect, analysis is similar to definition. This means that a necessary condition of any *good* analysis is that it reveal the constitution of the analysandum to the person or persons for whom it is intended. This requires that the analysis be adapted to his or their knowledge and particular needs.

The implications and applications of the foregoing discussion are both numerous and important. I shall, however, content myself with two related examples. We shall say more about these examples in chapter five.

[1] *The Concise Oxford Dictionary*, for instance, gives the following definition of 'analyse' and 'analysis': "*Analyse*, Examine minutely the constitution of; (Chemistry, Physics) ascertain the elements of (a compound); find, show, the essence of (treatise) and resolve (sentence) into its grammatical elements." "*Analysis*, Resolution into simple elements (in all senses of the vb.) ...."

The first example consists in the three well-known conditions which Moore lays down for anything to count as an analysis in his sense of 'analysis' (which he says is the analysis of concepts and not verbal expressions; or of both concepts and verbal expressions). Moore says:

If you are to "give an analysis" of a given *concept*, which is the *analysandum*, you must mention, as your *analysans*, a concept such that (a) nobody can know that the *analysandum* applies to an object without knowing that the analysans applies to it, (b) nobody can verify that the *analysandum* applies without verifying that the *analysans* applies, (c) any expression which expresses the *analysandum* must be synonymous with any expression which expresses the *analysans*.[1]

I shall limit myself to (a). If Moore is here enunciating a universal synthetic proposition, a uniform empirical generalization (i.e. if 'can' in 'can know' here means *actually can*), condition (a) would almost certainly be false; i.e., it would conflict with the nature of many actual *analyses qua analyses*. It is quite easy to present actual instances to the contrary. On the other hand, if 'can' is interpreted in a logical sense, condition (a) would be in conformity with our general principle of relativity; provided it is taken as a necessary condition of any *good, adequate* analysis, not of just any analysis (as Moore himself does), whether adequate or inadequate. On the latter interpretation, condition (a) would stipulate that in the case of any adequate analysis, the analysans would not be less familiar than the analysandum, to the person or persons for whom the analysis is intended. Thus, by the very meaning of 'good, adequate analysis,' it would be logically impossible for anyone to know that the analysandum applies without knowing that the analysans applies, if the particular analysis is adequate relatively to him.

A second example is afforded by Moore's view, put forth in *Principia Ethica*, than an analysis consists in the conceptual resolution of a complex into its constituent parts. One well-known consequence of this view is that "good" is unanalysable, since Moore claims that it is a simple property like yellow; whereas "the good," being a complex, *is* analysable into simple parts or constituents. Although Moore elsewhere states that analysis in his sense is the analysis of *concepts*, he confuses the analysis of concepts, objects and qualities. As a result, het fails to see that though the analysis of objects can be regarded as their resolution into simpler parts in a literal sense of 'parts,' the same is

[1] "A Reply to My Critics," *The Philosophy of G. E. Moore*, edited by P. A. Schilpp (Evanston, 1942), p. 663. Now published by The Open Court Publishing Company, La Salle, Illinois.

not true of concepts, in any literal sense of 'resolution into simpler parts.' We therefore see that, as a result of his failure to take into consideration the nature of the analysandum involved – in this case concepts – Moore fails to adapt the *ordinary* meaning of 'analysis' to this kind of analysandum. In other words, he fails to see that concepts are analysable in a different way from the way in which objects are analysable; that concept analysis is of a different form from object analysis.

In his *English Philosophy since 1900*,[1] G. J. Warnock criticizes Moore for taking "very seriously a suggestion that is implicit in his metaphorical name for his enterprise. The use of the word 'analysis' carries the suggestion that something complex, something constructed, is to be decomposed – that its component elements or parts are to be distinguished, and its mode of construction from these elements or parts made clear." [2] Warnock adds:

> There are certainly some cases in which it is natural enough to think of propositions in terms of this seductive metaphor. A cube . . . can be thought of naturally enough as a geometrical complex of planes in three dimensions; the proposition 'this is a cube' seems likely, accordingly, to be susceptible of analysis in terms of these planes, their number, their shapes, their mutual relations. . . . But now what of the proposition 'this is a hand?'" [3]

Warnock then suggests that the notion "being a hand" is not absolutely simple, and asks "what elements are there into which it can be analysed?" [4]

Although I am in partial agreement with the view expressed in the foregoing quotation, I cannot accept Warnock's thesis that to speak of analysis as the resolution into parts is to use the word 'analysis' in a metaphorical, pictorial sense; hence, that Moore was deceived by a metaphor. On the contrary, it seems to me that Moore was using 'analysis' in one very common, ordinary, literal sense of the term; and therefore that he was doing the proper thing in trying to conform to this sense. As I have suggested, Moore's error lay rather in his taking the ordinary *literal* sense of 'analysis' too literally; or more correctly, in his failure to adapt it to the nature of the different analysanda. Note that Warnock speaks of Moore's analysis of *propositions*. Here we have a further illustration of our point. For Moore did analyse propositions; but he does not appear to have seen clearly that the analysis of propo-

[1] (London, 1958), pp. 25ff.
[2] *Ibid.*, p. 25.
[3] *Ibid.*
[4] *Ibid.*, p. 26.

sitions is a different matter from the analysis of either concepts, objects, or qualities. This is true even if we disregard the possibility (Warnock believes that it is actually the case) that analysis may have a different character in respect to different propositions taken as analysanda.

Ernest Nagel makes a different criticism, as well as some criticiams that are similar to Warnock's. He claims that analysis, as understood by Moore, does not give us any important results.[1] In terms of the general conditions we lay down, Nagel's stricture may be construed as stating that analysis, as understood by Moore, fails to clarify the structure of the analysandum. Whether the criticism is cogent we shall not here inquire. But it is worth noting, in anticipation of our later discussion of it, that Nagel's stricture really rests on a different ground than Moore's failure to take into account the nature of the analysandum. Though the latter defect does prevent us from arriving at a proper understanding of the analysandum, it is not to be assumed that it is the only possible cause of such a state of affairs.

We now pass to a more detailed consideration of the nature of philosophical analysis, including the distinguishing of the various possible types and forms of philosophical analysis.

That at least an important part of what we call "doing philosophy" is the "logical clarification of thoughts," is, I think, universally acknowledged by philosophers. Indeed, for many philosophers this is a trite truism, especially at this late date; whether or not one is willing to go as far as to claim with Wittgenstein and the Wittgensteinians that "*The object* of philosophy is the logical clarification of thoughts ..." and that "the result of philosophy is not a number of 'philosophical propositions' but to make propositions clear." [2] The pronouncements and the practice of past philosophers too bear out our statement.

The logical clarification of thoughts (some may wish to say "ideas" instead of "thoughts"; but that is immaterial here) is at least *one* main task of philosophical analysis. Or, to put it differently, the logical clarification of thoughts may be achieved by conceptual analysis, in some sense or senses of 'analysis.'

Now I wish to maintain that there can be, and as a matter of fact philosophers have been practising and/or practise at present, different major types and forms of philosophical analysis. Note that I speak of *major* types and forms of philosophical analysis; since it is plain,

[1] Review of *The Philosophy of G. E. Moore*, *Mind*, vol. LIII (January, 1944), pp. 60–75.

[2] These quotations from Wittgenstein's *Tractatus Logico-Philosophicus* (4.112) are characteristically inscribed as mottoes at the beginning of a collection of essays entitled *Philosophy and Analysis* (Oxford 1954), edited by Margaret Macdonald. Italics mine.

particularly as a result of the very considerable amount of analysis that has been going on since the beginning of this century, that there are a number of specific or more or less specific ways of utilizing a given major type or form of analysis. In that sense, a given major form of analysis could be regarded as a family of particular "strategams," and a given major type of analysis, as a family of forms of analysis. In the present and in succeeding chapters we shall come across and say something about some of these "stratagems." [1]

I might, however, mention as an example Wittgenstein's now-famous "strategem" of imagining types of contexts which differ in some important respects from certain actual contexts, and attempting to discover how people would employ language, how they would play the different "language game," under these circumstances. That "stratagem" is one member of the family of "stratagems" which, borrowing Stephan Körner's phrase, I shall call "exhibition analysis."

The possible types of philosophical analysis fall into two broad categories. The first is a type of analysis to which I shall refer as "semantic analysis." As I envisage it, it consists of at least three major distinct [2] forms of analysis, which I shall discuss under the titles 'Semantic Analysis I,' 'Semantic Analysis II,' and 'Semantic Analysis III,' respectively. I shall also refer to the first as "Moore's form of Analysis" and, to the second, as "exhibition analysis." The third, which is chiefly associated with Bertrand Russell, includes some relatively specific types of what may be called "formal (logical) analysis," in the current sense of 'formal' and 'logical.' Insofar as the latter may consist in the *bona fide* analysis of such things as the *ordinary* concepts of entailment, implication, contradiction and other logical relations, it does not constitute a separate form of analysis. It is included in our second, or third, form of analysis, depending on the nature of the particular analysandum, and/or the manner of its analysis. On the other

[1] A clear and exhaustive presentation and discussion, with illustrative applications, of those cogent analytic "stratagems" which have hitherto been employed or have been brought to light in the history of philosophy, would, it seems to me, have considerable value. It would perform for the modern philosopher and student of philosophy a service analogous to that performed for the traditional philosopher and student of philosophy by the traditional text-book of formal logic in its presentation and classification of different forms of logical argument. It is not possible at any given moment to give all logically possible "stratagems," since that would require that the writer himself discover all those possible "stratagems" which are unknown at the time. The discovery of new "stratagems" is partly a matter of insight, like the discovery of new, fruitful scientific hypotheses, and cannot be taught or controlled.

[2] This qualification is important because there are, and it is always possible to envision, intermediate forms of philosophical analysis. One such intermediate form, which appears to combine elements of both our first and our second forms of analysis mentioned above, is the method advocated by John Wisdom in some of his writings.

hand, the formal logician's or the philosopher's *construction* of formal systems is not, and does not include, any form of analysis at all. This is true whether the resulting constructions are arrived at through the replacement of some ordinary concept by an allegedly more exact concept, or through free conceptual invention. But these matters will become clearer when we deal with them separately in their proper places in later chapters.

The second type of analysis I shall call, for want of a better name, the method of "extra-linguistic analysis." [1] I shall also refer to it as "empirical philosophical analysis."

"Extra-linguistic analysis," as I hope to show by the time we come to it, logically rests upon and carries analysis one step beyond semantic analysis. For this reason we shall deal which the former first in the appropriate place. As the same time, the synoptic or "speculative" function of philosophy logically rests upon and carries philosophical inquiry one step beyond analysis as a whole. Since philosophy, as traditionally understood, has no major positive functions besides analysis and synthesis, it would follow, if what we have said is true, that "semantic analysis" constitutes the first, "extra-linguistic analysis" the second, and philosophical synthesis the third and last logical stage of philosophical inquiry. The various forms of "semantic" and "extra-linguistic" analysis will be discussed in later chapters in the appropriate places.

The criticism of erroneous philosophical views, analyses, and arguments is undoubtedly one of philosophy's important tasks, and will probably remain so as long as philosophers continue to do philosophy. But the exposing or criticism of such errors is possible either on the basis of analysis, or of the synthesis it makes possible. At any rate, such criticism follows analysis – at least "semantic analysis" – logically speaking, as we shall see later in chapter six. This is clearly seen in the case of, say, contemporary criticism of "traditional" philosophical arguments, views or analyses.

The views, arguments and analyses of other philosophers can also be taken to task, of course, on purely logical grounds. On the whole, past philosophical criticism has appealed, at least explicitly, more to these and to what were regarded as empirical facts, than to linguistic grounds.

One last remark of a general nature. Philosophical analysis is

[1] The term was suggested to me by Professor Edmund Furlong of Trinity College, Dublin, Ireland.

conceptual in nature (unlike, say, chemical analysis); even where it is of the type I have called "extra-linguistic." That is, the "elements" of the analysandum are distinguished wholly by reflecting on the analysandum. These "elements" are obviously never separated, isolated; the analysandum is never actually "decomposed" into them. Our two major *types* of analysis are therefore distinguished by subject-matter, in kind of analysandum, and not by the nature of the activity of analysis itself. The kind of result obtainable through the process of analysis, analysis in the "product" sense, is determined by the purpose of the analysis and the kind of analysandum involved. Thus the kind of result – consequently the kind of proper analysans – is partly determined by whether the analysandum is a concept, the meaning of an expression, an expression's use, and so on ("semantic analysis"); or whether it is an actual object, quality, relation event or situation ("extra-linguistic analysis"). Finally, the different *forms* of philosophical analysis are determined by the different possible ways in which a particular kind of analysandum is conceptually analysed; which itself is partly determined by the objectives of the analysis and the generic nature of the analysandum.

CHAPTER TWO

ORDINARY LANGUAGE

It will be remembered that, in distinguishing the major forms of philosophical analysis in the previous chapter, I referred to "semantic analysis" as one of the two types of philosophical analysis there are. I said there that one major form of this type of analysis is "exhibition analysis" or "linguistic analysis." As we shall see in chapter six, which will be devoted to it, one major aspect of this form of analysis consists in the analysis of ordinary language. Indeed, for most, if not all of its present-day practitioners, that constitutes, positively speaking, the whole of "exhibition analysis." For this, if for no other reason, it is important that we devote some attention to the nature of ordinary language itself, in preparation for our later discussion of that form of analysis.

The value of such an inquiry is not confined to the foregoing. As a matter of fact, it extends to our entire discussion in the following nine chapters. The task of clarifying the nature of ordinary language is made more urgent by the fact that contemporary philosophy is full of misconceptions of it. At the same time, some of the critics of ordinary language have pointed out real problems or difficulties contingent upon its employment in philosophical inquiry. These problems or difficulties must be satisfactorily resolved before we can be certain of its utility in that endeavor.

Let me begin by saying that by 'ordinary' language I do not mean either "common sense" or the so-called "common sense beliefs" of the "average man," the "ordinary man in the street," the non-philosophical layman. I say this because there has been and there still is a tendency among some advocates of ordinary language and among some of its critics,[1] to identify – indeed, to confuse – ordinary language with the

[1] See for instance Bertrand Russell, "The Cult of Common Usage," *passim*, in *Portraits from Memory and other Essays* (London, 1956).

one or the other or with both. In a later part of this work I shall attempt to draw more precise distinctions between ordinary language and the so-called "common sense beliefs" of the "man in the street," as far as it is possible to distinguish the latter, very vague notion, from anything else! There I shall attempt to show the fundamental differences between ordinary language and these alleged beliefs, chiefly in order to bring out more clearly the nature of ordinary language and its use in philosophical inquiry. But it is, I think, clear, even from a superficial consideration of the matter, that ordinary language is not the same as any set of beliefs, be they of the sort called "commonsensical" or no. Ordinary language, by virtue of the simple fact that it is language, is not a set of beliefs. The "common sense beliefs" of the "ordinary man," whatever *they* may be, can be, and ordinarily are, expressed in ordinary language. Yet they remain a set of beliefs. Similarly, the results of an analysis of ordinary language are perhaps expressible in statements couched in ordinary language. These are not, however, ordinary language itself; and they may or may not agree with any "common sense beliefs." Even if some or all of them turn out to be in agreement with the "common sense beliefs" of the "ordinary man," ordinary language remains distinct from them.

Similarly, ordinary language is not the same as "common sense," whatever the obscure and vague term 'common sense' may mean. The *methods* of conceptual analysis which I have been referring to as semantic analysis, may be "commonsensical" methods – whatever that may mean. Or "common sense," understood as some sort of mental faculty, an attitude, or a method of answering philosophical questions in some sense of 'method,' may involve or include elements found in the methods of semantic analysis. Our judgment on this must await the discussion of semantic analysis in later chapters, if not also the formulation of a less obscure concept of "common sense" than the one hitherto employed by philosophers. In any case, "common sense" will have to be compared or contrasted with the methods of semantic analysis, not with ordinary language itself. The latter is neither a method nor a universal attitude of the human mind, the mental attitude of some but not all men, a mental faculty, or anything of the sort.

What then is ordinary language? Whose language is ordinary language? And how may we find out precisely what it is like? But first of all, is there such a thing as ordinary language?

The question: "Is there such a thing as ordinary language?" can also mean: "Is there such a thing as an (any) ordinary language in the sense of a homogeneous body of linguistic expressions and rules?" or it can mean: "Is a so-called ordinary language *a* language, or is it really only a *part* of Language?" In order to answer these questions we have to discover what constitutes a given ordinary language, say ordinary English.

In a sense, we all know the answer to this question, since we are all acquainted with, and constantly employ, one or more ordinary languages. What we want, however, is a somewhat careful analytical understanding, or at least a description of the salient features of any one ordinary language, *qua* ordinary language; without necessarily assuming that all ordinary languages have a common "essence" in the traditional sense.

The following is a rough general characterization of an *ordinary* language as I understand it. It is a set of conventional symbols, visual or auditory or both, used in manifold ways in daily life at a given time by a group of people in accordance with certain semantic and syntactical rules. The persons using the language may be only a few hundred or a few thousand in number. Or they may run into hundreds of millions. Moreover, it is language devoid of or freed from technical jargon, from unassimilated philosophical – and to some extent scientific – terminology.

We now pass to an explication and development of these statements.

First of all, the ordinary languages that are in daily use at present (the same applies to languages that are in daily use at any given time in history) are living, growing things, gradually changing with the passage of time. New or relatively new terms are constantly being introduced into a given ordinary language; and some old terms acquire new senses or meanings; while some of their old senses or meanings are sloughed off. At the same time, old words gradually begin to get out-moded, and some are left behind as language moves on; while other words enjoy a precarious existence as "obsolescent" or archaic words. Many of the terms coined nowadays are scientific terms; and after a while – particularly in a world being increasingly moulded by science and its applications – many of them will pass into ordinary discourse in their original or in modified senses. They will become part and parcel of ordinary language. In the same way, some philosophical words come into everyday use; sometimes so much so that people do not even suspect their exotic, technical descent.

Second, and in a similar fashion, new distinctions are constantly being added to ordinary language, often with the help of already present ordinary words. At the same time, some present distinctions are modified or obliterated, as a result of changes in the meaning of the terms used to draw the distinctions.

New scientific discoveries, the formulation of new scientific theories, or the rise of new philosophical ideas (particularly the first two) are, once more, the chief causes of these developments.

These and other types of changes in ordinary language necessitate an important qualification or specification in our description of it. Thus when I speak of technical jargon as not constituting part of ordinary language, I have in mind only those technical terms, distinctions and the like which, at any given time, are not, or are not also, in everyday use. These terms, distinctions, and the like which are in every-day use, whether or not they also continue to be used in technical works and specialized professional circles, form part of ordinary language.

Awareness of the dynamic, living quality of ordinary languages, besides being important for a clear understanding of ordinary language, should lead us as philosophers to a careful study of ordinary languages in their dynamic character. A study of the actual ways in which ordinary languages grow and change would enable us to get a better and more correct understanding of such important matters as how certain sounds or certain visual patterns become linguistic symbols, and how meanings change and develop. The importance of this knowledge to theory of meaning and other aspects of non-formal logic and the philosophy of language can be readily seen. But this sort of investigation falls within the general analysis of ordinary language, and will be more properly treated in the following chapters.

Any ordinary language – or at least any one of the ordinary languages with which the present author is acquainted – is a tremendously complex affair. One aspect of this complexity is the existence side by side of various dialects or patois in one and the same language, in addition to the literary speech and writing of the highly educated minority. Thus is English, even in the case of the Queen's English alone, leaving out American English, there are a considerable number of local dialects, apart from the language of the Eliza Doolittles, and over and above so-called Standard, "Oxonian" (or "Cantabridgian?") or "correct" English. And mixed with dialect or patois there is the constantly-changing slang of the uneducated. All these things are part of, and together constitute, ordinary language. These very commonplace facts, apart from other equally common facts, make it seem *prima facie* highly questionable that ordinary language can actually be utilized in philosophical inquiry. For one thing, some philosophers who are critical of what Russell calls the "cult" of ordinary usage, like to point out that the "ordinary language" which the "linguistic analysts" purport to speak about, is not ordinary language as a whole but only an unrepresentative slice of it. Russell illustrates this by giving a dialogue between a policeman and the bedmaker of a philosophy professor who has gone mad, in which all the words are used in accordance with what Russell regards as and calls common usage. He adds that these words are not so used by those philosophers who claim to believe in common usage. They do not really believe in common usage as determined by empirical methods. What they believe in is the usage of persons who are as educated as they are.[1]

This, in one sense, is a cogent criticism. What the linguistic analysts do in practice appeal to (and what, I must admit, the present author himself has appealed to in some of his published papers), is what they *think* is ordinary usage on the basis of a "sense of language" – which may or may not actually be ordinary usage. To say the least, the appeal to a "sense of language," to one's necessarily limited first-hand acquaintance with the way other people speak and write, is not very reliable. But those who are following this procedure have been forced into it because so far there have been no comprehensive empirical surveys of the linguistic habits of the users of a particular language. These practical limitations in actual practice are, of course, not an excuse for failure to do the proper thing. I fully agree that, in the absence of a proper empirical study of ordinary usage, the utility of what is regarded as ordinary language, for philosophical purposes, would always be an open question.[2]

It should be clear that the preceding does not mean or entail that ordinary language is a myth, an invention of philosophers; or that, in principle, it cannot be profitably used in philosophy. To jump to such conclusions would be as unwarranted as the assumption that ordinary language is exactly what any given philosopher may take it to be.

There is, however, a sense in which Russell's criticism misses its mark; even with regard to the actual practice of linguistic analysts at present. It is certainly true that a philosopher is not justified in identifying the linguistic habits of some of those who use a given

[1] *Op. cit.*, p. 155.

[2] The use of good, comprehensive standard dictionaries, such as *The Oxford English Dictionary*, is nevertheless of considerable value; particularly in the absence of such empirical surveys.

language with the language as a whole. But it is also true that philosophy would benefit from the utilization of these linguistic habits as a starting-point. The philosopher should, however, work wholly within the particular segment of the language which he chooses. He should not inconsistently (and particularly, not unwittingly) move back and forth between it and other segments of the language. Nor should he assume that the results of his limited analyses are applicable to the rest of the language. The particular usages he analyses may be those of a minority of people; but that would not detract from their genuineness as everyday usages.

So far I have concerned myself with stating what I think ordinary language is and involves. Since in the present work we are concerned with ordinary language in relation to philosophical inquiry, the important notion for us is that of *correct* ordinary usage. Correct ordinary usage is usage that conforms to the semantic and syntactical rules elaborated and stated in the standard books of the particular language by men who studied the ways in which eminent writers and linguists – in general, men who are presumed to know the language well – employ it. It is a trite truth that the rules of language set out in grammar books must be logically based on actual living languages, and should keep in step with any changes or modifications in them. Whether or not the standard grammar books of a given language ever correctly reflect actual *majority* usage is a moot question in the absence of thorough empirical surveys of the majority's linguistic habits. It remains, nonetheless, that standard grammar books, as a more or less faithful reflection of correct usage, function *prescriptively* as regards individual users of the language. But, as has been frequently pointed out,[1] ordinary usage is flexible; and a certain latitude in the employment of vocabulary and syntax (though less in the case of the latter, for certain important reasons) is not only inescapable but legitimate and desirable. Only extreme deviations, in ordinary discourse, from the prescriptions of standard grammar books or of what appears to be accepted ordinary usage, would constitute incorrect usage. But people differ in their estimate of the degree of a given deviation. This is perhaps one reason why some philosophers, even those who profess to be writing plain everyday English, have nonetheless (in my estimation) often journeyed far from it; giving rise to all sorts of ambiguities and confusions in their works and in the minds of their readers.

[1] For instance, by P. F. Strawson, in *Introduction to Logical Theory* (London, 1952), pp. 230ff.

It is essential to note that by "correct" ordinary English I do not mean "corrected" or "reformed" ordinary English in the sense of English which is consciously, deliberately modified by philosophers with a view to (allegedly) making it more consistent, more precise and rigorous. What I mean, and what the non-philosopher means, in using the expression 'correct ordinary language' is simply grammatically proper or correct *everyday*, current English: be it Standard English or the English of a given dialect or patois. The question whether or not correct usage – say correct English usage – is logically consistent, will be discussed in chapter seven.

Now it is possible to characterize ordinary language negatively by means of the concepts of contradiction, derivability, and their opposites. As Bar-Hillel rightly says, "... for a system of expressions to be called a *language*, as this term is commonly understood, it is necessary, though not sufficient, that logical relations such as derivability, contradiction, etc., should hold between at least some of the sentences of this system." [1] These relations are certainly a feature of ordinary or "natural languages," in relation to which the term 'language,' in its everyday uses, is in the first place applied. On the other hand, ordinary language is partially distinguished from "artificial languages" by, among other things, the fact that it does not constitute a system of expressions in the formal logician's sense of 'system.' This has been shown by the many analyses of ordinary semantics and syntactics undertaken by members of the Oxford School; for example by P. F. Strawson. As Strawson states the matter, "... ordinary language has no exact logic." [2]

The proposition that ordinary language is not a system of expressions in the formal logician's sense applies even more obviously to incorrect ordinary usage. At the same time, the notions of contradiction and non-contradiction apply to ordinary discourse which contains some incorrect, and some correct, sentences. And most correct ordinary discourse is perhaps limited to the discourse of university professors; while completely incorrect discourse is even theoretically impossible. Any "discourse" which is "completely incorrect" will be gibberish, not intelligible at all. If a string of words does convey some meaning as a whole, it cannot be said to be a completely incorrect discourse. Further, a set of "sentences" which are all semantically

[1] "Indexical Expressions," *Mind*, vol. LXIII, No. 251 (July, 1954), p. 378. Italics in original.

[2] "On Referring," *Essays In Conceptual Analysis*, edited by Antony Flew (London, 1956), p. 52. More about this will be said in later chapters.

and/or syntactically incorrect relatively to a given ordinary language can be regarded as correct sentences framed in accordance with the rules of a private code, limited to one individual or a relatively small group of individuals. If now any two or more of the "sentences" framed in accordance with this code assert anything at all, some or all of them will be either consistent or inconsistent with one another. If it is decided to call this code a language, it will not be ordinarily called incorrect English, French, and the like. These notions will be inapplicable to it as a whole. On the contrary, they will be applicable only in relation to *it;* and taken as a whole, *it* will provide its users with criteria of correctness or incorrectness peculiar to it.[1]

Our discussion of everyday usage in the preceding section brings us to an important distinction which we shall now consider. According to Antony Flew and other members of the Oxford School, an expression's everyday *usage* must be distinguished from its *uses;* though the two are crucially related. The latter is "language-neutral: if we enquire about the *use* of 'table' then we are simultaneously and equally concerned with the *use* of 'tavola' and the other equivalents in other languages; with, if you like, the concept of table." [2] The *usages* of a word, on the other hand, is "language-specific: if we enquire about the *usage* of 'table' then we are concerned with how that particular *English* word is (or ought to be) employed by those who employ that word, and not 'tavola.'" [3]

This distinction is of the utmost importance, as we shall see later on. I shall devote some attention to it here, insofar as it makes the notion of an ordinary language, and of correct ordinary usage, clearer and more precise. A somewhat detailed discussion of it is necessary because, for one thing, Flew's understanding of it does not seem to me to be completely adequate. To render his account of it completely acceptable, a number of qualifications must be attached to it.

(A) In the case of "material" general names, common nouns which denote something sensible, such as 'table' and 'tavola' in Flew's example, Flew's definition or description of the distinction comes, perhaps, closest to being perfectly adequate and true. The reason is

[1] For an interesting attempt to define 'ordinary language' and 'correct ordinary language,' see N. Malcolm, "Moore and Ordinary Language," in *The Philosophy of G. E. Moore*, edited by P. A. Schilpp (Evanston and Chicago, 1942), pp. 345–368. See also A. D. Woozley's comments on this in "Ordinary Language and Common Sense," *Mind*, vol. 62, No. 247 (July, 1953), pp. 301–2.

[2] "Philosophy And Language," *Essays in Conceptual Analysis*, p. 7. Italics in original.

[3] *Ibid.* Italics in original.

that these terms are referring expressions, and denote *sensible* things. There exists a common use, a common concept, corresponding to a particular usage of a given word of this type in one language and of its equivalents in other languages, precisely because these words name the same thing. We know from observation of ordinary English and Italian usage that 'table' and 'tavola,' say, refer to the same (kinds of) objects; and we therefore know that in ordinary discourse the word 'table' is used to *mean*, signify, the same things as 'tavola.' For, and I think this is true of all "material" *general* names [1] used in ordinary discourse, the sameness of the denotatum entails the sameness of the meaning of the expressions having that denotatum. Thus 'tavola' as much as 'table' implicitly involves in its ordinary applications (among other things) the notion of a certain use or function.[2]

(B) The situation is complicated by the fact that some, perhaps many, ordinary expressions – including at least some "material" words – suffer from "borderline indeterminacy" (the corresponding concepts are "open textured"): and the extent of this "indeterminacy" in the usage of a word in one language (say of 'table') may or may not coincide completely with the indeterminacy in the usage of its supposed equivalent in another language (e.g. of 'tavola').

However, it is quite likely that the uses of "material" words that name the same things are identical or near-identical, notwithstanding the foregoing complication.

With respect to names that do not denote anything *sensible*, the situation is more complicated and raises more problems. For there are not any sensible things which we could point out and thus use as general reference points in checking on the relevant concepts. This is notoriously true respecting many aesthetic, ethical, political and religious terms. While, significantly enough, it is with these and similar expressions that philosophy is mostly concerned.

(C) In the case of vague ordinary expressions (in the ordinary meaning of 'vague'), we have another type of situation in which the notion of synonymity of expressions in different ordinary languages raises problems and difficulties. Let us note here that the vagueness of expressions, in the ordinary sense, is distinct from "borderline inde-

[1] The above is not necessarily true in the case of "non-material" general names: words such as 'justice,' 'beauty,' 'nationalism,' 'intelligence,' 'emotion.' Also, it is definitely not true in the case of definite descriptions – which are not general names – occurring in the same language, and referring to the same denotatum.

[2] See my "Common Names and 'Family Resemblances,'" *Philosophy and Phenomenological Research*, vol. XVIII, No. 111 (March, 1958), pp. 341–358.

terminacy" [1]; although some philosophers have confused or identified the two. Some of the important expressions in philosophical currency (e.g. 'commonsense,' 'mystical,' 'philosophy of life,' 'culture,' 'liberal' and 'conservative') are vague ordinary expressions. Indeed, it is a significant if not also an ironical fact that the concepts from which the different traditional philosophies have arisen and on which they have thrived, are more often than not concepts expressed by vague expressions, i.e., are themselves vague concepts; and that the philosopher appears to have less use precisely for those concepts which are perfectly or almost perfectly non-vague in ordinary discourse! It is true that the different applications of some vague ordinary expressions involve what I call a "common core of meaning." [2] But the extent of this "common core" may vary with different expressions. Also, the "common core" in the different ordinary applications of one and the same expression in one language may not coincide with (may be more extensive or more restricted than) the common core in the different applications of its alleged equivalents in other languages. As for those ordinary expressions which are so vague as to lack any "common core" of meaning in their actual employment by different users (e.g. some of the expressions that we ordinarily call "extremely" or "hopelessly" vague), these expressions are so fluid and indeterminate in their employment that they practically mean what *a given user means* (purports to mean) by them. In these extreme cases the concept of synonymity becomes of doubtful applicability; and the view that the uses of an expression are language-neutral loses its cogency. It is obvious that unless there is some stability, some uniformity in the ordinary usage of a given expression, we cannot speak, except perhaps in an extremely loose sense, of any expressions in other languages as being equivalent to that expression.

(D) This brings us to another point. There are ordinary expressions to which nothing that can be called a literal equivalent, even in a very broad or loose sense, corresponds in other ordinary languages. For instance, expressions which have idiomatic uses do not, insofar as they are used idiomatically, have literal equivalents in other languages; even if and when we find expressions in the latter languages which, idiomatically, are equivalent or almost equivalent in meaning to them. And even in the latter type of case, the words composing the equivalent

[1] See chapter six, and my "Vagueness," *Philosophical Quarterly*, vol. 12, No. 47 (April, 1962) pp. 138–152.

[2] See *ibid.*

idiomatic expression in the one language will not be severally equivalent to the words composing the idiomatic expressions in the other languages. Apart from this, there are languages which are so restricted in vocabulary (e.g. "primitive" languages) that they simply do not possess any literal equivalents of expressions in richer (more "developed") languages in their *literal* non-idiomatic employment. One form of this limitation is the absence from one language of certain fine or subtle distinctions that are found in another language.

(E) We noted earlier that ordinary languages are dynamic in character. For our present purposes this means that the *actual uses* of an expression may change or be modified partly or even wholly with changes in their ordinary *usage*.

A given use that arises in relation to a given actual usage at a given time may become modified to a greater or lesser extent, or may completely cease to exist, as this usage is modified or abandoned with the passage of time.[1] In this sense, use is *not* language-neutral. Hence, when we wish to speak of a given use as an *actual* use, we have to specify the language or sub-language in which, or in relation to which, it obtains, *and* the period of time involved.

However, à propos of the present discussion, there is another important sense in which a given use *is* language-neutral; namely, as a possible and not merely as an actual use. Here its historical genesis – the language or languages in which it has first arisen – is quite immaterial. It is also immaterial in what particular languages it is an actual use; and even whether it is an actual use in *any* actual language. It is, I think, also theoretically possible for any human being with average intelligence to grasp any such use or concept independent of any particular ordinary language, and even perhaps (though this is a mere conjecture) independent of any ordinary language. I do not know, however, whether it is possible to do so without the help of any symbols at all, including mathematical and logical symbols, or any type of sensible representation, such as the visual or auditory representations of the fine arts.

The preceding distinctions are of the utmost importance, and we shall return to them in later chapters. They obtain in, and their validity extends to, "reformed" natural languages as well as to "unreformed" ones; and they are of great importance not merely in philosophy but in many other areas of human thought and action. For instance, the moral leader or reformer, as opposed to the moral philosopher, is concerned not only with the actual uses of ethical terms but also with the

[1] This is well brought out by Flew, *op. cit.*, pp. 7ff.

possible uses they can have – particularly their possible emotive and dynamic uses. Similarly, *mutatis mutandis*, with the art critic and even the artist.

(F) There is an important but rather obvious type of case where the distinction between "ordinary use" and "(correct) ordinary usage" arises without many of the complications we have hitherto noted. I mean the distinction as it arises within one and the same ordinary language or sub-language. Irrespective of whether the distinction validly cuts across different ordinary languages, it clearly holds and is of importance in respect to any one given language or sub-language. Here the notions of "language-relativity" and "language-neutrality" are inapplicable; but we can still speak of an ordinary use U as against a correct ordinary usage W. Also, as we shall see in chapter three, the meaning of an expression constitutes one type of use of the expression (it is not, as Flew holds, identical with use without qualification). Hence we may say here that a given use U (of a certain type) associated with a given usage W, is the (or a) meaning of an expression E that has that usage. Actual meaning, however, is language-specific in the sense that an expression has meaning in, or relatively to, a given language. That is, actual meaning corresponds to (one type of) *actual use;* whereas possible meaning, in one sense of this expression, corresponds to (one type of) possible use. I say "in one sense" because there is another sense in which possible meaning does not correspond to (one type of) possible use. Thus philosophers sometimes attempt to find the "possible meaning" of an expression as used in a given context by someone else, when they are in doubt as to the intended meaning.

In our first sense of 'possible meaning,' we certainly can *think* of the meaning of any given expression as a possible meaning; in the sense that we can mentally entertain this meaning independently of whether or not any actual expression in any given language has this meaning; and even when no actual expression does have it.[1] It is because this is possible that we can assign some, and also new, meaning to any sensible object or a part of it; that we can make new symbols or new signs.

[1] But, I think, we can do so only after some ordinary language, or some part of it, has come into existence through the more or less unreasoned actual employment of various sounds and shapes, spurred by the need for self-expression and communication.

CHAPTER THREE

MEANINGS, CONCEPTS, AND THE USES OF VERBAL EXPRESSIONS

In chapter two I frequently used such expressions as 'the meaning of an expression,' 'the concept of so-and-so,' 'the uses of an expression,' 'the expression X has the same meaning as the expression Y.' And we shall continue to meet these expressions in succeeding chapters. Although I did say something about "uses" in relation to the nature of "ordinary language(s)" (chapter two), I said little about concepts or synonymity. Nor have I hitherto attempted to deal with these in a separate section, at some length. In the present chapter we shall attempt to arrive at a clear understanding of the major *differences* and the *relations* between "meaning," "use," and "concept." The notion of synonymity will be clarified in chapter four. I shall not attempt to say what "meaning," "concept," "use" *are,* in the sense of providing definitions of the corresponding terms, in any usual sense of 'definition.' But some direct, explicit, as well as implicit, analysis – whether or not capable of terminating in a definition of some sort – of the concepts *meaning, concept* and *use* will of necessity be made in the course of the discussion.

I. MEANINGS AND USES

There are a number of current ordinary senses of 'meaning,' as well as a number which are now obsolete or obsolescent; as a glance through a good dictionary shows. Of the current senses and meanings with which alone we are here concerned, I might mention the following[1]:

(1) the signification or sense of an expression (word, phrase, sentence); e.g., "'*chien*' means "dog""; "'*Laissez-faire*' means "free enterprise.""

(2) The signification, sense, import of a phenomenon, action, or state

[1] These are based on *The Oxford English Dictionary*, but with considerable modifications and some additions.

of affairs; e.g., "What was the meaning of this man's laughter in the middle of my lecture?"

(3) The signification of a symbol – in the ordinary sense in which it includes verbal signs; e.g., "What does the sign of the cross mean?" "What does "+" mean?"

(4) "The intent, spirit as apart from the 'letter' (of a statement, law, etc.)" [1] e.g., "What is the meaning of 'Blessed are the poor in spirit?'"

(5) "That which a speaker or writer intends" [1]: (a) to express in words; the intended sense of (a person's) words; e.g., "You will be good enough not to misunderstand my meaning" [1]; "This is not what I mean!" (b) to convey non-verbally, by action (e.g., by gestures). Thus: "What did he mean by that strange gesture?" "He meant no harm by inviting your rival." (The use of 'meaning' in this sense in relation to what an *artist* may intend to convey by a part of a work or the work as a whole is not, it seems to me, an ordinary use of this term.)

(6) The significance, import (a) of a sentence, passage or work, literary or otherwise, or a part of a work (novel, play, poem, philosophical treatise etc.); e.g., "T. S. Eliot's "The Waste Land" is pregnant with meaning for the Twentieth Century." Also 'meaningful': "Keats' Beauty is truth, truth beauty' is tremendously meaningful!" Also 'full of meaning,' 'meaningless' (lacking in significance); (b) of an object, phenomenon, relation, and so on. Also 'meaningful,' 'meaningfully,' 'meaningless'; e.g., "A meaningful smile played on his lips as he spoke"; "My wife beckoned to me meaningfully"; "Macmillan's recent visit to the Soviet Union was utterly meaningless"; "Does Life have any meaning?" "Life is 'a tale told by an idiot, full of sound and fury, signifying nothing.'" [2]

There are obvious relations between these different senses, though some of them are more closely related than others. The interested reader can discover these for himself. I might just mention that there is an interesting relation between 'meaning' in senses (1)–(4) on the one hand, and sense (5) on the other hand; also between the latter and sense (6).[3]

It is clear that the sense of 'meaning' and 'to mean' which we met in chapter three – and with which we are concerned in relation to philo-

[1] *Ibid.*

[2] For a detailed discussion of various philosophical and other theories of the meaning of 'meaning' (before 1923), the reader is referred to C. K. Ogden & I. A. Richards; *The Meaning of Meaning* (London, 1923), *passim*; in particular, Chapter VIII & Appendices C & D.

[3] I have discussed some differences between senses (1), (5) and (6) in my *The Coherence Theory of Truth: A Critical Evaluation* (Beirut, 1961), Chapter VI, *passim*.

sophical analysis – the sense in which it is important to distinguish "meaning," "use" and "concept," is sense (1) above. This, again, is the sense involved when we speak of two expressions as synonymous or as non-synonymous; as having or as not having the same meaning. Consequently I shall (continue to) use the word 'meaning' and its cognates in sense (1) and that sense alone except where I indicate a different sense.

As regards the word 'use' in "the use of an expression A," which sense concerns us exclusively in the present context and almost exclusively in this work as a whole, it can again be readily seen that it admits of different senses or meanings. P. F. Strawson conveniently distinguishes three different "usages" (senses, meanings): "(a) the current usage in which 'use' (of a particular word, phrase, sentence) = (roughly) 'rules for using' = (roughly) 'meaning'; and... (b) my [Strawson's] own usage in the phrase 'uniquely referring use of expressions' in which 'use' = (roughly) 'way of using'";[1] and (c) the usage in which "*a use* of a sentence" = "an (one) *occasion* of the uttering or writing of a sentence." The last usage Strawson illustrates by the sentence 'the king of France is wise.' Now suppose that (1) two men utter this sentence, one in the reign of Louis XV and one in the reign of Louis XIV; and (2) two men utter the sentence simultaneously in the reign of Louis XIV. In this usage, the two men in (1) made different uses of the (same) sentence; whereas the two men in (2) made the same use of the sentence.[2]

It is clear that meaning in our first sense cannot be identified with either sense (b) or sense (c) of 'use.' The meaning of an expression is not, either exactly or roughly, a *way* of using the expression (sense b). An expression that has a number of (at least two) meanings or senses *is* used in one way rather than another when it is employed in a sentence in one of these meanings or senses rather than in another of its meanings or senses. But in Strawson's sense of 'way of using' an expression, this phrase designates *kinds* of uses of the expression of a more general nature than the use of an expression in one (rather than another) sense or meaning. For instance, the "uniquely referring use of expressions" which illustrates Strawson's usage, is a way of using a very large class of *different* expressions (e.g., singular demonstrative pronouns, proper names, singular personal and impersonal pronouns [3]) – expressions

1 "On Referring," *Essays In Conceptual Analysis*, p. 28, footnote 1.
2 *Ibid.*, p. 28.
3 *Ibid.*, p. 21.

many of which have different meanings or senses, in addition to meaning whatever they mean in different sorts of ways. It is not a way of using one and the same expression in one particular sense or meaning. Thus an expression may be used in one and the same way in Strawson's sense of 'use,' even when it is actually employed in two different senses or meanings; this is the case wherever an expression is employed, say, referentially, in two or more different senses or meanings (e.g., where the word 'man' is used in the sense of 'human being,' or in the sense of 'human race').

That the meaning – or a particular meaning or sense – of an expression is also not identical with sense (c) of 'use' above is immediately seen from the fact that the latter, as defined above, is restricted to sentences; whereas 'meaning' is of course not restricted in this way. Yet even if we limit ourselves to the meaning of sentences, the distinctness of meaning and the present sense of 'use' remains. It is clear that a sentence has to be a sentence, has to have meaning as a whole to begin with, before it can have a use in the present sense. For instance, there can be occasions of the use of "The king of France is wise" precisely because it has a meaning as a sentence. Now following Strawson, I am employing 'statement' to mean "sentence in use." Since the meaning of 'use' in this expression is actually sense (c) above, we can state the foregoing differently by saying that a string of words in certain kinds of arrangements can make statements only if it is meaningful as a whole; i.e., only when the words in it together form sentences – not excluding here tautological, self-contradictory or even "absurd" sentences. This does not mean or imply in respect to *ordinary* sentences, – and it is actually false – that the meaning of a given sentence is always or even perhaps sometimes completely determined or fixed in advance, in independence of all actual occasions of its use; in a contextual vacuum so to speak. It only means that a sentence will have *some* meaning before *any particular* occasions of its use arise: indeed, that it will not be (called) a sentence if this were not true of it.

And now, what about sense (a)? Anyone who is familiar with contemporary philosophy knows how widespread is the view – in particular among those who have been influenced by the later work of Wittgenstein – that the meaning of an expression is its "use." This view, epitomized by Wittgenstein's famous slogan, "the meaning of a word is its use in the language," deserves careful consideration because of its logical consequences and its far-reaching applications in the work of many eminent contemporary philosophers, as well as for its possible intrinsic merit.

The first thing to note is that Strawson speaks of 'use' as in one sense *roughly* equivalent to 'rules for using,' and roughly equivalent to 'meaning.' Also, that Wittgenstein himself states that "*For a large class of statements – though not all* – in which we employ the word "meaning" it can be defined thus: the meaning of a word is its use in the language."[1] But as David Pole [2] points out, Wittgenstein does not offer any other views of meaning to cover those cases in which, according to the foregoing quotation, meaning cannot be defined as use in the language. It is not unlikely, however, that Wittgenstein's meaning here is something else. It is possible that what he meant was that "use in the language" is the meaning of 'meaning' in *one sense or meaning* of it – which, if correct, would also mean that there is at least one other sense or meaning of it, not definable as "use in the language." Whatever Wittgenstein's actual meaning may have been, I shall attempt to show that 'meaning' in our first sense (which is the sense in which the advocates of the "use theory of meaning" identify "meaning" and "use") cannot be identified with use in the sense which Strawson has in mind in (roughly) equating meaning with "use," and with "rules for using."

The second point to note is that Strawson's usage of 'use' here – and the same remark applies to many if not all advocates of the view in hand – is the one I spoke about at some length in Chapter Two; in relation to the distinction Flew draws between (ordinary) 'use' and (ordinary) 'usage.' In this sense, however, the uses of an expression in an ordinary language are the rôles it plays in the language; and this is not even roughly identical with "rules for using" the expression. The latter are involved or are implicit in ordinary language; and the expression plays its rôles in the languages in accordance with them when, as we say, it is "correctly" used. Unless a distinction is drawn between the uses of expressions in ordinary language and rules for using them, the important distinction between just any and every usage of an expression and its "correct" usage would vanish. This, as I noted earlier, must not be taken to mean or imply the patently false proposition that the rules of any ordinary natural language come into existence before and in complete independence of *all* actual discourse in that language; before any expression in the language is actually used. The rules of a language, rather, come into existence in and by the employment of

[1] *Philosophical Investigations*, trans. by G. E. M. Anscombe (Oxford, 1953), 43. My italics.
[2] *The Later Philosophy of Wittgenstein* (London, 1958), p. 18, footnote 2.

expressions in certain more or less uniform ways (*partly*, in sense (b) of 'use' above), by a relatively large number of people usually living in relative proximity.

Whether or not "use in the language" may be roughly or exactly equated with "rules for using" an expression, the former cannot be equated with the "meaning of an expression."

The meaning of ordinary expressions is not the same as their "uses" in the ordinary language in which they occur; in the sense that, and because, the function of an expression that is labelled "meaning something" is, in many cases, only one among a number of (kinds of) functions or "uses" that it can properly have in the language. It is a commonplace that many ordinary expressions can be properly used emotively and dynamically: to express and to evoke emotion, and to stir to action – to mention two such extremely important kinds of uses of expressions. The reader can think of any number of such expressions by recalling the latest political speech he has heard or the latest Sunday-morning sermon.

But are an expression's particular emotive coloring and its particular dynamic aspect not part of its meaning in the present ordinary sense of 'meaning?' The answer, I submit, is No; even though a considerable number of philosophers hold that the answer is a clear Yes – at least with regard to the emotive uses of expressions – and accordingly speak of an expression's "emotive meaning" as against its "cognitive" or "semantic meaning."[1] It is simply not the case, it seems to me, that the meaning of an expression, at least in sense (1), includes either emotive coloring or the dynamic use of expressions. Stevenson defines the 'emotive meaning' of a word as a "tendency of a word, arising through the history of its usage, to produce (result from) *affective* responses in people. It is the immediate aura of feeling which hovers about a word."[2] Stevenson adds that "such tendencies to produce affective responses cling to words very tenaciously. It would be difficult, for instance, to express merriment by using the interjection "alas." Because of the persistence of such affective tendencies (among other reasons) *it becomes feasible to classify them as "meanings."*"[3]

There is no contradiction between all this and the view (which I hold)

[1] Cf. for instance C. L. Stevenson, "The Emotive Meaning of Ethical Terms," in *Readings in Ethical Theory* (New York, 1952), selected and edited by Wilfrid Sellars and John Hospers, Sections II and III, pp. 418–423; and Arthur Pap, *Semantics and Necessary Truth* (New Haven, 1958), pp. 172, 194, 362. etc.

[2] *Ibid.*, pp. 422–423. Italics in original.

[3] *Ibid.*, p. 423. My italics.

(a) that we can *discover* the *ordinary meanings* of expressions, as well as the other rôles they may play, by observing how they are concretely used in actual discourse; (b) that an expression's meaning is determined by the ways in which it is actually used; e.g., that 'cow' is literally used to mean a certain kind of quadruped and not an "admiral"; and (c) that, as Wittgenstein also holds, the ways in which we learn to apply an expression reflect its uses (including its meaning) in the language. However, the italicized portion in the above quotation from Stevenson indicates that the author is actually recommending an extension of the ordinary meaning of 'meaning' to include the emotive coloring of expressions; rather than giving us a description or an analysis of some ordinary meanings of 'meaning.' For I know of no expression that has a descriptive use – words such as 'cow,' 'dog,' 'mammal'; phrases such as 'green table,' 'acute angle'; sentences such as "What is the time?" "The lilacs are blooming" – in which we give the expression's emotive coloring as (even) part of the answer if anyone asks what the expression means; provided that the question and/or the context makes it clear that the 'meaning' in mind is (1), or even any of the other senses we distinguished except sense (6) and perhaps also sense (5) (a). The situation is less clear in the case of value terms like 'good,' 'bad,' 'right,' 'wrong,' 'wonderful,' 'beautiful,' 'pretty,' which some Emotivists claim to have no descriptive use but only emotive and dynamic uses. These words are certainly spoken of ordinarily as possessing meaning; and if these philosophers are right, the meaning they possess must be partly or wholly their emotive use. It would require a great deal of analysis, which would take us far afield in the realm of ethics, aesthetics and other branches of axiology, to arrive at a decision regarding this point.[1] Yet even if in these cases 'meaning' is identical with or includes emotive coloring as an element, what we said above about other expressions – and they are the vast majority – would still hold. Similarly if we regard interjections such as 'alas,' 'bravo,' 'My God,' 'ah me' as expressions which possess no cognitive use.

One main reason why in many cases at least emotive coloring is not

[1] I have tried to show elsewhere ("Common Names & 'Family Resemblances,'" *Phil. & Phen. Research*, vol. XVIII, No. III (March, 1958), pp. 354ff., that in the case of certain non-ethical uses of 'good,' 'very good,' 'poor' and the like, these expressions, used with the names of artifacts and human processes and activities – e.g., in "This is a good knife" – have at least an *implicit* cognitive reference. I mean that they *imply* certain things about the artifact, process or activity spoken of as good, poor, etc. The same applies to works of art; i.e., where these terms are used aesthetically. (Cf. my "Art Names and Aesthetic Judgments," *Philosophy*, vol. XXXVI, No. 136 (January, 1961).) All this is,ho wever, compatible with the absence of any *explicit* cognitive reference. It might still be the case that these expressions do not *express* (in a sense of 'express' contrasted with 'imply' or even 'suggest') anything.

ordinarily an element in an expression's meaning is not far to seek. It is the reason Stevenson recognizes in rightly regarding dynamic usage as *not* included in, or identical with, meaning; and the reason why he thinks, mistakenly, I submitted, that it *is* "feasible to classify" emotive coloring as "meaning." I mean that the notion of *relative* fixity or determinacy is implied in the ordinary meaning of 'meaning,' at least in sense (1). Thus Stevenson says: "we must not define "meaning" in a way that would make meaning vary with dynamic usage." (*Ibid.*, p. 422); whereas dynamic usage is variable, dependent in part on circumstances external to and independent of the expression itself. But what Stevenson does not recognize is that the same is true of the emotive coloring of many, if not all, words. His own example, 'alas,' is one of the relatively few exceptions – and even then, as we shall see presently, not a complete exception. An expression's tendency to produce a certain kind of affective response depends in large measure on the culture or age involved, or even on the individual who reads or hears the expression in use. It also partly depends on the logical content – really the meaning in sense (1) – of the particular expression, if and when it has such a content or aspect. To be more exact, an expression's emotive coloring in a given context is determined by the hearer's attitude to the objects, qualities, states of affairs, etc. that are signified and/or named by the given expression. Political and religious expressions are obvious and striking illustrations. One does not have to go to Moscow to become aware that 'red' and 'communist' have quite a different emotive coloring there from the emotive coloring they *generally* have in the United States. Nor does one have to live in Southern States of the U.S.A. to know that quite a different "aura of feeling" hovers about the word 'negro,' depending on the pigmentation of the hearer's or reader's, or speaker's or writer's, skin. It is significant, and really in harmony with what we are saying, that expressions such as 'good,' 'bad,' 'wonderful,' 'beautiful'; or 'alas,' 'bravo,' 'ah me,' – unlike expressions such as 'negro,' 'Jew,' 'Nazi,' 'red,' 'nationalist,' 'rich,' 'poor,' – do seem to have a persistent quality about their emotive, and to some extent dynamic, usage; whether or not this exhausts their usage. They seem to have been invented principally, if not solely, *in order to* fulfill emotive and dynamic functions. The persistence of their particular emotive and dynamic functions seems to be intended. It is part and parcel, and a requisite condition, of their proper functioning, use.[1]

[1] But note that even the emotive coloring of such words as 'good' and 'bad' is not abso-

Wittgenstein says in his *Philosophical Investigations* that "some expressions say nothing at all; they give us pictures." [1] Assuming this to be true in some sense of 'say nothing,' their "saying nothing at all" cannot be equated with "having no meaning at all" [2]; nor can we, as Virgil Aldrich does,[3] legitimately speak of these expressions' pictorial function or use – their giving us pictures – as a type of meaning in our first sense of this term. In speaking of "pictorial meaning" (as also, *mutatis mutandis*, of "emotive meaning," "cognitive meaning," etc.), one will be *extending* the ordinary meaning of 'meaning' to make it signify the pictorial uses of some expressions.

In saying that the pictorial, emotive and dynamic uses of expressions are not the same as, or are not included in, that use of expressions called "meaning," I certainly do not mean (intend to signify) that meaning and these types of uses are unrelated. All these types of uses of expressions are certainly related to one another. Thus the meaning of an expression partly determines its emotive and dynamic uses.

Since labels are useful if used cautiously and in small doses, I shall speak of meaning in sense (1) as "semantic use." All other types of uses of expressions I shall label "extra-semantic uses." We might even adopt Strawson's adverb 'roughly' and speak of meaning as roughly the same

lutely persistent. Calling a person a "good man" in the company of hardened criminals may, quite likely, evoke in them a "con-attitude" toward him; and a "pro-attitude" may, very likely, be evoked if he is spoken of as a bad man. Some criminals may regard it as an insult to be spoken of as virtuous or good men and will be flattered at being called bad men or badmen! Also – and this again shows the dependence of an expression's emotive coloring on the verbal and non-verbal context – the words 'wonderful,' 'magnificent,' 'bravo,' 'alas,' 'ah me,' can, of course, be used ironically. Where they are so used, their emotive effect will be the exact opposite of the usual one.

Let me here add another argument in support of my view that emotive coloring is not part or the whole of the meaning of expressions in our sense (1) of 'meaning': 'evil' and 'bad' are, in ordinary discourse, regarded as having the same meaning; yet 'evil' has a stronger negative emotive coloring then 'bad.' A clearer instance is afforded by 'bureaucrat' and 'public servant' which, as we ordinarily say, have the same meaning, though they generally have *opposite* emotive coloring.

[1] Page 112e.

[2] Aldrich gives 'above' and 'below' as illustrations of Wittgenstein's point. But these expressions certainly have meaning in the ordinary sense (sense (1)); and in one sense of 'say something,' do say something; though their use may be accompanied by certain pictures or images. Wittgenstein seems to be using 'say something' in a peculiar way, since he goes on to speak of a picture that is conjured up as seeming to "fix the sense *unambiguously*. The actual use, compared with that suggested by the picture, seems something muddled." (p.127e. Italics in original.) Therefore, for Wittgenstein, the expressions he has in mind do "say something"; but as Aldrich explains, not in the respect in which they evoke a picture or image.

Cf. "... The picture as an image is evoked by the expression, which in this respect "gives no information"; the expression just "calls up" the image." (*Op. cit.*, p. 100e. Quoted from Aldrich, "Pictorial Meaning, Picture-Thinking and Wittgenstein's Theory of Aspects," *Mind*, vol. LXVII, No. 265 (January, 1958) p. 71.

[3] *Ibid.*, pp. 70–79.

as use in the language, provided that the adverb is used to remind us of the distinction between "semantic" and "extra-semantic" uses of expressions.

We have distinguished "meaning" and "uses of expressions in the language" as a whole. Likewise we must distinguish a given expression's *particular* meaning(s) and the various *particular* uses it has: the particular picture(s) or image(s) it may evoke in the contexts of its use, the emotional and dynamic reactions it tends to evoke in hearers or readers; and so on. Using the word 'horse' to draw someone's attention to a certain member of the species *Equus caballus* involves its application to some state of affairs in accordance with one of its ordinary meanings ("correctly," "properly" as we say); and this *way* of using or applying the expression is a "semantic use" of it. The meanings of 'horse' – and though we have spoken of meaning in the abstract as a type of use of expressions, *a* meaning is always particular – are actually *determined* by the way in which the majority of English-speaking persons employ the word in sentences; by the class of actual and possible *occasions* of its application (that is, by the class of uses in Strawson's sense (c) of 'use'). And the word's "semantic use" is one kind of way in which the word's individual applications are applications of it. Yet the meaning of 'horse' in the sense of *Equus caballus* is itself not any one *particular* use, employment or application of it; nor any number of such particular uses, instances of employment or applications. Nor is it a characteristic or feature common to all (i) actual and possible instances of these; or (ii) actual and possible *sentences* in which 'horse' is or may be correctly used in the sense of '*Equus caballus*.' Nor is it, finally, certain "family resemblances" of the things falling under (i) or (ii).

Does this imply that an expression's particular meanings or senses, in sense (1) of these terms, cannot be identified with 'uses' in a sense intermediate between "use" in Strawson's sense (c) and our "semantic use" of expressions? The answer is No. Yet it is also the case that we cannot identify any meaning that an expression has with just any of its uses in the suggested intermediate sense. Once more: the word 'horse,' besides possessing different meanings or senses, can be used "extra semantically." It has more or less specific "extra-semantic uses" as well as more or less specific "semantic uses" (in the intermediate sense). That is, an expression's particular meanings constitute one particular intermediate type of use, not just any (and every) type of use of it.

II. MEANINGS AND CONCEPTS

The view that the meaning of an expression is an idea in the mind in the sense of a concept (or alternatively, an image), is I think still widely held, despite its difficulties and the many cogent criticisms that have been levelled at it. This view, as I hinted before, I do not subscribe to at all, though there is a close logical relation between the meanings of expressions and concepts. We could, if we wanted, show the distinctness of the two by criticizing the view that meanings are concepts. But instead of doing so, I shall concentrate on pointing out, with appropriate reasons, the relation between meanings and concepts; in the course of which some of the differences between the two will I hope emerge.

Before we begin, let me make it clear that in speaking of concepts I do not mean *thoughts*, in the sense of certain alleged psychic entities, or processes, in individual minds; though some of the advocates of the theory that meanings are ideas may be using the term in that sense. What I mean, rather, is what is usually meant by the word 'concept': the logical content of individual thoughts, what many thoughts can and may have in common. In this sense, the present account or meaning would not be open to Ayer's criticism that the view that "words are the signs of ideas" ("and ideas are identified here with thoughts or images"), "if it is taken literally, ... implies that we never do, or indeed can, talk about anything except our own *mental processes* ..." [1] Similarly it can escape his criticism that "people very often use words significantly without engaging in any processes of thinking other than those which are embodied in their intelligent use of words." [2] For whether or not concepts are regarded as independent of the actual thinking processes of human beings, the advocates of the view can very well claim that concepts are involved precisely in and only insofar as such processes of thinking arise in the intelligent use of words. Ayer's third criticism is however more germane. "The appeal to ideas," Ayer maintains:

> So far from serving to explain how words have meaning, merely brings in a second set of symbols, which have in many cases a dubious title to existence and in no case fulfil any function that is not already fulfilled by the corresponding words. We can say, if we like, that words are used to express ideas, though even this will be incorrect if it implies that having an idea necessarily precedes or accompanies the significant use of words as a separate mental process; but we must not say that they mean them.[3]

1 "Meaning And Intentionality," *Proceedings of the 12th International Congress of Philosophy*, Venice, 1958, vol. I, p. 144. Italics mine. The modified view would still be open, however, to the criticism that, if it is taken literally, we can never talk about anything except *concepts*.

2 *Ibid.*

3 *Ibid.*

It is perfectly correct that the appeal to concepts does not serve to explain how words have meaning, as our discussion will make clear. However, the word 'idea' is a perfectly good ordinary word, and in one sense of it means what 'concept' has been designed to mean. And it does convey a meaning which cannot be conveyed merely by using the corresponding expressions. Thus when we speak of the idea of democracy, we mean something which cannot be conveyed merely by our referring to the meaning of 'democracy' or to the conventional connotation(s) of this term; nor merely by any statements in which 'democracy' is used. This is precisely because, as we shall see in some detail, a concept is *not* identical with the meaning or with the connotation of an expression (if and when it has a connotation). We do not need, however, to hypostatize concepts in order that we may legitimately speak of them. Finally, concepts cannot be regarded as mental *processes:* and of course we cannot say that words *mean* concepts. There is a world of difference between saying (as the advocates of the view under consideration do say) that the *meaning* of a word is the concept "expressed" by the word, and saying that words *mean* concepts. Obviously, if the *meaning* of a word is a concept, the word cannot mean a concept.

Let us now note that the concept theory of meaning, as we might call it, is inapplicable in its above form to sentences, even if it is applicable to single words or phrases. For a sentence does not express *a* concept – when or if it does express anything at all – but a *thought* in a logical sense of this term analogous to the normal use of 'concept.' That is, a thought consists of a number of concepts logically related in certain ways. To cover sentences as well one must reformulate the above view to read: the meaning of a word or phrase is a concept; the meaning of a sentence is a thought – a set of concepts (at least two or three) logically related in certain ways.

The usual way in which philosophers speak about the logical relation between expressions and concepts is that an expression "expresses" a concept. In a similar fashion we ordinarily speak of a sentence as "expressing" a thought or an idea (e.g., that "Man is mortal" expresses the idea that all men are mortal). We also ordinarily speak of a phrase (e.g., "Taller than the Eiffel Tower") as "expressing" an idea. But although philosophers usually regard a phrase as "expressing" an idea in the sense of *a* "concept" and not a "thought," it is *prima facie* not clear which of the two the term 'idea,' as applied to phrases, is intended to convey in ordinary usage. But more of this later. The point now is that an expression, if and when it does "express" a concept or a thought, does so *by virtue of its meaning.* A string of nonsense-words or a jumble of meaningful words expresses no thought just because it is meaningless as a whole. Similarly with words that do "express" concepts. And at least in the case of sentences, we do not merely mean by this that a sentence cannot express an idea or a thought unless it has some meaning. We also mean that the nature of the particular thought it expresses is determined by its specific meaning. These considerations show that meanings and concepts are different, but related, things. If A possesses a feature *Y* by virtue of its possessing a feature X, it is obvious that *Y* cannot be identical with *X*.

Further, there are certain *words* of various sorts which, though perfectly meaningful, cannot be properly said to express concepts. Some examples are 'is,' 'but,' 'and,' 'or,' 'also,' 'too' (the last, at least in the sense of 'also'); also 'oh!' 'ah!' 'alas!' (the last as used in its current, not etymological sense), and other interjections.[1] Even in the case of words which appear to be legitimately classifiable as concept-expressing words, the concept theory of meaning faces serious difficulties. I shall not say anything here about vague ordinary words, since I shall speak about them in later sections. But take a perfectly precise, non-vague and innocent word such as 'man' or 'bird' (I am using 'precise' and 'non-vague' in their *ordinary* senses). 'Man' has several meanings; but take any one of them, say "male human being." We hear everybody saying that 'man' expresses the concept *man*, which, in the case in hand, is the same as the concept *male human being*. Now what is the alleged concept *male human being?* A possible answer is that it is not *one* concept but rather a complex of concepts. A second possible answer is that it is a concept "composed" of other concepts, in some sense of 'composed'; just as, though in a different way from the way in which a thought is "composed" of concepts. Nevertheless, only the latter is open to us if we wish to speak of the concept *man* as *a* concept.

But what is the nature, the content of the "concept" *male human being?* To answer this we must ask, first, what the nature, the content of the concepts *male* and *human being* are. What now is the content of the concept *male?* The usual, if not the inevitable answer, is that *male* is the concept of what we call "maleness"; which consists in certain characteristics and capacities, possessed by the class of things ordinarily called "males." Similarly with *human being*. In general, the question: (i) "What is the content of the concept *X*?" is usually translated into:

[1] I am not including value terms because the question as to whether they express concepts is still a matter of controversy.

(ii) "What is *X* the concept of?" which in turn is translated into: (iii) "What is it to be an "*X*"? '(What is it to be an instance of the kind of thing to which *X* properly applies?) or (iv) "What sorts of features, etc. must a thing possess to be properly called an "X"?" Question (i) would be usually regarded as logically equivalent to a question asking for 'X's' *conventional connotation* (iii & iv); and, in some cases, as equivalent to a question asking for 'X's' denotation.

Now let us notice, first, that *X* is the concept of a kind of existent that possesses certain features and capacities associated with the meaning of the expression 'X.' This is seen if we consider ordinary discourse. The question, "What is the idea of "male organism"?" is ordinarily answered by, "It is the idea of organisms that possess such and such characteristics."

Second, a concept *X* is not identical with 'X's' conventional connotation; though both are determined by 'X's' meaning. The following considerations should suffice to show this: 'X's' connotation is a set of characteristics, in the sense of *kinds* of qualities and properties (including dispositional properties) which are exemplified by all things that are, or can be, properly called "X's," by virtue of being called "X's." [1] It is clear that *X* can only be identical, if at all, with the characteristics comprising 'X's' connotation, *qua* kinds of characteristics, as "universals": it cannot be identical with any set of instances of these characteristics. For *X*, like all other concepts, is a general idea, by virtue of which it applies to all members of *class X*. If it were a set of instances of the characteristics we are speaking about, it would be a member of class *X*, along with all other things each of which exemplifies one particular set of instances of these characteristics – which is absurd. For then it cannot possibly *apply* to any member of the class at all; since it would be logically in the same boat as the "other" members of *class X*. This is another way of saying that if concept *X* is a member of *class X*, it cannot logically determine that class; whereas *class X* is determined by the logical content of concept *X*.

Is concept *X* then identical with 'X's' connotation as a set of *kinds* of characteristics? The answer is again No. This is clear where 'X' does express a concept but cannot be properly said to have a connotation in our present sense. Thus such words as 'green,' 'yellow,' 'hard,' 'soft,'

[1] I am ignoring, for the sake of simplicity, the fact that with respect to many (perhaps all) ordinary expressions, "connotation" can only consist in a set of criss-crossing "Family resemblances." But this fact does not adversely affect our argument. On the contrary, it makes the identification of a concept with the connotation of the expression which expresses the concept even more difficult to maintain.

'length' express concepts. But they cannot be said to have a connotation in our present sense; since they name individual qualities. In order that the notion of connotation may apply to them and like expressions, we must broaden the concept of connotation by defining 'connotation' as a characteristic or set of characteristics which something must have, or which something *must be,* in order that a given expression may properly apply to it. Yet even in this broader sense, the connotation of an expression 'X' cannot be identical with concept *X*. Suppose we take any kind of characteristic, say greenness, which is or may be exemplified in some (green) object or objects. We can now form a *concept of* this characteristic, just as we can form a concept of the object(s) in which it is or may be exemplified. But if the concept of greenness itself is the characteristic greenness, the concept and the thing of which it is the concept – greenness – would be one and the same thing. But this is impossible! The concept of something itself cannot ever be numerically the same as the thing of which it is the concept. If a concept is something, it cannot be literally (numerically) identical with what it is about; otherwise we can never possible conceive of anything. But now, if there is such a thing as the quality greenness as a universal, it either exists in green things and does not exist apart from them, or it exists ("subsists") in a Platonic world of forms apart from actual green things. In both cases the concept which is (supposed to be) something mental, existing in relation to the mind, cannot itself be the characteristic existing objectively. The only alternative, then, is to suppose that the concept is an instance of the characteristic greenness, existing in the mind. But this cannot be the case; since we saw earlier that a concept cannot possibly be an instance of a characteristic, or instances of a number of characteristics. To conceive of greenness, to have a concept of greenness, is then simply another way of saying that the mind becomes *aware* of the quality greenness which is in the world outside or in a Platonic "heaven"; but that to be aware of something is not, literally, to have what one is aware of "in" the mind (awareness of it does not make it mental). Since the meaning of an expression 'X' is what gives concept *X* its logical content, and it also determines 'X's' connotation, we might be tempted to say that concept *X* is some kind of entity which contains some sort of copy or duplicate of the characteristics comprised in 'X's' connotation; hence that to conceive of greenness, say, is to have some mental copy, called a concept, by means of which we apprehend the quality greenness.

In contrast to this, what our foregoing analysis shows, it seems to me, is that a concept is not something, an entity. To say "I have an idea or concept of something" is merely another way of saying that I am aware of that thing; and it would not add anything useful to say that the awareness of something can only take place through some second thing, which somehow copies what one is said to be aware of.

However, as long as we do not think of a concept as some kind of entity, the locutions we have used about it in the present chapter and elsewhere can be quite useful. In that manner of speaking we can now say that a concept is not identical with the connotation (wherever it obtains) of the expression which expresses the concept. It can also be readily shown that a concept is also not identical with the class of things which are named by that expression (its comprehension, in C. I. Lewis' use of this word).

In the light of this discussion, our earlier statements about the connotation of an expression 'X' and its relation to 'X's' meaning on the one hand and concept *X* on the other hand, can be simply restated as follows: If and when we understand the meaning of an expression 'X,' and if we analyse this meaning, we find that it provides us with a condition or set of conditions for 'X's' correct application. This condition or these conditions (sometimes) stipulate(s) that for anything to be an (unquestionable example of) "X," to be a member of class *X*, it must possess, or it must itself be, a certain characteristic or a set of characteristics.

When we conceive, when we form a concept of X we fix our attention on this characteristic or set of characteristics; assuming that 'X' involves some characteristic or characteristics by virtue of its meaning. What we have in mind when we conceive of X can be called the logical content of concept *X*; and where 'X' is an expression of the present type – where, as we say, it has a connotation – we can add that *X*'s logical content is determined by 'X's' connotation, and therefore by 'X's' meaning, which determines 'X's' connotation.

It must be added, however, that a number of difficulties arise in relation to the traditional unextended concept of conventional connotation, and even the broader concept of it which we ourselves employed. For one thing, it is sometimes quite difficult to determine what the connotation of a given expression is, or can be, from an examination of the expression's meaning. Moreover, and more important, there are a number of serious limitations to the applicability of this notion of connotation in relation to ordinary expressions and ordinary concepts. (See footnote 1, page 36; also, chapter four page 46, footnote 1).

These limitations show that this concept is an oversimplified, ideal scheme approximated only in various degrees by ordinary expressions and concepts; that it finds its best and most complete applications in the case of the rigorously defined expressions and rigorously delimited concepts of pure mathematics and, to a lesser extent, the more-or-less rigorous and precise expressions and concepts of the various empirical sciences. As a matter of fact, it is not unfair or untrue to say that those philosophers who have whole-heartedly embraced this notion have taken mathematical, rather than ordinary terms and concepts as their models or paradigms. I shall return to these and to related points in later chapters.

CHAPTER FOUR

SYNONYMITY

Our preliminary discussion in this part of the present work would be quite incomplete without a somewhat detailed consideration of sameness of meaning or synonymity of verbal expressions. This is particularly true in relation to our analysis and evaluation, in the next chapter, of what I shall refer to as Form I of semantic analysis. For as we shall there see, any form of words that purports to express a correct analysis of a given analysandum must be, in that form of analysis, synonymous with the verbal expression expressing that analysandum. An inquiry into the conditions and criteria of synonymity of expressions is also useful in relation to our entire discussion of semantic analysis in Part Two. It also ties in with the preceding two chapters, and throws further light on the nature of ordinary languages.

The drawing of logical distinctions is an important part of philosophical analysis; and I shall start my discussion of synonymity of expressions with such a distinction. In raising questions about synonymity of the type we are here interested in, we should distinguish the question as to (a) the nature of synonymity or the correct analysis of the notion of synonymity; and the related question as to (b) how we can discover whether or not any two given expressions are synonymous; i.e., the question of the criteria of synonymity. The correct answer to question (a) helps us to arrive at the correct answer to question (b), by defining the goal to be achieved by the application of the relevant criteria of synonymity. It may turn out, however, that the actual utilization of a given criterion of synonymity arrived at with the help of our answer to (a) is impracticable. Although that alone would not rule it out as an answer to question (a), it would naturally arouse our suspicions concerning its correctness as an answer to that question.

Our discussion of synonymity in this chapter, like our discussion of meanings, uses and concepts in chapter three, is intended to help clarify notions which we have been and will be increasingly using in the course of our discussion of the different types and forms of philosophical analysis. A clear understanding of synonymity is necessary for our purposes because the analysis of the meanings of philosophical expressions, or of the concepts expressed by them, sometimes requires the employment of criteria of synonymity. I mean, whenever the results of the analysis are expressible in one relatively brief statement which, in order to convey the analysans correctly, must be synonymous with the expression conveying the analysandum. The major form of semantic analysis referred to will be dealt with in the next chapter, and the application of the following discussion will become more apparent when we pass to it. It is useful and convenient to combine the two aims of this chapter by attempting to discover the *criteria-features*, as we might call them – whether determinate or relatively-determinate common characteristics and/or various "family resemblances," etc. – that obtain in each class of synonymous expressions. The "criteria-features" are the defining features of pairs of synonymous expressions, whose presence or absence in a given instance indicates the synonymity or lack of synonymity, respectively, of the particular pair of expressions involved. I must add, however, that it is theoretically possible to arrive at criteria of synonymity without analysing the ordinary concept of synonymity.

It is nowadays customary to begin a discussion of synonymity with the true statement that no completely satisfactory account of synonymity has hitherto been given. Because of this, and it is due to the difficulty of the subject-matter, it will not be expected (nor am I presuming) that a completely satisfactory account will be found in the pages that follow; especially in view of the limited space and time we are here devoting to it. It is only hoped that some progress will be made in the right direction, which may eventually lead to an account that satisfies the majority of reflective minds.

There is not, and, to my mind, there cannot be, a single completely adequate or completely precise analysis of synonymity, holding true of *all* pairs of synonymous expressions – not even one which holds true of all words, or all phrases, or all sentences alone.[1] All the accounts or analyses with which I am familiar suffer from some fatal flaw. For one thing, they purport to hold good for all synonymous words, phrases, or sentences; and some purport to hold good for all these kinds of expressions. Even the question which Nelson Goodman asks in his "On

[1] Unless we are to consider "sameness of function(s)" in a given language as a completely adequate or completely precise account of it.

likeness of Meaning," [1] i.e., "Under what circumstances do two names or predicates in an ordinary language have the same meaning?" does not have a single correct answer. One thing seems certain: two names or predicates in an ordinary language have the same meaning under *different* circumstances, depending on the kind of names or predicates they are. Similarly with words other than names or predicates, with phrases, and with sentences.

A number of accounts of synonymity which at various times have been formulated by philosophers are satisfactory in respect to particular, limited classes of expressions. And a considerable part of our task will lie in assigning each account its legitimate sphere. But as I hope we shall see, there are classes of expressions to which, in my opinion, no account that I am familiar with actually does justice. A part of our task will therefore also consist in the attempt to remedy this deficiency as far as possible. I do not quite agree with Benson Mates when he expresses doubts "that any adequate definition of "synonymity" – at least for languages sufficiently complex to make the problem interesting – will ever be found by means of the usual arm-chair methods of philosophizing." [2] His reason is that "We need empirical research regarding the ordinary language in order to determine which expressions are in fact synonymous, and with the help of these data it may be possible to find an acceptable definition of "synonymity" for some language which has a determinate structure and which closely resembles the ordinary language." [3] Without minimizing the importance and the need for the empirical study of ordinary language (see chapter two), it is not an exaggeration or incorrect to say that we *do* know that certain (though perhaps not many) pairs of ordinary expressions are synonymous. For we often speak of this or that word as being synonymous with this or that other word, in the same way that we speak of this object as being a table, or of that object as being a chair. And we do the latter as much in the absence of empirical research as the former. Moreover, of the instances of synonymity given by those of us who have a good knowledge of the particular language(s), some must surely be paradigm cases of it. This is true both where the synonymous expressions occur in the same language and where they occur in different languages.

[1] Reprinted in *Philosophy And Analysis*, edited by Margaret Macdonald (Oxford, 1954), p. 55.

[2] "Synonymity," in *Semantics & the Philosophy of Language*, edited by Leonard Linsky (Urbana, Illinois, 1952), pp. 118–119.

[3] *Ibid.*, p. 119.

A. SYNONYMITY OF GENERAL NAMES AND PREDICATES

There is a well-known view, advocated by Nelson Goodman, that two terms are synonymous if they have the same extensions in the sense that "(a) they apply to exactly the same objects, and (b) each compound term constructed by combining certain words with either of the terms in question applies to exactly the same objects as the compound term constructed by combining the same words in the same way with the other of the terms in question." [1] This view, despite the skill and ingenuity with which it has been elaborated and defended against the many criticisms it has provoked, seems to me to break down when applied to names of non-existent things, such as 'centaur' and 'unicorn.' Its treatment of such terms as these has indeed occasioned many objections, but apparently none of these objections – at least none of those dealt with by Goodman in his reply to them – has attacked what seems to me to be the essential point: namely, that Goodman applies the notion of extension to such terms. Goodman, like some other contemporary formal logicians (e.g., C. I. Lewis) speaks of these terms as having zero or null extension. He does not speak of them as lacking any extension at all; or, better, regard them as expressions to which the notion of extension is inapplicable. As a consequence, he is faced with a problem which threatens to undermine his account of synonymity; namely, that "there are certain clear cases where two words that have the same extension do not have the same meaning. "Centaur" and "unicorn," for example, since neither applies to anything, have the same (null) extension; yet surely they differ in meaning." [2] He adds immediately, "I do not mean to suggest that identity of extension with difference of meaning occurs only where the extension is null, but such cases are enough and are the most striking." Because of this difficulty Goodman introduces clause (b) above – the identity of "secondary extensions" – to his definition or criterion (it is not quite clear whether he is offering us the former or the latter, or both). The odd consequence, logically traceable to his introduction of the restrictive clause (b) and hence to his attempt to overcome the difficulty mentioned, is, in Goodman's words, that "no two different words have the same meaning." All that we can say, strictly speaking, is that two names or predicates

[1] "On Some Differences About Meaning," reprinted in *Philosophy And Analysis*, pp. 63–64. See also "On Likeness of Meaning," *passim*.

[2] "On Likeness of Meaning," p. 69.

have a greater or lesser degree of *likeness* of meaning. This consequence is odd, for one thing, because Goodman's final conclusion contradicts what he, by his own admission, sets out to do; i.e., to tell us under what circumstances two names or predicates in an ordinary language have the *same* meaning. For the datum from which he starts, and from which anyone trying to do what he attempts has to start, is that there *are* words in ordinary language which have the same meaning. Otherwise, what sense can we attach to our use of the expression 'having the same meaning' in ordinary discourse; and what would any philosopher be doing if, in his analysis of synonymity, he is not analysing the notion as we have it? Goodman, instead of giving us an analysis of the ordinary notion of synonymity, in a straightforward sense of 'analysis,' really modifies that notion by replacing it by a somewhat different notion. And this itself is a result of his drawing too fine a distinction between "same" and "not same," as a consequence of his too-restrictive and stringent clause (b).

The point on which I want to dwell here, however, is that though the notion of null extension (as well as Lewis' infinite extension) may be very useful for purely logical purposes, it is positively misleading and a source of difficulties when used in our present context. Its possible usefulness elsewhere should not blind us to the fact that it is nothing more than a logical, conceptual device, and does not in fact describe or stand for anything actual in an ordinary sense of actual. (Perhaps it is not an exaggeration to compare it to the equator line and the latter's use in geography.) Further, as we shall see, we can characterize synonymity of such terms as 'centaur' and 'unicorn' more successfully by means of the notion of conventional connotation or intension, along with other classes of expressions to which the notion of extension is altogether inapplicable.

A. Sameness of (primary) extension, as far as I can see, is a sufficient as well as a necessary condition of synonymity of pairs of names of existent things, consisting of *single words* (e.g., 'table,' 'chair,' 'man'). The same applies to the names of ordinary predicate-*words* (e.g., 'green,' 'heavy,' 'triangular'). The addition of a further requirement does not seem to be necessary; though it is probable that pairs of words which satisfy this condition would also satisfy Goodman's clause (b), at least in many compounds. As far as I can see, all pairs of (single) words which name the same thing(s), hence have the same extension, also have the same meaning.[1] However, even in the present type of case, "naming"

[1] This does not exclude the possibility we mentioned in chapter two, in relation to the

and "meaning" are distinct functions of words; and even here, the meaning of a word logically determines what it names, not the other way round.

I just spoke of name-*words* and predicate-*words*. This is intended to exclude (i) *phrases* that name some existent thing, such as 'featherless biped' and 'rational animal'; (ii) definite descriptions, some though not all of which – e.g., 'The Evening Star' – are called "names" in ordinary language; and (iii) compound predicates, predicates in the form of phrases; e.g., 'taller than the Eiffel Tower,' 'whiter than snow.' I shall deal with the latter two types of expressions later on; but it is clear that our adopted condition is not a sufficient condition in regard to (i). It is clear that 'man' and 'featherless biped' or 'rational animal' are not synonymous class names; though they are extensionally isomorphic or identical. Similarly, extensional isomorphism is not a sufficient condition of synonymity of pairs of expressions falling under (ii) above. As Goodman, following Frege, points out, the definite description 'The Evening Star' applies to the same object as "The Morning Star'; yet the two expressions do not have the same meaning. The addition of Goodman's clause (b) perhaps enables us to deal extensionally with synonymity in the case of (ii) and (iii); but I shall not inquire whether or not this is so; or whether some other extensional stipulation can achieve our objective. As we shall see presently, we can get at least an equally satisfactory, but more widely applicable, analysis of synonymity with the help of the notion of intensional identity. We must, however, discuss the synonymity of proper names before we pass to that; for reasons which will now be stated.

ordinary applications of 'table' and 'tavola.' I mean the possibility that the marginal indeterminacy involved in the case of 'table' may not coincide with the marginal indeterminacy involved in the case of 'tavola'; though these two words name the same thing and are synonymous. For when we speak of two expressions as being synonymous or non-synonymous, we refer exclusively to those applications of them as are more or less fixed or determinate; not, or not also, to those situations in which the applicability or inapplicability of the expressions is indeterminate. The – or at least one – reason for this was already stated in chapter three, in our discussion of the reasons why, in many cases at least, the emotive coloring of words is not ordinarily considered as a part (or a form) of their meaning in our sense (1) of this word. I mean that the concept of meaning in this sense involves the notion of relative fixity or determinacy. (A further illustration of this fact is provided by the way in which we ordinarily speak about the meaning of *vague* expressions: expressions whose usages in general are fluid and variable.)

In contrast to meaning, the marginal indeterminacy of some of the applications of an expression that involves marginal indeterminacy is part of its ordinary *use* or *uses*. And this entails that the ordinary use(s) of two synonymous expressions, say 'table' and 'tavola,' will be identical only if the marginal indeterminacy involved in the two cases coincide. Here we have one important type of situation in which "meaning of an expression" and "use of an expression" diverge or do not coincide. Similarly with "sameness of meaning" and "sameness of use(s)."

B. SYNONYMITY OF GENERAL NAMES, PREDICATES (SIMPLE OR COMPOUND), DEFINITE DESCRIPTIONS, VERBS AND ADVERBS

So far we have seen a general feature of a limited – though a very large – class of synonymous expressions. We now come to a characterization of synonymity which to my mind is the most comprehensive and, in that sense, the most satisfactory characterization of it; though even this characterization has its limitation. It states that two expressions have the same meaning if and only if they have the same conventional connotation or intension. That is, that intensional sameness is a necessary and sufficient condition of sameness of meaning. This account takes care of the synonymity of general names, which, as we stated earlier (under A), can be adequately dealt with along extensional lines. It can also take care of names of fictitious things, definite descriptions, and predicate-terms (whether consisting of single words or phrases), none of which can be adequately dealt with purely extensionally.[1] Among possible characterizations of synonymity of expressions it appears to come closest to the ideal – logically unattainable, however – of a single all-embracing characterization. Since intension determines extension in C. I. Lewis' sense of 'comprehension what I myself refer to as *possible*, as opposed to actual extension (or denotation) – expressions which have the same intension will have the same possible extension: if they have a possible extension at all. (The converse of this is not always true, however; e.g. in the case of 'The Morning Star' and 'The Evening Star.') If now intensional sameness supplies us with a correct characterization of certain classes of expressions, extensional sameness would, as a logical consequence, constitute a *necessary* feature of – and hence may be taken as a necessary condition for – the synonymity of expressions that possess an extension. But since extensional sameness does not entail intensional sameness, the former cannot, even in the case of expressions that have extensions, *always* constitute a sufficient condition; though there are perhaps some

[1] Here, and in all future references to connotation or intension, I shall include in this notion any criss-crossing "family resemblances" that may determine the correct non-marginal applications of a given expression as it is actually employed in a given period of time. I shall not limit it to common characteristics that may constitute necessary and sufficient conditions of the correct application of an expression. Indeed, in the case of most or all ordinary, or even scientific, expressions connotation will consist wholly of criss-crossing family resemblances rather than of common characteristics.

expressions that have the same extension and also, as a matter of fact, the same intension.

That intensional identity is a necessary and sufficient explication of the synonymity of pairs of general names that have an extension – names such as 'table,' 'chair,' 'book,' 'tree,' 'forest' – is, I think, clear. Thus 'book' and '*livre*' are synonymous inasmuch as they have the same intension. The same applies to names of geometrical figures and scientific names. Here we must distinguish the ordinary meaning(s) and the mathematical or scientific meaning(s) of these terms. For the technical meanings of many such expressions are different from their every-day, non-technical meanings. The words 'triangle,' 'circle,' 'acid,' 'salt,' 'fish' easily occur to the mind. This does not materially affect our characterization of synonymity, however; and in many instances of this type, an expression A is synonymous with another expression B both in its technical and in its ordinary meanings. (The reasons for this are not very hard to discover; but they do not concern us.)

Our explication easily applies to such expressions as 'centaur' and 'unicorn.' These words are not synonymous because they do not possess the same intension; whereas 'centaur' and 'a fabulous creature, with the head, trunk, and arms of a man, joined to the body and legs of a horse' are synonymous (or more or less synonymous), and have the same (or more or less the same) intension. Similarly with definite descriptions. 'The Morning Star' and 'The Evening Star' are not synonymous; and they do not have the same intension, due to the difference in the meaning of 'morning' and 'evening.' Whereas 'The Morning Star' and 'Der Morgenstern' have the same intension and are synonymous.

Similarly, *mutatis mutandis*, with predicates, simple (such as 'rectangular') or compound (such as 'stronger than Goliath'). The common formulation of intension in logic textbooks as the set of characteristics which a thing must have in order that the given expression may properly apply to it, must however be slightly modified in the case of predicates that denote simple sensible qualities; such as 'red' or 'hard.' To make the notion of intension applicable to them in a straight-forward sense, we shall reformulate it as follows: the intension of an expression is the characteristic or characteristics, or the relation or relations, that a thing must have or a quality must be in order that the expression may properly apply to it. As reformulated, the notion of intension readily applies to predicates that express relative concepts in one common sense of 'relative'; e.g., 'bright,' 'dim,' 'dense,' 'light,' 'tall,' 'short.'

Coming to compound predicates, such as 'taller than the Eiffel Tower,' 'stronger than Goliath,' the situation is seen to be similar to that which obtains in the case of definite descriptions, indefinite descriptions, and other types of phrases. In each of these cases [1] what we might call the "phrase-intension" of the expression is wholly and solely determined by the meaning of the expression as a whole; paralleling the way in which the intension of an individual word is wholly and solely determined by the word's meaning. But the expression's meaning as a whole is, in the same way, determined by the meaning of the individual words composing the expression, together with the syntactical rules in accordance with which they are conjoined.[1] It follows that these two factors also determine, wholly and solely, the expression's "intension" as a whole. That is, they determine the characteristics which a thing must have in order that such an expression may be applicable to it. Accordingly, two or more compound predicates, definite descriptions, indefinite descriptions and the like will be synonymous if and only if they have the same "phrase-intension."

The legitimacy of speaking of the intension of an expression of any of the present kinds can be readily seen by considering 'taller than the Eiffel Tower.' "Having a height of more than 984 feet," which is a necessary and sufficient condition for any object's being properly said to be higher than the Eiffel Tower, is a *bona fide* characteristic, in an ordinary sense of this term. Similarly with 'stronger than Goliath,' 'The Evening Star,' 'The present king of France' and all other definite descriptions.

The concept of "phrase-intension" appears to break down in the case of phrases containing personal or relative pronouns; for example, in relation to the compound predicate 'holier than thou.' For the pronoun 'thou' in this expression does not refer to any particular person. Hence the *degree* of holiness which a person must possess in order that the expression may be applicable to him depends on, and varies with, the degree of holiness or unholiness of the person with whom he is compared. That is, the degree of holiness which a person must possess in order that the expression may apply to him depends on, and varies with, the particular *statements* in which the expression may be used in particular

[1] I am excluding, as we must, so-called idiomatic phrases. For the above does not hold in their case. Unlike non-idiomatic phrases, the idiomatic meaning of such a phrase as a whole is different from its literal meaning. The sameness of meaning in which we are usually interested in their case is the sameness of idiomatic meaning. For that purpose we can utilize the logical expedient of "idiomatic intension" to parallel "idiomatic meaning," on the analogy with non-idiomatic phrases, and say that two idiomatic phrases are synonymous if and only if they have the same "idiomatic intension."

contexts. Whereas, the meaning of 'thou' and of the phrase as a whole is *not* dependent on the contexts in which that phrase may be used, in the same sense of 'dependent' (more exactly, its cognate, 'depends') as above. Therefore the synonymity or non-synonymity of 'holier than thou' with some other expression is similarly independent of any contexts in which either expression may be used.

It might seem that we can dispense with the notion of "phrase-intension" in relation to all non-idiomatic phrases, and say that two phrases are synonymous if and only if the following two conditions are satisfied: (a) that for every word – and by 'word' I mean either a simple or a compound, in the sense of a hyphenated, word – in the one phrase there is a corresponding word in the second phrase which has the same intension as it; and (b) that the syntactical rules in accordance with which the words in the one phrase are strung together correspond to, play the same role as, the syntactical rules in accordance with which the words in the second phrase are strung together. If the phrases concerned occur in the same language, the syntactical rules should, it appears, be numerically identical in both cases. Condition (a) unfortunately raises at least one difficulty which makes it impossible to accept it in its present form. Consequently, the analysis of synonymity of phrases in terms of the notion of "phrase-intension" seems to be more acceptable.

The difficulty I am alluding to is that two synonymous phrases may differ in length. In the cases of phrases that do not occur in the same language this is usually due to differences in word-economy. Examples can be readily found by comparing English phrases with, say, German phrases that are synonymous with them. The attempt to remedy the flaw by adding 'or a corresponding phrase' immediately after "in the one phrase there is a corresponding word" in our statement of it above would merely re-create the original problem: for what is a phrase which "corresponds" to a given word? As for condition (b), we can, I think, delimit the notion of the "correspondence" of the syntactical rules of different (natural) languages in terms of the parts of speech to which the constituent words belong, and the nature of the phrases as a whole. I mean, in terms of the fact that a given phrase is a definite description, a noun phrase, an adjective phrase, or some other type of phrase. But I have a strong suspicion that the attempt to define either 'part of speech' or 'noun phrase,' 'adverb phrase,' etc., or both, will inescapably result in circularity. My suspicion may be unfounded, however. In any case, I shall not here attempt to see what can be done with the notion in hand; and I shall not pursue further the question of the synonymity of phrases.

Our intensional criterion is inapplicable to proper names, most conjunctions, certain verbs such as 'is' and 'are' (in all their tenses), 'has' and 'have' used as auxiliary verbs, and interjections such as 'oh!' and 'ah!' In the case of proper names and interjections, this is not due to any limitations in the criterion itself but, as I shall show, to the fact that, in its ordinary uses, the notion of synonymity is not applied, and is inapplicable, to them.

(*1*) *Proper names*

All proper names as proper names have a certain common function – that of referring to, of naming things. Some but by no means all proper names also have certain specific meanings (in our first sense; chapter three). These are acquired in various traceable ways. These proper names, whenever they are employed *qua* possessing such meanings, can be said to function as general names rather than as proper names. Usually the specific meanings which proper names may possess as words are indifferent to, do not affect, their naming function. Independently of this, and even where the specific meaning of a proper name plays some role in relation to its naming function, the two are logically distinct and not identifiable. This is by no means a novel view. Its correctness could readily be shown by an examination of the way in which we ordinarily talk about proper names. But such an inquiry falls outside the scope of our present discussion. The important point here is that the notion of synonymity is, ordinarily, not applied to a proper name *qua* proper name. It is also not applied to it *qua* functioning as a general name, wherever it does have some specific meaning. Consider 'Mary' and 'Marie.' We ordinarily say that these two names are the *same*, or that 'Marie' is the *French form of* 'Mary' (and vice versa). We do not say that they are "synonymous," that they "have the same meaning." (This itself is a good indication of what we have just said: that naming is not a form of, or the same as, meaning.) Similarly, we do not say that 'Mary' and 'Peter' have different meanings, but rather that they are two different names. Now consider 'Plato' and 'broad.' Here we say that, *in Greek*, the *word* (not the name) 'Plato,' or 'πλατων,' means "broad." Nor do we say that 'Plato,' as a proper name, occurs in the Greek language. Whereas we do speak of it in this way *qua* functioning as a general name. We do not say that 'Plato' and 'broad' "have the same meaning." Let me add that the notion of intensional identity could readily take care of "synonymity" in relation to proper names *qua* functioning as general names (where they do so function), were the concept of synonymity applicable to them.

Finally consider 'Venus' and 'The Morning Star.' We ordinarily say that the two expressions name the same thing, "Venus"; but we do not say that they are synonymous or *not* synonymous. The notion of synonymity, here also, does not apply.

(2) *Interjections*

Questions of meaning do not normally arise in respect to interjections – we do not ask, say, what 'oh!' means – except when we do not know that a given interjection *is* an interjection. If an interjection has, or has had, some meaning as an ordinary expression, it would be proper to ask for this meaning. But then we would not be asking for the expression's meaning *qua interjection*, but *qua* general name. Thus we might ask for the meaning of 'alas' in the sense of asking for its derivation or etymological meaning. As for 'O God!,' we can properly ask what 'God' *names;* but it would be improper to ask what 'O!' or what 'O God!' means. Further, the notion of synonymity seems to arise only in respect to interjections that have some meaning as a whole (e.g., 'Sblood!') or are etymologically derived from a word which has, or has had, a specific meaning (e.g., 'alas!'); or that contain words that have a specific meaning (e.g., 'Ah me!'). We can therefore properly say that 'alas!' and 'hélas!' are *synonymous*. These and similar cases can be adequately dealt with extensionally or intensionally, either as we have hitherto understood these notions, or with some modifications. To illustrate: 'alas!' and 'hélas!' can be regarded as synonymous *qua* having a certain etymological meaning, because both originally named the same object, God. We cannot, however, speak of the *extension* of these two words as being the same, since we cannot really speak of extension in relation to proper names. For it does not make sense to speak of the class of all actual and possible things named by a given proper name, in any straight-forward sense of 'class.' Theoretically speaking, and frequently also a matter of fact, practically any given proper name can be given to almost anything actual or possible. Hence there cannot be a class of things named or nameable by it, since nothing is theoretically excluded from it. Stated in other words, there are no characteristics or "family resemblances" – certainly none that are specific in any degree – the possession of which makes something nameable by a given proper name, and the absence of which makes it not nameable by it.

On the other hand, we can deal intensionally with interjections such as 'Sblood!' and their etymological synonyms, without recourse to any modification of our concept of intensional identity.

(3) Verbs, prepositions and conjunctions

The synonymity of pairs of verbs, transitive and intransitive, with the exception of 'is' and auxiliary verbs in all tenses, can also be adequately dealt with intensionally, in terms of our broader formulation of intension. The same is true of many prepositions (e.g., 'up,' 'down,' 'above,' 'below,' 'over,' 'under,' 'against,' 'in,' 'out'). The exceptions in both cases cannot be dealt with extensionally either. Similarly, conjunctions are not amenable to extensional or intensional treatment. And yet it goes without saying that the ordinary notions of synonymity and non-synonymity are applicable to all verbs, prepositions and conjunctions.[1]

The inapplicability of our two conditions of synonymity to these expressions is not surprising, as the function of the latter is to *relate* two or more expressions in phrases, clauses or sentences. It is to be expected that in order to discover the necessary and sufficient conditions of synonymity in their case, we must consider the synonymity of pairs of sentences and of pairs of clauses. To this we now turn, by considering an alleged condition of synonymity for all classes of expressions, including sentences, proposed by Benson Mates in an essay entitled "Synonymity." [2] This condition states that "*Two expressions are synonymous in a language L if and only if they may be interchanged in each sentence in L without altering the truth value of that sentence.*" [3] This condition refers only to synonymity between pairs of expressions occurring in the same language, as Mates explains. Mates does not give us the "different and more general criterion for the synonymity of expressions occurring in different languages." [4] Also, his condition is intended to apply to "languages which do not contain names of their

[1] It might be thought that we can characterize synonymity with respect to verbs, prepositions and conjunctions – indeed, all the different parts of speech – in terms of the notion of identity of use. In this characterization, two expressions will be synonymous if and only if they have the same uses in the language or languages in which they occur. The trouble with this, however, is that the notion of 'use' is too broad. What we need is a way of distinguishing clearly the particular kind of use called "meaning," from the other kinds of uses an expression may possess. This in turn requires a thorough discussion of the nature of meaning as against the other kinds of uses of expressions: something which we have briefly touched upon in chapter three.

[2] Reprinted in *Semantics and the Philosophy of Language*, pp. 201–226.

[3] *Ibid.*, p. 119. Italics in original.

[4] *Ibid.*, pp. 119–120.

own expressions and semantical terms like "true," "denotes," and so forth. In particular, it is important that the language L not contain the semantical term 'synonymous in L.'" [1]

It is clear, I think, that if the above condition of synonymity is to be satisfied at all, L cannot be an ordinary language – at least not English, French, German, Arabic, Armenian, to mention the few ordinary languages with which I have some acquaintance. Mates points out that L will be a "language in which the formation rules do not prevent the interchange of expressions of the same type. Thus, the fact that "humanity" and "human" are not interchangeable in English does not indicate a difference in meaning, for syntax alone prevents their interchange." [2] This statement is not completely true, since 'humanity' and 'human' do differ somewhat in meaning: "human' means "possessing humanity," in some sense of 'humanity,' not "humanity" itself. However, only some expressions that are of the same logical type cannot be interchanged in a language such as English. It may be true as a *matter of fact*, though, that English (say) does prevent the interchange of some expressions of the same logical type which are also synonymous. Whenever this occurs, if at all, Mates' condition will be of restricted application. Moreover, as a condition of synonymity, it does not apply to most, and even perhaps all, advanced natural languages – such as European and many Asiatic languages – *in their entirety*, for a reason Mates himself gives. These languages contain terms like 'true,' 'denotes,' 'synonymous with,' if not also names of their own expressions. I therefore find it surprising that Mates regards his condition as a "guide for conducting research to determine which expressions ('presumably in *natural* languages) are in fact synonymous for given persons..." [3] and illustrates his principle by examples drawn from ordinary English.

Mates' condition of synonymity, apart from the foregoing restrictions on its application, suffers from the fact that Mates ascribes truth-values to sentences, as a result of his failure to distinguish sentences and statements. If modified in the light of this distinction, it will read: "Two expressions are synonymous in a language L if and only if they may be interchanged in each statement, or sentence-in-use, in L, without altering the truth value of that statement." In this form, it gives us a true condition of synonymity of pairs of expressions. It is

[1] *Ibid.*, p. 120.
[2] *Ibid.*, p. 129 footnote 7.
[3] *Ibid.*, p. 119.

doubtless true that two expressions are synonymous if they can be interchanged in each statement in a natural language without altering its truth value. It also seems likely that, contrary to Mates' view, *all* synonymous expressions may be interchanged in each sentence, at least in the natural languages I am familiar with, without resulting in a syntactically improper sentence. In the light of my personal knowledge of a number of natural languages, it seems to me that two really synonymous expressions – at least in the languages referred to – tend to be of the same part of speech, and so may be interchanged without violation of syntax. If this is true, the above condition will also provide us with a necessary and sufficient condition of non-synonymity: two expressions then cannot be synonymous (i.e., will be non-synonymous) if (a) they can not be interchanged in each sentence in a natural language without violating the syntax of that language; *or* (b) if they can be interchanged in each sentence in a natural language without violation of syntax, but not without altering the truthvalue of at least one statement that these sentences would make in actual or possible contexts. In any case, even if (a) is not true in some natural languages, (b) is, I think, definitely true.[1]

What is the merit of Mates' condition of synonymity relatively to the two conditions we discussed earlier? It can be easily seen, I think, that it is of wider applicability than the condition of extensional isomorphism. The more important question is how it fares in relation to the condition of intensional isomorphism. Here the following may be said:

(1) The latter is of wider applicability than it in respect to synonymity of pairs of expressions occurring in different natural languages. This should be evident from our earlier discussion.

(2) As regards expressions occurring is in the same language, it is seen that it is positively applicable wherever (but only wherever), in respect to any given word or phrase 'X,' the particular language concerned contains another word or phrase 'Y' which is synonymous with it. Such synonyms are practically non-existent – at least in the languages with which I am familiar, such as English, French, Armenian – in the case of conjunctions and interjections, and those verbs to which the condition of intensional isomorphism is inapplicable (e.g., 'is,' and auxiliary verbs such as 'has been'). As regards these classes of expressions, therefore, the present condition of synonymity does not, as a positive condition, fare better than the condition of intensional isomorphism. It nonetheless has an advantage over the latter as a *negative*

[1] For arguments in support of Mates' condition of synonymity see *Ibid.*, pp. 120ff.

condition of synonymity. For instance, the fact that no word or phrase is synonymous with 'is' or 'has been' in English can be shown [1] by substituting as many other words or phrases as we please, one at a time, for either of them in each sentence in which they occur. If we do this, we discover that the truth value of at least some of the statements which the resulting sentences (when they are well-formed) can make will be different. Similarly we can employ this criterion to show that, for example, the word 'book' is not synonymous with, say, the word 'cat,' or the word 'table' with the word 'chair.' Further, our two conditions are of almost equal applicability in respect to another class of expressions – pronouns. Here, both conditions have only a negative application (this, as in all cases where either condition can only be negatively applied, is due to a peculiarity or, if you like, limitation of the language to which they are applied, not to any defect in the conditions themselves) for the same reason that makes them only negatively applicable to conjunctions, interjections, and the like. Despite this, Mates' condition has an advantage over the other condition: the notion of intension ceases to be applicable in relation to the pronouns 'he,' 'she,' and 'you,' and even of 'it' and 'they.' It is difficult to see what property or properties, or what "family resemblances," in any non-Pickwickian senses of these words, a thing must have to be properly referred to as 'it.' Similarly with 'they.' Mates' condition, needless to say, is not open to this difficulty.

A third major ground of comparison between Mates' condition and the condition of intensional isomorphism arises in relation to the synonymity of sentences. With this we have not dealt so far, and to it we now turn.

C. SYNONYMITY OF SENTENCES

Mates' condition of synonymity, as it is stated by its author and in the modified form in which we have utilized it, is not directly applicable to sentences unless we state it in the following way: "Two single, compound or complex sentences, in the grammatical sense of these terms, are synonymous in a language L if and only if they may be interchanged in each single, *compound* or *complex* sentence in L, as the

[1] To show with *logical certainty* that no word or phrase in English is synonymous with (say) the word 'is,' we would need to substitute for that word *every* other English word or phrase, in the sentences in which it ('is') occurs or can properly occur. Since this is impossible in practice, our condition can only give us, in practice, a high degree of probability of the non-synonymity of 'is' with any other English word or phrase.

case may be, without altering the truth value of that sentence." But even if it is stated in this form, in does not hold universally. It does not hold in respect to *all* compound or complex sentences in which two or more sentences may be interchanged, unless we exclude certain sentences containing modal operators and indirect discourse about *names* of expressions. (We have seen how Mates excludes names of expressions from the language L to which his condition is intended to apply.) If this exclusion is not made, we could frame sentence forms such as (1) "A believes that 'X' means the same as 'X,'" (2) "A knows that 'X' means 'X'" (3) "It is necessary that A believes that 'X' means the same as 'X.'" And it is clear that the truth values of the corresponding statements may change if we substitute, say, "'X' means the same as 'Y,'" in (1), "'X' means 'Y'" in (2), and "'X' means the same as 'Y'" in either the first or the second clause, but not in both clauses, in (3); where 'Y' is an expression synonymous with 'X.' It is a commonplace that a person may not know that two particular expressions are synonymous. He may not even know whether or not a given expression has a synonym in the same language; especially, though not only, where the synonyms occur in different languages. This may be true even if he knows the meaning of one of the expressions.

Mates' condition on the other hand comes out with flying colors, though Mates shows this only negatively, in respect to sentences which contain indirect discourse, with or without modal operators. But it breaks down in respect to sentences which contain *names* of expressions together with the expressions 'synonymous with,' 'has the same meaning as,' or 'means the same as.' Thus take the sentence "Whoever believes that D believes that D." (I am borrowing this from Mates, where 'D' is the abbreviation of a sentence, e.g., "John is curious.") Now substitute for D any other sentence D′ which is synonymous with it (e.g., "John is inquisitive"). The statements which the resulting sentence makes will all be true, like the statements which the original sentence makes; and this, we will notice, is independent of anybody's beliefs or knowledge. For example, it is always true that, whoever believes that John is curious believes that John is inquisitive, whether or not he knows or believes that 'curious' means "inquisitive" or 'inquisitive' means "curious," etc. The truth of the statement depends on the *meaning* of 'John is curious' and 'John is inquisitive' (on "D" and "D′") . However, Mates' rejection of G. I. Lewis' condition that synthetic sentences are synonymous if and only if they are logically equivalent, is based on an invalid argument. His argument is also invalid as applied to intensional isomorphism in relation to sentences; as it fails to show the alleged inadequacy of this condition of synonymity. Contrary to his contention, these two conditions do not break down in relation to sentences involving modal operators, for the same reasons which I just gave: the same reasons that make *his* own condition applicable to such sentences. Thus, if Jones – anybody – knows that he has one nose, he will also know that the number of his noses is equal to-($e^{\pi i}$), even if he does not know the value of the latter expression or even what the symbols in it stand for. For knowing that he has one nose is tantamount to knowing the state of affairs "having one nose"; which is also the state of affairs "having a number of noses equal to-($e^{\pi i}$)." Hence it cannot be validly argued that "(He) has one nose" and "the number of his noses is –($e^{\pi i}$)" are *not* synonymous because the statements which can be framed from the sentences "Jones knows that he has one nose" and "Jones knows that the number of his noses is –($e^{\pi i}$)," do not always have the same truth value.

The same is true, in a sense of 'believe' to be explained, if Jones – anybody – believes that he has one nose; though this necessitates a distinction which is concealed in the case of the notion of knowing. For perhaps in one ordinary sense of 'believe,' it is not the case that whoever believes that he has one nose believes that the number of his noses is equal to-($e^{\pi i}$). When I therefore say that whoever believes that he has one nose *believes* that the number of his noses is equal to-($e^{\pi i}$), I am thinking of the existence of a concept in the particular person's mind which may be indifferently characterized as the concept *having one nose* or *having a number of noses equal to-($e^{\pi i}$).* If, however, by "believing X" or "having an idea X" we understand something psychological rather than logical, Mates will be right in holding that the sentences considered "might well have opposite truth values." The same remarks are seen to apply to Mates' criticism of the condition of intensional isomorphism, if we consider the sentences "Whoever believes that D, believes that D," and "Whoever believes that D, believes that D́"; where 'D' and 'D́' are abbreviations of two intensionally isomorphic sentences. But let us note that these things do not invalidate the conditions of logical equivalence and intensional isomorphism as conditions of synonymity of sentences. Moreover, if they did invalidate them, they would also, and to the same extent, invalidate Mates' own condition of synonymity. Our contention that our condition is applicable to sentences involving modal operators and indirect discourse is based on the fact that we have understood the words 'believe,' 'know,' 'hold,' etc. in a logical and not a psychological sense. But – and this is the essential point – the inapplicability of the three conditions where 'believe,' 'know,' etc. are understood in a psychological sense, is not a result of any flaw in these conditions (this is not to say, however, that they are flawless). It is due to the fact that, in one sense, one may know that D is D without knowing that D is D́ – where 'D' and 'D́' are synonymous sentences – because of the nature and limitations of one's *knowledge*. The following consideration shows that the limitation in the applicability of these conditions is extraneous to their general adequacy or inadequacy in relation to *other* classes of sentences. Suppose that a sentence 'D' is synonymous with another sentence 'D′.' Now substitute 'D́' for 'D' in its second occurrence in "Whoever believes that D, believes that D." On our present interpretation of 'believe,' the resulting sentence will sometimes give us a false statement; whereas the original sentence will be true in all instances of its use. The conclusion is then either (i) that there are no synonymous sentences at all occurring in the same language or even in different languages – which is absurd; or (ii) that the outcome of the substitution rests on some other ground than the synonymity or the non-synonymity of 'D' and 'D́'; or (iii) that it rests on an untenable interpretation of 'believes.'

It is true, notwithstanding all this, that logical equivalence is not a sufficient positive condition of synonymity of sentences. But it is a necessary, i.e., a (sufficient) negative condition of synonymity. Not all logically equivalent sentences are synonymous; but all synonymous sentences, excluding sentences which involve model operators and indirect discourse, are (also) logically equivalent sentences. An example of logically equivalent sentences which are non-synonymous is "The Evening Star is a planet" and "The Morning Star is a planet." Intensional isomorphism, by contrast, does seem to give us, within the same limits as those just noted, a sufficient as well as a necessary condition of synonymity. As in the case of phrases, the meaning of a sentence as a whole – the state of affairs it signifies – can be characterized in terms of the meaning, hence the intension, of the individual words that compose it. For the meaning of a sentence is a logical function – in the same sense as an ordinary literal phrase – of the words that compose it, and of the syntactical relations between them.

So far we have concerned ourselves with the discovery of necessary and sufficient *conditions* of synonymity in regard to the different classes or ordinary expressions: with features which are common to and characteristic of one or more classes of expressions. None of the conditions we have discovered through an analysis of the uses of the term 'having the same meaning as,' however, furnishes us, as such, with a definiens; with an explication of the ordinary meaning of these terms. For if the meaning of an expression is distinct from extension and intension, even where an expression can properly be said to have the one or the other or both, neither extensional isomorphism nor intensional isomorphism can be identified with the meaning of 'has the same meaning as.' It is also clear, I think, that Mates' condition of synonymity is no different in this respect from the other conditions. The meaning of a sentence partly determines the truth values of the statements it can make in various contexts. Nevertheless, a sentence lacks a truth value, even though it has some meaning as an expression. Indeed, a sentence cannot make statements, which have a truth value, unless it has some meaning to begin with. Let me add here that Mates' condition, as stated by its author and as I have discussed it, is applicable only to declarative sentences; it is inapplicable to interrogative, imperative and other classes of non-declarative sentences. Whereas, I need not add, the majority of sentences of the latter type (those which are non-absurd) do possess meaning as a whole. That condition can however be extended to non-declarative sentences; perhaps without much difficulty. This can be done, for instance, by stipulating that two interrogative (imperative, etc.) sentences are synonymous if and only if the declarative sentences "corresponding" to them satisfy Mates' condition of synonymity. Its logical adequacy would then depend on the success with which we can give an appropriate characterization of a declarative sentence "corresponding" to an interrogative (imperative, etc.) sentence. But however successful such an attempt may be, synonymity and Mates' condition as extended would remain distinct.

The next major question we have to ask is to what extent, if at all, the three conditions of synonymity we have discussed can supply us with workable *criteria* of synonymity of expressions. Since we do sometimes attempt to discover whether or not two given expressions in ordinary language are synonymous, and sometimes declare that this or that expression is or is not synonymous with another given expression, we could perhaps answer our question by considering what criteria of synonymity we actually use. If we do so, we find, I think, that we frequently use different criteria in relation to different types of expressions. In the case of individual words which refer to or name existent things, we sometimes employ the notion of extensional isomorphism or non-isomorphism; though even here, I think, we more often employ, in effect, the notion of intensional isomorphism. Similarly we appeal to this latter notion in respect to phrases which name existent things, and expressions which name non-existent things (centaurs, satyrs). In other cases, where either of the two notions cannot be utilized, we appeal to some extent to Mates' condition.

There are at least two rather important differences between the former two conditions and Mates' condition as furnishing us with criteria of synonymity. First, there are definite ways in which we can discover whether or not two expressions have the same extension or intension. That is discoverable, for instance, by finding out how these expressions are actually employed in ordinary contexts. In contrast to this, there does not seem to be a handy and reliable way of discovering whether or not a given expression in a language L can be interchanged with some other expression in each sentence in L *without* altering the truth value of the statements that can be made by that sentence. Second, and this is connected with our last point, we can never actually be sure, on Mates' condition, that two synonymous expressions are *really* synonymous; since we can never actually exhaust the number of sentences, and hence statements, in which the two expression can be interchanged. In contradiction to this, our two other conditions enable us to determine with greater – I would not say perfect – assurance, in respect to a certain type of expression, that two given actually synonymous expressions *are* synonymous. The type of expression I have in mind are expressions which refer to and mean *sensible* things. Where the expressions are not of this type, the degree of assurance actually attainable will be less; reaching its lowest point in respect to vague (better, "extremely" or "hopelessly vague expressions of this type). This is certainly one main area where philosophy in general and philosophical analysis in particular can satisfy a real need; for many of the expressions with which philosophy traditionally deals name or mean nothing sensible; and some of these are also vague in one degree or another.

PART TWO

CHAPTER FIVE

SEMANTIC ANALYSIS I

In the first part of the present work we considered some important topics by way of preparing the ground for a critical study of philosophical analysis. With that we pass to a detailed consideration of the major types and forms of philosophical analysis themselves, as we have outlined them in chapter one. The type of analysis to be considered first is "semantic analysis"; and we shall begin with that form of it which we have labelled "Semantic Analysis I." The other forms of "semantic analysis," as well as the major forms of "extra-linguistic analysis," will be taken up in turn in succeeding chapters.

It will be generally agreed, I think, that the analysis of individual words, purely as symbols, does not concern philosophy. The study of the morphology of words forms part of the subject-matter of linguistics: of philology, phonetics, and prosody. The analysis of phrases and clauses into their components and the tracing of their relationships in the analysed expression, is also a part of linguistics. Grammar, which is a branch of the latter, is interested in the roles which words, phrases and clauses play in sentences. (What grammarians call "grammatical analysis" and "parsing" are two forms of this.) But grammatical analysis is one form of the analysis of *sentences* into their component clauses (in the case of compound and complex sentences), phrases and, ultimately, component words (in the case of simple, compound and complex sentences). And the composition of sentences is certainly of interest to philosophy. But philosophy is interested in the meanings and other types of uses of words in sentences (or stated in terms of concepts, in the concepts they express), and in the logical relations between them. Similarly philosophy is concerned with the meanings and other types of uses of sentences themselves, in actual and possible contexts of discourse. In contrast to this, linguistics is concerned with the usage of words and combinations of words, including sentences, and in their syntactical relations.

I said that the analysis of verbal expressions purely as symbols is not a form of philosophical analysis. This does not preclude the possibility of there being a form of philosophical analysis which is about *both* non-verbal objects – for instance concepts – *and* verbal expressions in some sense of 'about.' As a matter of fact, we shall see that there is at least one form of philosophical ("semantic") analysis which is both about non-verbal objects and verbal expressions.[1]

The view that in philosophical analysis, or in one important form of it, the analysandum is a concept (or a group of concepts related in certain ways, a proposition) or a meaning, has been widely held in the history of philosophy. G. E. Moore, a great contemporary advocate and practitioner of analysis, goes as far as to claim, in speaking about his own conception of it, that "... I never intended to use the word 'analysis' in such a way that the *analysandum* would be a *verbal expression*. When I have talked of analysing anything, *what* I have talked of analysing has always been an idea or concept or proposition, and *not* a verbal expression ...."[2]

Moore's conception of analysis which will be the subject of this chapter, and to which I shall henceforth refer as "reduction analysis,"[3]

[1] C.H. Langford, in "The Notion of Analysis in Moore's Philosophy," *The Philosophy of G.E. Moore*, pp. 321-342, presents a view of philosophical analysis where the analysandum and the analysans are allegedly verbal expressions. An example he gives is: "'X is a small Y' means what is meant by 'X is a Y and is smaller than most Y's.'" For our discussion of and reply to this, see the latter part of this chapter.

[2] *The Philosophy of G. E. Moore*, p. 661. Italics in original. It should be mentioned that Moore identifies a concept and the meaning of a verbal expression.

[1] A. R. White, in his *G. E. Moore* (Oxford, 1958), Chapter V, shows that Moore envisions three different conceptions of analysis: analysis as inspection, as division, and as distinction. The second of these is the form of analysis with which I am concerned in this chapter. Analysis as inspection essentially consists in the introspective inspection or scrutinizing of a concept or proposition before the mind; while analysis as distinction consists in "*either* (1) ... drawing attention to, pin-pointing, and enumerating the various meanings of a given ambiguous expression and of other expressions considered relevant to it; or (2) ... saying, or describing, how one particular meaning of an expression which interests us is to be distinguished from and related to other meanings both of the same expression and of other expressions." (*Ibid.*, pp. 74–75). This last activity can be regarded as an aspect, or the first stage of what I refer to as "exhibition analysis," and is accordingly discussed in chapter six. As for "analysis as inspection," White's discussion convincingly shows, it seems to me (*Ibid.*, pp. 66–72) the fatal flaws from which this view suffers; and I can do no better in the present context than to refer the reader to it. Apart from this, "inspection" or "scrutiny" in Moore's sense does not really constitute a form of (philosophical) *analysis*. "Holding something before the mind," if this expression can be given any literal meaning, can perhaps be preparatory to its analysis, say by division. It itself can hardly be regarded as analysis, either in the ordinary meaning of this word or in any philosophical meaning that, with the necessary changes, conforms to the former. Nevertheless, it would be analogous to analysis to some extent if it is considered as the direct mental apprehension (what some writers would call the "intuition") of the *contents* of the concept "held before the mind." This is the way in

is too well known, at least in outline, to require a detailed exposition of it here. His writings are also full of actual instances of analysis. Moreover, his conception and practice have been discussed or criticized so often and so extensively that, for our purposes, we can do no better than to refer the reader to them. In the main, I shall concern myself with Moore's conception, and his practice of analysis as providing us with an important actual formulation and application of the form of analysis constituting the subject-matter of the present chapter. There are other forms of reduction analysis in contemporary philosophy, such as the form of it advocated and practised by the logical atomists. But we shall not discuss these at all in this chapter or elsewhere in this book. Enough has been written about them, and they have been sufficiently criticized for us to attempt that here. For a somewhat detailed study and criticism of them the reader is referred to J. O. Urmson's *Philosophical Analysis*.[1] But the chief reason for our neglecting them in the present work is that these forms of reduction analysis are inextricably tied up with a particular conception of language, of philosophy and (in the case of the form of it held by logical atomism) with the relation between language and the world ("facts"). Whereas I am concerned in this work with what I believe are methods of analysis that can be usefully employed by many philosophers, even by those with widely divergent preconceptions and approaches to philosophy. Thus in the case of Moore's form of reductive concept-analysis, for instance, we have something which can be employed – to the extent to which it can be usefully employed at all – independently of Moore's (or any other) form of the sense-datum theory; or of his other specific epistemological or metaphysical views. This is true despite the fact that the sense-datum theory is complementary to his conception and application of reduction analysis. In some cases, the method cannot be properly employed without effecting certain changes in it, to suit the particular

which Moore himself thinks of this activity; for example, in his discussion of "good" in *Principia Ethica*. Since Moore identifies the meaning of an expression with the concept it expresses or is presumed to express, this activity is tantamount, for Moore, to an inspection of the meaning of an expression; and the apprehension of the contents of a concept held before the mind is therefore an awareness, or a full awareness, of the meaning of the expression which conveys that concept. But we must add that for such an awareness to have objective validity, it must rest on the particular person's knowledge of the ordinary meaning of an expression, of how the expression is customarily used in ordinary discourse, if it is an ordinary expression; and how it is used by experts in the particular field, if it is a technical expression. But this itself may involve analysis as "discrimination," or even full-scale "exhibition analysis." It logically carries us, therefore, to these forms of analysis. (See also later in this chapter, and chapter Six.)

[1] (Oxford, 1956).

philosopher's orientation or presuppositions. But it can always be readily adapted in this way.

In dealing with Moore's conception of reduction analysis, I shall attempt to point out certain features of his theory and practice which have tended to be overlooked or to be insufficiently emphasized, but which are important for an understanding of semantic analysis as a whole, apart from their value within the general framework of Moore's philosophy.

As is well known, Moore attempts in his celebrated *Principia Ethica* to show that "good" is indefinable, in the sense of not being reducible into simpler constituents (qualities). For he regards goodness as a simple quality, like yellow. From this, and from what Moore says and does in the rest of that work and in other writings, it is seen that he frequently conceives analysis (in the process-sense) as the conceptual breaking down or reduction of a complex *quality*, *object* or *state of affairs* into its simpler elements, in some sense or senses of these words to be discovered. In the case of physical objects, Moore's sense-datum theory provides the necessary analysis (or, at least, one main way in which they may be analysed). He regards physical objects as partly analysable in terms of sense-data; and correspondingly, statements about physical objects, such as "This is a hand," as partly translatable into sense-datum statements. These sense-data are the ultimate simples with which the analysis of sensible objects, carried far enough, will terminate; or the ultimate subject of statements about sensible objects. But the precise ontological relation between physical or sensible objects and sense-data is a question to which Moore does not succeed in giving an unequivocal answer. It is a question with which he wrestled to the last. Suffice it to note here, however, that Moore holds that the sense-data of a physical object may perhaps sometimes coincide with a part of the latter's surface. In any case, the sense-data are not parts of the object, in any sense of 'part.' Their relation to the object concerned is therefore different from the relation which obtains between, say, the head, trunk, legs, etc. of a horse and the horse as a whole.

That Moore frequently conceives of analysis as the reduction of a complex *thing* into simpler elements is clearly seen in the way in which Moore illustrates a real definition; which is what he supposes analysis is concerned to arrive at. Taking 'horse' as an example, he says, "... We may [when we define 'horse'] mean that a certain object, which we all of us know, is composed in a certain manner: that it has four legs, a head, a heart, a liver, etc., etc., all of them arranged in definite relations to one another." [1] This also indicates that, in this particular instance or sort of analysis, Moore is thinking of the analysis as decomposition into qualitatively differentiated quantitative parts; in contrast to the (partial) analysis of physical objects in general in terms of sense-data. As for "good," it is to be presumed that Moore is thinking of qualitative and not, or not also, of quantitative analysis in stating that "good" is unanalysable; since he regards "good" as a quality. For it is meaningless to speak of a quality as quantitatively unanalysable. That he is thinking of "good" as unanalysable into other qualities is also seen from the fact that he speaks of it as a "simple quality." He does not, however, tell us what it would be like for a quality to be a "complex," a "non-simple" quality; and he certainly does not give us any examples of such presumed qualities.

Yet, and whatever his actual view may have been, Moore does as a matter of fact *distinguish* "good" from other alleged simple qualities, such as "yellow," by regarding it as an "intuitively" apprehended, non-sensible, non-natural unique quality. These distinguishing features – or the more positive of them – together with its character as a "consequential property," can therefore be properly regarded as features of "good" itself. Insofar as it allegedly possesses these features, it *can* be regarded as analysable, as "complex" instead of "simple"; and we can regard Moore himself as giving us an analysis of it in giving us these features, however much he may insist that it is really unanalysable.

We should note in fairness to Moore, however, that though there is a possible sense in which we can speak of analysing the "simple" quality "good" (supposing it to be a quality), and even perhaps such sensible qualities as yellow and red, this analysis differs from the (really) quantitative-qualitative analysis of horses and hares, and from the purely qualitative analysis of complexes of qualities (or "complex qualities," if we wish to use such a locution). The alleged features of "good" are features of *a quality*, are second-order characteristics; whereas the qualities composing a complex of qualities are themselves

[1] "The Indefinability of Good," *Readings in Ethical Theory* (New York, Appleton-Century-Crofts, Inc., 1952), edited by Wilfred Sellars and John Hospers, p. 71.

Moore is quite inconsistent in his use of quotation marks and indifferently speaks of the definition of 'good' and of "good." He thus fails to distinguish the definition, or the meaning, of the expression 'good' and the analysis of the alleged quality "good" ("goodness"). As a matter of fact, using 'definition' in a philosophical and not in an ordinary sense, he speaks of defining, and the indefinability of, the quality "good." Whereas we would ordinarily speak of defining, and of the definition of, words; and of analysing, and the analysis of, (a) words – though as we saw, it is meaningless to speak of the *philosophical* analysis of words–, (b) uses, meanings or concepts, and (c) objects, states of affairs, and the like.

qualities of *objects*, are first-order qualities, not qualities of qualities. Similarly with the qualities which differentiate one quantitative part of an object from its other quantitative parts. Moore speaks of "good" as unanalysable (as "simple") because he does not appear to regard the distinguishing of the features of single qualities as a form of analysis. Nevertheless, insofar as his "scrutiny" or "inspection" of the concept of goodness enables him (as Descartes thought intuition enabled him) to *distinguish* "good" from any other qualities, such as all natural qualities, Moore is actually practising analysis as discrimination. It is noteworthy that this latter, at least in this and similar cases, seems to be an aspect, or at least an outcome of the "scrutiny" of the concept *good*. It is clear, however, that analysis as discrimination can be thought of as a logically separate activity, independent of "analysis" by inspection.

The import of Moore's view of analysis as reduction or division is clearly seen if we consider an alternative way of looking at it. That way of looking at it is sketched by Bertrand Russell in his early essay, "The Elements of Ethics," written under Moore's influence. To say that a concept is simple or unanalysable is to say that it is logically ultimate; that while other concepts can and may be analysed in terms of it, it itself cannot be analysed in terms of any other concept. An important consequence of this is that no propositions not containing that concept can have consequences which do contain it. For instance–to take Russell's own example – if the concept *good* is simple, "no propositions not containing this notion can have consequences which do contain it."[2] So if *good* is a simple concept we cannot, unless our premisses contain it, "... prove that the world is good, or indeed any other result containing the notion of good ...."[1] The significance of this for Ethics – specifically for the logical relation between statements about matters of fact and ethical statements – is evident to any student of that subject. If Moore's view concerning *good* is correct, then the attempt to deduce ethical conclusions from non-ethical premisses would result in what has been variously labelled the "factualist fallacy" or the "valuational fallacy."[2] (Indeed, it would also follow from this that a logically illicit process would be involved in any attempt to deduce consequences about "good" from *ethical* premisses that contain other ethical concepts, such as *right* or *ought*, but not *good* itself: were it not for the fact (according to the

[1] In *Philosophical Essays* (London, 1910). Reprinted in *Readings in Ethical Theory*, pp. 1–32.
[2] *Ibid.*, p. 7.
[3] *Ibid.*
[4] See W. K. Frankena, "The Naturalistic Fallacy," *ibid.*, p. 106f.

present view) that these concepts themselves logically presuppose the concept *good.*) But this is only one major consequence of Moore's view that *good* is a simple concept. For to say the latter is, for Moore, tantamount to saying, first and foremost, that *good* is the central or fundamental concept of ethics; in terms of which other ethical concepts (e.g. *right*) must be understood or analysed. Hence to attempt to define 'good' in terms of any other concept(s) would be to commit an error. It is important to note here that this does not mean or entail that the meaning of 'good' cannot be explained in terms of such ethical concepts as *right* or *ought*; for there is a definite logical relation between *good* and these other concepts, since the latter themselves are analysable in terms of the former. Thus Russell, in the essay cited earlier, says: "To explain what we mean by Good and Bad, we may say that a thing is good when on its own account it ought to exist, and bad when on its own account it ought not to exist." [1] But as Russell says, this (on Moore's own grounds) cannot be a definition of 'good.' Similarly if we take Moore's definition of 'right' (or instrumentally good) acts as those acts whose consequences, on the whole, are good. We can reverse this definition by saying that good consequences are those states of affairs which are produced by right acts. But this would not be, or contain, a definition of 'good': though, like a proper definition, it would be – or rather, can be made – an analytic statement. The crucial point is that for 'good' to be definable, there must exist concepts that are simpler than the concept of good itself, in terms of which 'good' is to be defined (or the concept good is to be analysed); but if that were the case, *good* would be complex, not a simple concept, contrary to Moore's view.

The upshot is that, on Moore's form of reduction analysis and his corresponding understanding of definition, a statement containing a given concept *A* may be stated in other words not containing any reference to *A*; in terms of other concepts *C* and *D* (say); and yet such a translation may not be regarded as a definition (or as containing a definition) of 'A' or an analysis of concept *A*. Such translatability is a necessary but by no means sufficient condition of a definition of 'A' or an analysis of *A*.

Returning to the concept *good*, we said that any attempt to "define" *good* in terms of other concepts would commit an error. If the latter concepts are non-ethical ones, the Naturalistic Fallacy is committed in one of the several distinct but related meanings of this phrase as employed by Moore. An error would also be committed – even if Moore

[1] *Op. cit.*, p. 4.

would not call it (a form of) the Naturalistic Fallacy – if the defining concepts are ethical in nature: *if* and *when* the attempt to "define" *good* means the identification of the property "good" with some *other* (here a non-natural) quality or property, or relation. Thus for Moore, if "good" is a *simple* property; hence if *good* is a simple concept, (1) all attempts to define 'good,' whether in ethical, non-ethical of partly ethical, partly non-ethical terms, would commit an error; to wit, the error of defining what is indefinable. But (2) since "good" is a (simple) *property*, it follows that all attempts to "define" "good" in terms of some quality, property, relation or something else would be tantamount to identifying "good" with some *other* quality or property, or confusing a property with a relation, etc. This is a consequence of Moore's conception of (real) definition as the logical outcome of reduction analysis. It should be emphasized, however, that the logical error of identifying "good" with something else is independent of the simplicity or complexity of the property "good": the error is equally committed if some "complex" quality or property is identified with something else, whether "simple" or "complex."

Our discussion of the concept *good* in relation to reduction analysis above applies, *mutatis mutandis*, to all other concepts that Moore does, or would, regard as simple or unanlysable; for example, to the concepts of sense-data. It should therefore give us a fair idea of the significance of Moore's reduction analysis; to the extent to which it can be usefully employed in philosophy.

Moore's conception of analysis, insofar as it relates to the analysis of objects, events, complexes of qualities or states of affairs, does not really concern us in the present chapter; since it is one conception of the type of analysis we called "extra-linguistic analysis," rather than of semantic analysis. I mention it, however, because Moore himself does not distinguish it – or does not distinguish it clearly – from the latter type of analysis [1]; and because, though different, it is essentially related to reductive concept-analysis. These points are illustrated by what Moore says concerning the notion or concept of "good" in the following characteristic passage:

> My point is that 'good' is a simple notion, just as 'yellow' is a simple notion; that, just as you cannot, by any manner of means, explain to any one who does not already know it, what yellow is, so you cannot explain what good is. Definitions of the kind that I was asking for, definitions which describe that real nature of the *object* or *notion* denoted by a word, and which do not merely tell us what the

[1] Cf. C. H. Langford, "The Notion Of Analysis In Moore's Philosophy," in *The Philosophy Of G.E. Moore*, p. 342.

word is used to mean, are only possible when the object or notion in question is something complex.[1]

The same point is also seen in the way in which Moore passes immediately from the foregoing passage to the "definition" of a horse (an object) in terms of its "many different properties and qualities," all of which can be enumerated but which, he believes, cannot be defined. "They are simply something which you think of or perceive, and to any one who cannot think of or perceive them, you can never, by any definition, make their nature known."[2]

The shift from objects to concepts or vice versa, or Moore's reference to them in the same breath, is no accident. It results from and indicates the relation that exists between Moore's (form of) reductive concept-analysis and one form of "extra-linguistic analysis." Thus there is a correspondence between the complexity or simplicity of a concept, or its analysability or unanalysability, on the one hand, and, on the other hand, the complexity or simplicity, the analysability or unanalysability of the *things subsumed* under it as a class-concept or universal. A complex concept is complex, hence analysable, because things subsumed under it are complex and hence analysable; or things subsumed under a concept are complex and analysable because they are subsumed under a complex and analysable concept. The same applies to the simplicity or unanalysability of concepts and of things. Logically it makes no difference which way we look at the relation between concepts and the things subsumed under them. But in the type of case in hand, we must regard the complexity or simplicity, the analysability or unanalysability of *things* as primary or basic, and the complexity or simplicity, analysability or unanalysability of the corresponding concepts as derivative. It is because a horse is a qualitatively (and quantitatively) complex thing that the concept *horse* is "complex"; hence the latter is analysable because the former is analysable. In the same way the concept *yellow* (or *good*) would be "simple" and unanalysable in Moore's sense because, for Moore, yellow (or "good") is qualitatively simple, unanalysable.

So far so good. But – and here the differences between the analysis of concepts and the analysis of objects begin to appear – the constituents of a given object in the present sense are qualities or properties literally possessed by its "constituents," its quantitative parts. In contrast to this, the less complex or the completely simple "terms" of

[1] "The Indefinability of Good," *Readings in Ethical Theory* (New York, Appleton-Century-Crofts, Inc., 1952), edited by Wilfrid Sellars and John Hospers, p. 70. Italics mine.

[2] *Ibid.*

a "complex" concept are themselves other concepts; and they are not in any straightforward sense possessed by the original, " complex" concept. The concept *horse* is not literally analysable into the concepts *four legs, head, heart, liver,* etc.; and these, in turn, are not analysable into other, "simpler" concepts of the same sort – such as the concepts of the various kinds of cells of which the head, the heart, the liver, etc. are composed; and so on. But Moore ultimately analyses concepts of, and propositions about, physical objects (partly) into concepts of, and propositions about, sense-data. Since the sense-data of an object may or may not be identical (indeed, Moore is not sure at all whether or not they are ever identical) with a part of its surface, the relation between a horse and the sense-data of the horse is a very complicated and different relation from the kind of relation obtaining between the horse on the whole and its head, legs, liver, and other anatomical parts.

What then is the precise relationship between the concept constituting the analysandum and the concept(s) constituting a given stage of analysis, the analysans at that stage of analysis? And what is the precise relationship between the analysans at one stage of analysis and the analysans at another, say a further, stage of analysis? To answer these questions, it is necessary to turn to verbal expressions and their meanings. The ordinary concept *horse* is what it is because the word 'horse' ordinarily *means* (is used to mean) a four-legged animal of a certain description. The ordinary meaning of a verbal expression determines the nature of the concept which comes to be ordinarily expressed by it. Similarly, a given technical meaning of a verbal expression *gives rise* to and determines the nature of the technical concept which it expresses in certain contexts. My point now is that the concepts *animal, four-legged, long-necked, hooved,* etc., in *certain logical relations to one another* – the relation expressed by the phrase "a four-legged, long-necked, hooved ... animal" – constitute an analysans of *horse* because the word 'horse,' in ordinary discourse, has the *same meaning* as the phrase "four-legged, long-necked, hooved ... animal,"[1] which expresses the concepts *four-legged, long-necked, hooved,* etc.

In the same way, the "simpler" concepts, related in a certain logical manner, constitute the analysans of the concept *horse* at a further stage of analysis, S_1, because they are concepts that are similarly expressed by a phrase synonymous with the phrase "four-legged, long-necked, hooved ... animal." In other words, the analysans of 'horse' at stage S of analysis can be regarded as a new analysandum in relation to which

[1] I am assuming that this phrase is tightened to describe a horse uniquely.

certain concepts, connected in a certain manner, constitute an analysans. The final stage of analysis will be reached when the last analysans is composed of "simple," ultimate concepts that are thermselves incapable of further analysis (i.e., concepts of single qualities or properties).[1]

It is clear that the present account would escape circularity only if the (ordinary) meaning of an expression 'X' is not identical with the (ordinary) concept expressed by 'X.' It is, thus, not open to Moore himself; since he does identify a concept with the meaning of the expression which conveys that concept. The foregoing discussion itself implies that a meaning is not the same as a concept, since it assumes that a given verbal expression ordinarily expresses a given concept *by virtue*, or *as a result*, of its having a given ordinary meaning. But I have already attempted to show in chapter three this *is* true: the meaning of an expression and the concept conveyed by it are distinct. I have also attempted to trace the precise logical relation between the two.

I stated that in any proper analysis the expression conveying the analysans *Y* must be (by the very nature of reduction analysis as understood by Moore) synonymous with the expression conveying the analysandum *X*. That is, that the synonymity of 'X' and 'Y' is a necessary condition of *Y*'s being a proper analysans of *X*. This, as a matter of fact, is Moore's own view. I shall now elaborate on this matter in some detail.

(a) Let us note, in the first place, that I am *not* asserting that if two ordinary verbal expressions have the same meaning, then the concept ordinarily expressed by the one can, *ipso facto*, serve as an analysans of the concept ordinarily expressed by the other. In other words, I am not asserting that synonymity of 'X' and 'Y' is a sufficient condition of Y's being a proper analysans of X. For though what I *have* said seems to me to be true with respect to the sort of analysis we are dealing with here, the statement that synonymity is a sufficient condition of a proper analysis seems to me to be false except if duly limited or qualified. For one thing, it is false if the verbal expression expressing the proposed analysans is a single word, i.e., is a synonym of the verbal expression expressing the analysandum in the sense in which the word 'synonym'

[1] The following passage, quoted from Paul Marhenke's "Moore's Analysis Of Sense-Perception," gives us a clear picture of the different stages involved in the analysis of perceptual propositions partly in terms of sense-data: "... The stages in the analysis of the proposition "I see an A" can be sketched very rapidly. (a) "I see an A" is equivalent to "I see_1 $this_1$ and $this_1$ is an A." (b) "$This_1$ is an A" is equivalent to "$This_2$ is a part of the surface of A," or, alternatively, "The thing which has a surface of which $this_2$ is a part is an A." (c) "$This_2$ is a part of the surface of A" is equivalent to "$This_3$ (i.e., the sense-datum) stands in a certain relation to $this_2$ (i.e., the surface)." (*The Philosophy of G.E. Moore*, pp. 260–261.)

is used in ordinary discourse and in standard grammar books. For example, the concept *evil* does not constitute an analysans, hence does not provide us with an analysis of the concept *bad*. We cannot, with its help, construct a real definition of the expression 'bad'; whereas the proper analysis of a concept, of the present form, does seem to yield a real definition. The verbal expression representing the analysans should be a set of words related in some manner or other.[1] In this way we would attain one form of clarity, one way of understanding the analysandum. And clarity and understanding are one major aim of analysis. C. H. Langford stipulates that:

> The analysans will be more articulate than the analysandum; it will be a grammatical function of more than one idea. One who uses the verbal expression representing the analysandum will mention objects of a certain class; one who uses the verbal expression representing the analysans will mention these same objects, but will mention them descriptively by reference to other kinds of objects.[2]

The last sentence is true only where the verbal expressions conveying the analysandum or the analysans are referring expressions. Where they are otherwise, the verbal expression conveying the analysans may mention, or may imply a reference to, nothing at all.

(b) The second point we should note is that our account implies that if two expressions 'X' and 'Y' are not synonymous, the concept(s) expressed by 'Y' cannot constitute, jointly or severally, an analysans of the concept expressed by 'X.' Thus the concept expressed by the definite description 'The Evening Star' does not constitute an analysans of the concept expressed by 'The Morning Star' because, among other things, 'The Evening Star' does not have the same meaning as 'The Morning Star' in the relevant ordinary sense of 'meaning.'

D. S. Shwayder, in his "=," says the following about the statement "The Morning Star is the same as The Evening Star":

> If I say that the Morning Star is the same as the Evening Star what I say is *not* that "The Morning Star" and "The Evening Star" have the same meaning or even refer to the same object; what I do say is that the brightest heavenly body different from the moon which is sometimes seen to precede the rising of the sun in the east is the same as that heavenly body which is at other times brightly seen in the west after the setting of the sun. From what I say it certainly does, in some sense or other, *follow* that the two expressions considered may within a limited variety of sentence contexts, be substituted one for another. But what I say or

[1] This does not mean, as we shall see later in this chapter, that the analysans is to be regarded as composed of at least two concepts.

[2] *Op. cit.*, p. 326.

assert is an empirical fact about heavenly bodies, it is not an assertion about language....[1]

I agree that the statement referred to by Shwayder does not *assert* that the 'The Morning Star' and 'The Evening Star' have the same meaning, or that they refer to the same object. But I do think that the statement "The Morning Star is the same as the Evening Star" logically *implies* that the two descriptions it contains refer to the same object(s). That is, the proposition that the two descriptions refer to the same object follows deductively from the (true) proposition expressed by the foregoing statement, together with the (true) tacit assumption that the "Morning Star" and the "Evening Star" are the referents of 'The Morning Star' and 'The Evening Star' respectively. (However, "The Morning Star is the same as the Evening Star" does *not* imply that 'The Morning Star' and 'The Evening Star' have the same *meaning*. This can be easily seen by considering that that statement is true, whereas it is false that our two definite descriptions have the same meaning.) Moreover, I cannot share Shwayder's view that the statement, as it stands, states or asserts that the "brightest heavenly body different from the moon which is sometimes seen to precede the rising of the sun in the east is the same as that heavenly body which is at other times brightly seen in the west after the setting of the sun." [2] This is what an astronomer, a man who knows to what *object* 'The Morning Star' and 'The Evening Star' refer, who knows that the object concerned is bright and is sometimes seen to precede the rising of the sun in the east, and so on (i.e., knows the actual empirical characteristics of the object) *may* have in mind, may intend to mean, by the statement. But the statement, as such, says just what it says, means what it says: that the Morning Star is the same as the Evening Star. Let us note further, that the concepts expressed by 'the brightest heavenly body different from the moon ... in the east' (call them M), do not and cannot constitute an analysans of the concepts expressed by 'The Morning Star.' Similarly with the concepts expressed by 'the heavenly body which is at other times ... the setting of the sun' (call them E) and 'The Evening Star.' The first two expressions, and the latter two expressions, respectively, certainly refer to the same object. They are, nonetheless, not synonymous, just as 'The Morning Star' and 'The Evening Star' are not synonymous (see chapter four). As the same time – and not accidentally – M and E do not provide us with a clarification of the

[1] *Mind*, vol. LXV, No. 257 (January, 1956), p. 18. Italics in original.
[2] *Ibid.*

concepts that *are expressed* by 'The Morning Star' and 'The Evening Star,' respectively. M and the concepts expressed by 'The Morning Star' are about *different* features or aspects of Venus; similarly with E and the concepts expressed by 'The Evening Star.' This last point indicates that in a correct analysis of a concept expressed by a *referring* expression, the expression expressing the analysans must describe (a) the referent of the expression expressing the analysandum; and (b) the same features or aspects of the referent that are named by the expression conveying the analysandum. The second condition, (b), seems to be required only where the expression expressing the analysandum is a definite description. For instance, it is not required where the expression expressing the analysandum is a single word (general name), or even, perhaps, an indefinite description. For in these cases, the expression would refer to its referent as a whole, not to any specific feature or aspect of it; hence the analysans, if it describes the particular referent, will, *ipso facto*, clarify the analysandum.

(c) Semantic analysis of concepts, of the form we are concerned with in this chapter, and as we envision it, is by no means limited to concepts expressed by referring expressions, or even referring-type expressions in general. This form of analysis is equally applicable to concepts expressed by non-referring types as expressions. Moore, in his own understanding of concept-analysis, unnecessarily restricts its scope, in effect, to concepts expressed by referring-type expressions. His constant use of the concepts *horse* and *yellow*, which are of this type, and *good*, which he regards as of this type, illustrates this. The reason, as we have seen, is that his conception of concept-analysis as the reduction of a "complex" concept to its "simple" constituents, is thought of by him as – and necessarily involves – the conceptual decomposition or division of complex things, such as objects, into qualitatively differentiated parts, constituents or elements. Let us note, however, that concept-analysis, envisioned in this fashion, is really applicable to concepts expressed by referring-type expressions that do not name anything actually existing (e.g., to the concepts *centaur* and *satyr*), as well as to those that do. This is the reason why I said that concept-analysis in his sense is restricted to concepts expressed by *referring-type* expressions, and not to those expressed by referring expressions. For whether or not Moore would concur with this, it is certainly possible to analyse a concept such as *centaur* by conceptually decomposing the imaginary being, "centaur," into qualitatively differentiated parts – head of a man, trunk and legs of a horse, etc. (It is also possible to think of a centaur in terms of certain theoretically possible sense-data; even though a "centaurish patch" has never been actually perceived by anyone – at least not by psychologically normal people.) It is clear, nevertheless, that this cannot be done on the basis of empirical observation of any members of the class of centaurs, as one can do by observing horses, say; since centaurs are not to be met with in our actual world. On what basis, then can we analyse concepts such as *centaur* and *satyr* – and, indeed, concepts that are not expressed by referring-type expressions at all; i.e., concepts expressed by non-referring-type expressions, if such concepts exist? The answer to this question, as will become clear in the following chapter, leads us to a different form of concept-analysis. For the answer is: by analysing the meanings of the expressions that convey these concepts. That form of analysis, as a philosophical method, is different from reduction analysis. But as we shall show in chapter six, there is a close logical relation between the two methods. Since this constitutes the subject-matter of the following chapter, I shall not pursue the matter here. However, we shall say something about it in later parts of the chapter.

Our view (which is also Moore's view) that the expression expressing the analysans (call it 'A') must be synonymous with the expression expressing the analysandum (call it 'C'), brings us face to face with the so-called Paradox of Analysis stated by C. H. Langford in the essay earlier alluded to. According to it, if 'A' has the same meaning as 'C,' the analysis will be trivial as stating a "bare identity"; if 'A' and 'C' do *not* have the same meaning, the analysis will be incorrect.

In order to deal with this Paradox, I shall take as my point of departure Max Black's attempt to resolve it.[1] Taking Moore's favorite example of analysis: the analysis of the concept *brother* into the concept(s) *male sibling*, Black expresses the Paradox in the following way:

"(1) The concept 'being a brother' is identical with the concept 'being a male sibling.'" This statement, if true, seems to be saying exactly the same thing as (2) "'To be a brother is the same thing as to be a brother.' But it is obvious that these two statements are not the same; and obvious also that nobody would say that by asserting 'To be a brother is to be a brother' you were giving an analysis of the concept 'brother.'" [2]

Concentrating on the chief points in Black's resolution of the Para-

[1] "The 'Paradox of Analysis,'" *Mind*, vol. LIII, No. 211 (July, 1944), pp. 263–267.
[2] *Ibid.*, pp. 263–264.

dox,[1] my first comment is that an (any) analysis of concepts cannot be properly expressed by an *assertion* of identity between the concepts involved, as Black holds. We consequently cannot express it by some such statement function as "the concept C *is identical with* the concept A" (in Black's example: "The concept 'being a brother' is identical with the concept 'being a male sibling'"). A proper analysis of concepts, for instance the analysis of *brother* into *male sibling*, may take the form: (3) "A brother is a male sibling," or, consequently, (4) "To be a brother is to be a male sibling," or (5) "Being a brother is identical with being a male sibling." But these do not assert or express a numerical identity of any *concepts*, but rather the numerical identity of the *referent* of the verbal expressions 'brother' and 'male sibling,' referred to by the concept *brother* or *male sibling*. The identity of the concepts concerned is logically implied, not asserted or stated, in the sentences expressing the results of the (process of) analysis. The sentence "the concept *Being a brother* is identical with the concept *being a male sibling*," (1), is not equivalent to (3), (4), or (5) – the three variant formulations of the results of the analysis. It states what is only implied in these sentences; it makes explicit what is implicit there. The meaning of a sentence, in the ordinary sense of 'meaning' relevant here (sense (a)), is neither identical with, nor includes, nor is a part of what is implied by the sentence. "Mean" and "imply" here are contradistinguished, contrasted.

The same holds if the analysandum and the analysans are expressed by non-referring, and not as in the above example, by referring, expressions: whether they are non-referring types of expressions, or referring-type expressions that do not actually refer to anything existent. For example, it applies to such concepts as *existence* [2] and *centaur*, respectively.

Further, *if* we speak of a concept as the meaning of an expression, as Moore does, we can substitute 'meaning of' for 'concept' (together with the appropriate changes) in sentence (1). We would then get the sentences "the meaning of 'brother' is identical with the meaning of 'male sibling'" (6), or its logical equivalent, " 'brother' means the same as 'male sibling'" (7). Obviously, however, (6) and (7) do not express an analysis of concepts; and what is more important, they cannot be properly regarded as expressing any philosophical analysis at all – not even, we might add, of the verbal expressions 'brother' and

[1] The reader can readily see that Black presents the Paradox somewhat differently from Langford; also that Black's implied final conclusion differs slightly from Langford's conclusion.

[2] See my "On Existence," *Methodos*, vol. 9, Nos. 33–34 (1957), pp. 65–76.

'male sibling.' Moore makes the cogent remark that sentences of type (6) and (7) should not be considered as instances of analysis, since they merely assert that two expressions have *some* the same meaning. They do not mention the meaning of either expression, or say what the meaning of either is. This indicates, among other things, that, for analogous reasons, Moore would rightly not regard (1) as expressing an analysis.

Let us add that there is no contradiction at all between this and our account of the analysis of concepts where the expressions representing the latter are non-referring expressions. For I only maintained there that in a correct analysis of the kind under consideration, the verbal expressions representing the analysandum and the analysans, respectively, must have the same meaning. I did not say, and as just stated, I do not hold that the analysis must be stated in either of the general forms represented by (6) and (7) above.

My second comment is that even if (1) is true, (1) and (2) do *not* have the same meaning in *any* sense of the term 'having the same meaning'; hence the paradox, in the form Black puts it, does not arise at all. The reason has already been stated in relation to (1) and (3), and the latter's equivalents; namely, that (2), in contrast to (1), does not state or even mention anything about concepts, let alone about particular concepts. It simply says what it says: "To be a brother is the same thing as to be a brother." This sentence, and the same applies to all "tautologies," *can* "say" something, perhaps even different things, and does serve a function or make a point, when and if it is employed in actual contexts of ordinary discourse – despite what formal logicians would say about it. (Imagine, for instance, how Moore could use this sentence in a lecture, to illustrate or emphasize his point that "something is what it is and not something else" – whose famous application, the "Naturalistic Fallacy," has become so influential: "Gentlemen," he might say, "to be a brother *is to be a brother*." And he could add: "Nothing more, nothing less.") But what it "says," or can say, in its actual uses is obviously quite different in meaning from what (1) says. This sentence is also different in meaning from (3), (4) and (5). The transition from (3), (4) and (5) to (1), and the transition from (1) to (2), cannot therefore be effected. Hence the supposed triviality of (3), (4) and (5), and their not expressing any analysis at all, is not logically established by Black's form of the Paradox.

The triviality of (3), (4) and (5), their not expressing any analysis at all, *is* what has to be shown. For the Paradox of Analysis, as formulated by Langford, arises on the assumption that the meaning of (1) is the same as that of (3), (4) or (5). Now sentences (3), (4) and (5) are more or less the same in meaning; they are not exactly identical, due to the use of 'to be' in (4), and 'being' and 'identical with' in (5), etc. But suppose we ignore the relatively slight differences in meaning: does (3), (4) or (5) have the same meaning as the trivial and "tautological" (2) – "To be a brother is to be a brother"? On the face of it, the answer seems to be Yes; since 'male sibling' is synonymous with 'brother.' If the former is replaced by the latter, we clearly get (4); and we get something very close in meaning to (2) if we do the same with (3) or (5). Stated generally, if we use the sentential function "x is yz" in place of "A brother is a male sibling" and other sentences of the same sort, including (roughly) (3), (4) and (5), it may be thought that " 'x is yz' is identical in meaning with 'x is x' " validly follows from the function "x is yz." For 'x' can be validly substituted for 'yz' in "x is yz," without change of meaning, giving us "x is x." As against this prima facie plausible but nonetheless erroneous view, the following should be said:

In the first place, the substitution of 'x' for 'yz' would be legitimate if, but only if (a) 'x' and 'yz' have the same meaning in *all* the senses or meanings of the expressions that happen to take their place (if each has two or more senses or meanings); or if (b) the one expression is substituted for the other in the sense or senses in which they are identical; assuming that they are identical in at least one but not all their senses or meanings. The expressions 'brother' and 'male sibling,' for instance, have the same meaning in one sense of 'brother' and in the one and only meaning of 'male sibling': since 'brother' can also mean "friar" as well as "male sibling." Hence 'male sibling' can only be properly substituted for 'brother' in certain occurrences of the latter.

Secondly and more importantly, the symbols in the function "x is zy" are all "used" and not "mentioned": the function is about "x" and "zy" – whatever these may be in any particular substitution in the function – not about 'x' or 'yz,' which name "x" and "yz" respectively. Whereas in the sentential function "' x is yz' is identical in meaning with 'x is x,'" something different obtains. Here all the symbols in the function "x is yz" (also "x is x") are mentioned. It follows that from "x is yz" – at least from it alone – the desired conclusion, "' x is yz' is identical in meaning with 'x is x,'" cannot be logically derived. This does not, of course, mean or even show that the last sentential function cannot be used to make true statements; that if someone asserts that, say, "'A brother is a male sibling' *is* identical in meaning with 'A brother is a brother,'" he would be making a false assertion. Further but related considerations, however, show that all assertions of this form would be false, whatever examples we may choose.

This brings us to our third point. In the propositional function "x *is* yz," where " x is yz" is asserted, the function does not state, mention or even imply the sameness of *meaning* of 'x' and 'yz' – of any symbols, for that matter. If 'x' and 'yz' have the same meaning, it would logically follow that "x" *is* yz"; but the opposite is not necessarily true. "x is yz" may be true even when it is false that 'x' and 'yz' have the same meaning. The following are therefore involved in asserting "x is yz":

(a) The function *states* (but it may *mention* other things as well) that any object, quality, occurrence or state of affairs signified by 'x' is identical with any object, quality, occurrence signified by 'yz.'

(b) The function logically *implies*, in a sense of 'implies' which is different from "entails," that the characteristics and other features "yz-ness" are numerically identical with the characteristics and other features "x-ness" (or vice versa).

However, the reason why Moore himself regards a sentence such as "A brother is a male sibling" as providing us with an (a correct) analysis of the meaning of 'brother' or the concept *brother* is not the fact that 'brother' and 'male sibling' *name* or *refer to* the same things, with all its logical consequences. It is the fact – among other things – that 'brother' and 'male sibling' *mean* the same thing: which is the reason why they also name the same things. Hence in our further consideration of "x is yz," we must add the stipulation that 'x' and 'yz' are to be understood as synonymous expressions. From this stipulation, it logically follows (it is implied) that these two expressions *express numerically one and the same concept*. In other words, the logical conjunction "x *is* yz" *and* "'x' and 'yz' are synonymous" implies that 'x' and 'yz' express the same concept.

Further, the notion of the identity of the meaning of 'x' and 'yz' implies that the symbols said to be identical in meaning are distinct as "types" and not merely as "tokens"; since the expressions '... has the same meaning as ...,' '... is identical in meaning with ...' are ordinarily used, hence have meaning, only in relation to symbols of different "types." [1] Hence "'x' means the same as 'yz,'" or the conjunction of this and "x *is* yz," implies that 'x' and 'yz' are symbols of different

[1] Thus it would be odd to say, for instance, that 'x' has the same meaning as 'x'; for instance, that 'brother' has the same meaning as 'brother'! Note also that 'type' in its present employment has a different meaning from 'logical type.' For many, if not absolutely all synonymous expressions belong to the *same* logical type.

"types." On the other hand, "x *is* x" neither states and/or mentions what "x *is* y" states and/or mentions, nor logically implies what it implies – whatever "x *is* x" might imply (e.g. that something is identical with itself).

It follows that even if "'x is yz' *is* identical with 'x is x'" were true in some sense of 'identical,' that would not mean, entail or imply that "x *is* yz," as expressing the results of an analysis, is trivial; provided that it satisfies Moore's own conditions of correct analysis (even if only the synonymity condition). As a matter of fact, "x *is* yz" would be the basis of a correct *definition* of 'x' (or 'yz'). The definition would state part of what "x *is* yz" logically presupposes for Moore as a correct analysis – namely that 'x' is synonymous with 'yz.' It would also logically imply (a) that characteristics, etc. "yz-ness" are numerically identical with characteristics, etc. "x-ness"; and (b) that 'x' and 'yz' express numerically the same concept. For[1] "x *is* yz," *ex hypothesi*, logically presupposes the synonymity of 'x' and 'yz'; it thus *explains*, by implication, what 'x' means. It tells us what characteristics or other features "x" has. The function "x *is* yz," hence the particular analysis whose expression it is, would only be trivial if the features implicitly referred to are themselves "non-defining" features relative to the ordinary meaning of 'x.' This would be the case if knowledge of these features does not enable us to identify situations in which 'x' may be properly employed.

The foregoing discussion also shows that there is a sense in which conceptual analysis of the form we have been dealing with is both about concepts – the analysandum and the analysans – and the verbal expressions used to convey the analysis. As we have seen, a sentence expressing a correct analysis in Moore's understanding of this necessarily includes the synonymity of the verbal expressions expressing the analysandum and the analysans respectively. But we also saw in chapter three that the logical content of a concept is determined by the meaning of the verbal expression conveying it. From these two premises it logically follows that a sentence expressing a correct analysis logically implies that the analysans and the analysandum, in Moore's use of these terms, are really one and the same concept. It is therefore in the sense of "logically imply," not in the sense of "state," that a sentence expressing an analysis is both *about* certain verbal expressions and the concepts expressed by them.

[1] In the case of the other usual form of (reported) definition, which states that 'x' means "yz," the situation partly resembles and partly differs from the above.

Moore believes that the suggestion that an analysis is about both concepts and verbal expressions would be open to the difficulty that –

> This ... would be compatible with its being the case that ... (an assertion such as) "To be a brother is the same thing as to be a male sibling" is merely a *conjunction* of the assertion "The verbal expression '*x* is a brother' has the same meaning as the expression '*x* is a male sibling'" with some other assertion which is merely an assertion about the *concept* "*x* is a brother" and not an assertion about any verbal expression. But I do not think this can possibly be the case: what would the second assertion in this supposed conjunction be? [1]

It is readily seen that our suggestion is not faced with this difficulty, if it is a difficulty. In our view, "To be a brother is the same thing as to be a male sibling" is not a conjunction of the sort Moore gives above. For in order to be so, it has to state or affirm something about the verbal expressions '*x* is a brother' and '*x* is a male sibling,' and about the concept, if it is *a* concept, *x is a brother*. Whereas what it actually "says" about these things is only logically *implied* by it, hence cannot give us an equivalent sentence, whether simple, complex or compound. Also, Moore thinks that there cannot be a conjunction of the sort he mentions because he implicitly identifies the *meaning* of '*x* is a brother' with what he regards as the *concept x is a brother*. If these two are not identified – and on the basis of our discussion in chapter three they cannot be identified – the second assertion in the supposed conjunction *could* be "The concept *x is a brother* is numerically identical with the concept *x is a male sibling*." For then, that statement would not be a mere repetition of the first assertion in the conjunction; that is, "The verbal expression '*x* is a brother' has the same meaning as the verbal expression '*x* is a male sibling.'"

I shall now make some remarks about Black's way out of the Paradox of Analysis, by way of rounding off the present discussion.

Black attempts to resolve or dissolve the paradox by showing that Moore's example of analysis, i.e., "A brother is a male sibling," involves a certain relation between the concepts *brother, male* and *sibling*. This relation might be expressed by speaking of the concept *male sibling* as the "conjunct" of the concepts *male* and *sibling* – analogously to a mathematical *product* in the numerical example ("$21 = 3 \times 7$"). The three concepts in Moore's example involve a relation which holds between three concepts whenever the first is the conjunct of the other two. This shows that "A brother is a male brother" cannot be justifiably regarded as expressing the same proposition as "A brother is a brother." The relation between our three concepts is a "non-identical

[1] "A Reply To My Critics," *op. cit.*, pp. 665–6. Italics in original.

relation" (I presume Black means a relation of non-identity); whereas "A brother is a brother" asserts a mere identity. This "way out" of the Paradox seems to me to be correct as far as it goes. However, Black's notion of a "conjunct," which is left unexplained, produces a sense of uneasiness: except if we regard the analogy to a mathematical product, to which he appeals, as an explanation. For in many respects the concept *male sibling* is quite different from "3 × 7" or any other mathematical "product"; and though one may perceive that "A brother is a male sibling" involves a relation between the concepts *brother, male* and *sibling* which is absent in the case of "A brother is a brother," one cannot see the precise nature of this relation unless what Black calls a "conjunct" is clarified. Furthermore, it appears that Black assumes that three concepts are involved in "A brother is a male sibling," and not two concepts only: the concept *brother* and the concept *male sibling*. If that assumption is made, Black's view that ". . . even if we interpret Moore's example of an analysis as being *only about* 'concepts' there is no good reason for regarding the analysis as issuing in an *identity* between concepts . . ." [1] obviously follows. For *a* concept (in our case the concept *brother*) cannot be numerically identical with *two* concepts (*male* and *sibling*)! And if it has been shown that an analysis does *not* issue in an identity between concepts, it would follow that ". . . no further measures are needed to take care of the 'paradox of analysis.'" [2] Our point, however, is that only two concepts are involved in the example in hand, and in similar examples. The "conjunct" of *male* and *sibling*, to use Black's expression, is one new concept – the concept *male sibling* – which is logically resolvable into the concepts *male* and *sibling*. It is, I think, misleading or incorrect, or perhaps even meaningless, to speak of the concepts *male* and *sibling* as forming a new concept, the concept *male sibling*, by becoming logically related in a certain manner. A more proper way of putting the matter is that the verbal expressions 'male' and 'sibling' which, individually, express *male* and *sibling* respectively, come to express the one concept, *male sibling*, when they are grammatically related in a certain manner. That is, when 'male' is used as an adjective qualifying 'sibling.' This notwithstanding, and notwithstanding the identity of the concepts *brother* and *male sibling*, the sentence "A brother is a male sibling" is not trivial; as I earlier attempted to show. The discursiveness of 'male sibling,' and its ability to clarify, are not prejudiced by the identity of the concept

[1] *Op. cit.*, p. 265. Italics in original.
[2] *Ibid.*

which it and 'brother' both express. The concept *male sibling* is not more complex, more "discursive," more "explicit" than the concept *brother*; since it is identical with that concept. The one concept, expressed in different words, is clarified by the use of the verbal expression 'male sibling,' which points out, be employing 'male' and 'sibling,' certain features in the object it names. Whereas 'brother' does not point out any features at all.[1] In this way 'male sibling' plays a clarifying role and expresses an analysis. We might say that it indicates or exhibits how 'brother' is correctly *used* in ordinary discourse; to what objects it is applicable. In this way of putting it, analysis consists in the discovery of the linguistic uses of any given verbal expression 'x'; which also means the discovery of the expression's uses in the *non*-linguistic contexts in which language as a whole is employed. A sentence of the form "x is a yz" may then constitute one way of exhibiting or indicating a use of 'x' that has been noted. This manner of speaking about analysis anticipates our discussion in the next chapter, and for the present I shall say no more about it.

Our solution of the Paradox of Analysis, it can be readily seen, is in perfect accord with Moore's own conception of reductive concept-analysis; and this, if true, is of considerable importance since the Paradox was first pointed out in relation to and as a result of Moore's own conception of analysis: in particular, the condition of synonymity which he lays down for any correct analysis. (Since the synonymity condition may form part of other, non-reductive forms of analysis, the Paradox is not confined to Moore's form of concept-analysis.) To see this, let us revert to our earlier example about the analysis of the concept *brother*. As we saw earlier, Moore analyses this concept in terms of the concepts *male* and *sibling*; which he considers as the simpler concepts to which the concept *brother* is "reducible." However, our view is – and this, it will be remembered, is our solution to the Paradox – that the phrase 'male sibling' as a whole expresses the same concept as the word 'brother.' Thus what Moore calls a process of "analysing the concept *brother* in terms of the two concepts *male* and *sibling* related in a certain way, is, in effect, and much more simply, the substitution for the *expression* 'brother' of another, more extended expression, 'male

[1] It is interesting to note that Black's analysis of "To lave inertia is the same thing as to have mass" is closer to our analysis here than his analysis of "A brother is a male sibling," since he regards the former statement as about both concepts and verbal expressions. But he speaks of the statement as "indicating," rather than as "implying," that 'having inertia' and 'having mass' are synonymous; and that this is achieved by the statement's mentioning or asserting, rather than implying, the concept *having mass* or *having inertia*, which both expressions express.

sibling,' which *means the same thing* and *hence expresses the same concept*. That it must necessarily express the same concept is a logical consequence of its being, for Moore, the expression conveying the correct analysans of the concept *brother*; by virtue of Moore's own stipulation that the expression expressing the analysans must be synonymous with the expression expressing the analysandum. Since Moore also identifies the meaning of an expression with the concept which it conveys, the identity of the concept expressed by the two expressions is immediately seen. (It is clear, however, that the identity of the concept conveyed by both expressions follows from the synonymity condition, whether or not the meaning of an expression is identical with the concept it expresses. This will be true, of course, provided that the meaning of an expression logically determines the concept conveyed by it. This, it will be recalled, was our position in chapter three.) One probable reason why Moore tended not to see this rather simple fact is his confusing use of the words 'analysandum' and 'analysans' to refer to concepts, rather than to verbal expressions: to the expressions which convey what Moore calls the analysandum and the analysans, respectively. (One main reason for this itself is Moore's identification of the meaning of an expression, which he regards as the object of analysis, with the concept conveyed by it.) For this means, or at least gives one the (false) impression – by the use of two different words, 'analysandum' and 'analysans' – that these words refer to different concepts. Further, it is possible and even likely that Moore's use of these expressions in the way he does itself is a consequence of his conception of analysis as reduction or division.[1]

The gain in understanding resulting from our way of looking at the relation between "analysandum" and "analysans," and therefore the relation between the expressions which convey them, lies in the fact that 'male sibling' brings out the meaning of 'brother.' So, instead of describing reductive concept-analysis as Moore does, in the very misleading language of division or reduction of a "complex" concept into "its" "simple constituents" – into *other* concepts related in a certain way – we can now say (in the light of our solution of the Paradox of Analysis) that "reductive" concept-analysis aims at bringing out the

[1] Let us emphasize here that the synonymity of the expression conveying the analysandum and the expression conveying the analysans is a necessary but by no means sufficient condition of a proper analysis. Another necessary condition, resulting immediately from Moore's conception of reduction analysis as "division" or "reduction," is the greater "simplicity" of the concepts constituting the analysans. Stated in this way, it necessarily follows that the analysans must be composed of at least two concepts, related in a certain way. And it is this which has given rise, or seemed to give rise, to the Paradox of Analysis.

meaning of a particular expression by discovering an extended (usually, a more extended) expression synonymous with it, which makes this meaning explicit. If the expression whose meaning is to be analysed is a referring or a referring-type expression, the expression which provides us with the analysis will be a phrase which names or refers to the same things that the former expression names or refers to. But the analysis is not, and need not be, confined to the analysis of these types of expressions. It applies – and our general statement of it ensures that it will apply – to the analysis of the meaning(s) of any verbal expression; whether it is a referring, a referring-type or a non-referring-type expression; and whether or not it is the kind of expression that expresses some concept. The fundamental question which remains, of course, is precisely how we can realize the goal of "reductive" concept-analysis understood in this general way; how we can discover or uncover what is involved in the meaning (or the uses) of whatever expressions we are concerned with. Or, in terms of Moore's own formulation of (reductive) concept-analysis, the question is how we can discover or uncover the "simple" concepts which constitute an analysis of our "complex" concept; and the precise relation between them. One major, and to my mind the most general and most adequate answer, which we shall elaborate in chapter six, is – by "exhibition analysis." [1] This means that, if our thesis is correct, reductive concept-analysis, in the case of any type of expression with which it may be concerned, must have recourse to "exhibition analysis" (and in that sense it must rest on it) in order to achieve its aims in the most complete way.

In the preceding section I stated one condition that any correct analysis of the form under discussion must fulfill: I mean that any expression conveying the analysandum must be synonymous with any expression conveying the analysans. This is one of the three conditions of correct analysis which Moore himself lays down. The second of these conditions, i.e., that "nobody can know that the *analysandum* applies to an object without knowing that the *analysans* applies to it," [2] we have already discussed in chapter one; and so I shall not say anything about it here. The third condition is that "nobody can verify that the *analysandum* applies to an object without verifying that the *analysans* applies." [3] This condition, like the second, is misleadingly phrased; and

[1] For Moore's own alternative answer to this, and for a discussion of the difficulties it encounters and the limitations that are imposed on it, see chapter ten.
[2] *Op. cit.*, p. 663. Italics in original.
[3] *Ibid.*

like it, it appeals to epistemological concepts that are irrelevant to an analysis' being or not being a proper analysis. Instead of being a necessary condition of a proper analysis, it really envisions a method for discovering whether any given analysis is a correct analysis.[1] The condition of correct analysis it implies is, I take it, that the features of an object X which ordinarily make the analysandum applicable to it (i.e., the conventional connotation of the expression 'x') must be qualitatively indentical with the features which ordinarily make the analysans applicable to given objects. Or, in other words, that the logical content of the analysans is identical with the logical content of the analysandum. If this is taken as the condition implied by Moore's "condition," it is certainly cogent in the light of our earlier discussion of the present form of analysis. For if the logical content of the analysandum and the analysans is identical, the analysandum and the analysans would also be numerically identical concepts (see chapter three). And the numerical identity of analysandum and analysans is, it will be remembered, a major feature, hence a necessary condition, of any proper analysis of the form under discussion. Indeed, it itself is a logical implication of our necessary condition: the synonymity of the expressions expressing the analysandum and the analysans respectively. Nevertheless, Moore's "condition" does not provide us either with a sufficient or a "necessary" criterion of a proper analysis. The same is true of it as a criterion of analyticity, in respect to the relevant class of statements. We can determine whether the concepts expressed by any given analysandum and any given analysans are identical by discovering whether the connotation of the verbal expressions expressing them is the same: therefore, whether these expressions are synonymous expressions. But this method is not the only one possible in the circumstances. It is also possible to find out the foregoing by observing how these verbal expressions are employed in actual discourse. Indeed, the former method itself logically rests on the latter method, as our discussion in chapter six will, I hope, show.

Further, as we have seen in the early sections of this chapter, the identity of analysandum and analysans is not a *sufficient* condition of a proper analysis.

[1] It also purports, therefore, to provide us with a method for testing the analyticity of one class of analytic statements: those made by subject-predicate sentences in which the grammatical subject and predicate are synonymous. It would be interesting, in this connection, to note the similarities between it and a criterion of statement synonymity advocated very recently by George Krzywicki Herburt in "The Analytic and the Synthetic," *Philosophy of Science*, vol. 26, No. 2 (April, 1959), pp. 104–113.

The upshot of the foregoing discussion is that Moore's third "condition" does not provide us with any new necessary or sufficient condition of correct analysis. We are still left with our old conditions. I might add that though we have concentrated so far on the synonymity condition, as we might call it, we can properly regard its four logical implications (i–iv) discussed earlier as providing us with four more necessary conditions of correct analysis. Or, more conveniently, we can regard all *five* conditions as merely different aspects of one and the same necessary condition.

The conditions of correct analysis which Moore lays down, and which we have discussed, have been severely criticized by many philosophers. I shall mention only a few of the more important criticisms. Thus G. J. Warnock maintains that Moore "... involved himself in some trivial embarassments by laying down conditions that any successful analysis must satisfy, which unluckily are partly too stringent, and partly too vague, for any analysis on these conditions to turn out successfully." [1] These, for Warnock, are minor difficulties, however, and he proceeds to state what he regards as two difficulties of a more serious nature. The second of these is that –

Moore involved ... himself ... in difficulties resulting from the unquestioned assumption that any analysis must be of a standard pattern. It was always to consist in providing a verbal paraphrase of what was to be analysed, in the form of a longer, more explicit, but strictly synonymous phrase or sentence. ... But the fact is that very many of our words and phrases are not thus tightly related to any more explicit synonyms, and can only be made to seem to be so by artificial devices. It is also true, and not less important, that this sort of analysis may sometimes leave out exactly what is of most philosophical interest.[2]

Warnock then illustrates these things by taking up Moore's "struggles with the concept of goodness."

Ernest Nagel criticizes Moore in much the same vein as Warnock. He expresses doubts about the importance and the clarificatory power of analysis as Moore conceives it. He holds that on the condition laid down by Moore –

It seems clear that whether an anlysis of a concept is possible depends very largely upon the accidents of the language one is using. Is the concept *goodness*, for example, analysable: Not if every expression for it (presumably in the English language) is not *synonymous* with any expression which may be used for the alleged analysans: ... Moreover, many expressions for concepts are highly vague, and it is most unlikely that more complex expressions can be found which are synonymous with the first in a given language. It is undeniable, nevertheless,

[1] *English Philosophy since 1900* (London, 1958), p. 25.
[2] *Ibid.*, p. 27.

that those concepts can be clarified in important ways, and that Mr. Moore has often given us a clarified view of some of them in spite of the absence of synonyms for them.[1]

The criticism levelled at the synonymity condition is particularly important, since that condition, hence all that it implies, is essential to the present form of analysis. The elimination of that condition, as a way of avoiding the criticism, is therefore not open to us. The only proper course to take is to concede that the present form of analysis is of limited value or utility in philosophy. Its usefulness is mainly confined to relatively uncomplicated cases of analysis; in general, to those cases where the results can be expressed in a relatively short and simple formula. Other limitations of the present form of analysis will be mentioned in the next chapter. We must, however, point out here that the difficulty which Nagel thinks is due to the supposed vagueness of many expressions for concepts, arises relatively infrequently in actual fact; since most ordinary expressions are not vague in the ordinary meaning of this term. However, the "marginal indeterminacy" of many ordinary expressions does raise a serious difficulty in respect to non-referring-type, and may sometimes raise a difficulty – a less serious one to be sure – in respect to referring-type, expressions. This and other difficulties or problems created by "marginal indeterminacy" have already been discussed (in chapter two) in connection with Flew's notion of "use" and "usage."

Although the analysis of individual concepts in the manner I have outlined in this chapter is of limited applicability, the analogous analysis (a) of a set of propositions constituting a "view," "doctrine" or "theory," into its component propositions, and (b) of an individual proposition into its "component" concepts (in a different sense of 'component,' however), has very considerable philosophical utility. The former is, indeed, a stage of analysis which may be practised in relation to any form of semantic analysis in philosophy; while the latter is a stage of analysis which often precedes the analysis or individual concepts in the manner described at some length in the present chapter. In both (a) and (b) analysis consists first in distinguishing the individual propositions or the individual concepts in the analysandum and then in tracing their logical relations to one another. In these respects the analysis is similar to the analysis of individual concepts.

[1] Review of *The Philosophy of G. E. Moore*, *Mind*, vol. LIII, No. 209 (January, 1944), p. 73.

CHAPTER SIX

SEMANTIC ANALYSIS II

In the preceding chapter I discussed in some detail one form of philosophical analysis – the analysis of concepts – which I had earlier classified under "Semantic Analysis." In the present chapter I shall discuss a second, related form of "Semantic Analysis." This form of analysis, it will be remembered, we have referred to as "exhibition analysis," borrowing a convenient phrase from Stephan Körner. Some, perhaps many, of the method's salient features, as set out and advocated by me here, are derived from or inspired by the pronouncements and especially the practice of the so-called later Wittgensteinians or Oxford (or Linguistic) Analysts. I am not, however, concerned with an exposition or analysis of the methods associated with these philosophers; nor do I claim that these thinkers would agree with the views here set out any more than the present writer accepts their own methods in their entirety. Similarly, my employment of the phrase 'exhibition analysis' is not intended to imply complete agreement on my part with Körner's understanding of what he calls "exhibition analysis."

The form of analysis which I discussed in the preceding chapter, in addition to the shortcomings I mentioned there, has the important shortcoming of not specifying *how* a "complex" concept is to be resolved into "simpler" concepts. To be able to do so, the method must appeal to something other than concepts themselves; which means that, as a method, it logically rests upon or requires some other form or forms of analysis without which it itself cannot function.

The concepts of empirical entities, whether physical or mental, can be analysed in the light of an *empirical* examination of either the quantitative parts and/or the characteristics possessed by the entities concerned, depending on their nature. This examination, depending on the manner in which it is performed and on the items it takes as elements, will result in different, or even different types of, "simples." And the manner in which the examination is performed, and the elements attended to, partly depend on the purpose of the analysis in any given instance. The purpose of the analysis also partly determines the point to which the conceptual resolution into elements is actually carried. On the other hand, the nature of the particular entity involved and the nature of the elements attended to determine the point to which this conceptual process *can* be carried.

The concept *horse* – taking one of Moore's favourite examples – can be analysed in terms of a horse's gross anatomy (head, legs, torso, etc.), its histological or physiological structure, and so on. In each case the process necessitates the employment of a form of analysis whose immediate subject-matter is not concepts but things; that is, a form of "extra-linguistic analysis." The precise nature, scope and value of this form of analysis will be discussed in its proper place in chapter eleven.

The foregoing remarks apply in general to such concepts as *justice, goodness* and *badness, rightness, wrongness, democracy, communism, humanism, time, red, green, hard* – and many other concepts of interest to philosophers.[1] For we can analyse these concepts by examining the particular entities which are subsumed under them. Thus we can analyse the concept *rightness* by examining particular acts that are, at a given time and in a given place, generally regarded as right acts. What is more, we can use this method whatever our view regarding the status of universals may be. The analysis of particulars in the manner indicated does not commit us to nominalism or preclude any form of logical realism.

So far I have indicated the logical dependence of the method of analysis discussed in the previous chapter on "extra-linguistic analysis." But – and this is the important thing here – the analysis of concepts is also dependent on "exhibition analysis," though in another way. Whether or not a given concept can be analysed by means of the method of "extra-linguistic analysis," it can certainly be analysed by means of the method of "exhibition analysis." This will become clearer when both methods have been discussed. Let me say here in anticipation that "extra-linguistic" analysis itself is logically, or methodologically, posterior to "exhibition analysis."

As I said in chapter five, the content of a concept is logically determined by the uses (actually, the meaning) of the verbal expressions which convey that concept in the language, ordinary or technical, in

[1] The above does not apply to logical and mathematical concepts. These concepts are analysable purely logically, conceptually.

which the expressions occur. From that it follows that a concept's content can be discovered and analysed if we discover and analyse the (ordinary or technical) usage of the expressions conveying it. But the method of "exhibition analysis" consists, broadly speaking, in the discovery of an expression's uses through the discovery and analysis of its usage in the language in which it occurs. Insofar as this is true, therefore, the analysis of concepts is logically posterior to and is based upon "exhibition analysis."

But this is not all. I said a little earlier that the analysis of certain types of concepts can be effected through an empirical examination and analysis of the corresponding empirical entities. This is true, but only in one sense. The content of an ordinary concept is logically determined by the uses – actually, that particular kind of use of it which we call the meaning – of the expression that conveys it. Where the expression refers to some empirical entity, an examination of its denotata will reveal the common features and/or "family resemblances" which they possess, including the features and/or resemblances comprised in the expression's connotation. And the latter features or resemblances constitute the logical content of the corresponding concept. Here a knowledge of the expression's meaning (which as we saw, is one kind of use of expressions) is necessary on two counts. We cannot know whether an expression refers to anything actual, and, if it does, precisely to *what* it refers, unless we first know the expression's meaning or meanings. We also cannot know what the connotations of the particular expression are without a knowledge of the expression's meanings.

An examination of parts of an expression's denotation, particularly of a large number of them, may reveal a part of the expression's comprehension; but only a knowledge of the expression's connotation can tell us which of the features in its comprehension form part of the content of the corresponding concept, and which do not. The analysis of the denotata of a referring expression cannot be of any help in the determination and the analysis of the corresponding concept, in the absence of prior knowledge of the expression's connotation, hence of its meaning.[1] Whereas a knowledge of the expression's connotation, arrived at through an analysis of its meaning, is sufficient for the determination of the logical content of the corresponding concepts.

To illustrate the foregoing points, let us again consider the concept *horse*. The actual observation of horses will reveal to us some of their

[1] For the way in which the proper employment of the method of "extra-linguistic analysis" itself depends on a prior utilization of the present method, see the beginning of chapter ten.

constituent parts and some of their features, which, as far as they go, can constitute "simples" in terms of which the concept *horse* may be, purely theoretically, understood. But not all these parts or features are "simples" in terms of which the ordinary (or the biological) concept *horse* that we have can be analysed. For example, we cannot analyse the ordinary concept *horse* in terms of the colors of different horses, their sizes, speeds, temperaments, or the shape of their eyes, ears, muzzles, and a host of other variable features.

The present method of analysis – and here I broadly follow the later Wittgenstein and the Oxford School – may be briefly or simply described as a method that attempts to clarify ideas, whether philosophical, scientific, mathematical or otherwise, through the discovery and the analysis of the ways in which we employ linguistic expressions in actual, concrete contexts. In the case of ordinary concepts, this is achieved through the discovery and analysis of the various everyday applications of the expressions which convey them. In the case of mathematical, scientific or other technical languages, this is achieved through an analysis of the way in which the experts in the particular field employ the relevant language. In terms of the narrower notion of meaning, the present method may be described as aiming at the discovery and analysis (the "exhibition," to use Körner's term) of the meanings of ordinary, mathematical, scientific or other kinds of expressions, through an analysis of the ways in which these expressions are actually employed. This involves or includes the discovery and analysis of the syntactical relations between individual expressions in sentences, and the logical relations between different sentences. It also includes the discovery and analysis of the possible relations between the different meanings or senses of one and the same expression, whenever an expression has more than one sense or meaning, and between each of these and the meanings of other expressions. In short, the analysis may be both semantical and syntactical in nature. Thus the analysis of the ordinary applications of 'right' (say) includes (a) the discovery and analysis of the different meanings and/or senses of the word; (b) the relations between these different senses or meanings: for instance, the relation between the moral and the legal uses of the word; and (c) the logical relation between its moral use(s) and the corresponding (moral) use or uses of such words as 'good,' 'ought' and 'duty.'

John Holloway, in a critical notice of Antony Flew's *Logic and Language*, First Series, distinguishes two movements or inquiries which have gone under the name of the "linguistic movement" in philosophy.

He regards the two movements or inquiries as "radically different in approach and method; perhaps also in permanence." [1]

> The first of these [which is our present method] might be called an empirical study of language in use, so as to discover what is done with it; and the characteristic method of this enquiry is to *differentiate* expressions from each other. The second is quite different: it is an enquiry deploying some of the discoveries made in the first enquiry to give controversial though perhaps correct solutions or dissolutions to known philosophical problems, and (though it may differentiate expressions to begin with) its characteristic method is ultimately to *assimilate* expressions.[2]

As described by Holloway above, the first method is gravely onesided. Whether or not it has actually been used only to differentiate expressions from one another, the method as I envision it includes the discovery and analysis of the relations between the uses of various words, phrases, sentences and groups of sentences. And this necessitates the differentiation of expressions whose uses are different, and the grouping together of expressions whose uses are similar or identical. (If the latter is what Holloway refers to as "assimilation," then his second inquiry is really a part of our method.) The same applies to the uses of the expressions themselves. Further, the differentiation of the uses of different expressions has a positive side. One cannot differentiate two or more things without, in so doing, learning something positive about them: not merely that a thing A is not thing B or that relation X is not relation Y, but also, to some extent, what A and B, X and Y are in themselves, as things or relations. This is again illustrated by our earlier example about the moral uses of 'right' and 'good.' In distinguishing between these uses of 'right' and 'good' (hence between right acts and morally good things *qua* right or good), we obviously discover at least some of the characteristics of morally right acts as opposed to good things, or of good things as opposed to right acts. We will also discover, if we wish to differentiate these as clearly and completely as possible, some of the relations between right acts and other things, such as good or bad motives; or the relation between morally good things and (say) other things that have goodness of some kind (e.g. good paintings, or good poems; good knives, chairs, cars, etc.). Thirdly, since the concepts of right acts and morally good things are logically related, the differentiation of right acts from morally good things may also, in the present case, throw light on the exact relation between the two.

[1] *Mind*, vol. LXII, No. 245 (January, 1953), p. 100.
[2] *Ibid.* Italics in original.

Various questions and problems arise in relation to "exhibition analysis." Some pertain to the mode of its employment or other specific aspects of it; others have a more general character, and concern its nature as a whole. One way of dealing with them would be to attempt to meet some of the many criticisms that have been levelled against it. For there is perhaps no single aspect of it that has not been criticized. Part of our concern will be to show that this method is a *philosophical* method of analysis; that it is not verbal or grammatical analysis, the type of analysis which a linguist would be interested in making. We shall have to show the philosophical *point*, as some philosophers put it, of this form of semantic analysis. The importance of this is difficult to exaggerate since many philosophers, I have observed, are indifferent or positively hostile to the method because they feel that it is purely verbal, linguistic analysis. This, I may say, was my own feeling only a few years ago, when I first came into contact with Wittgenstein's *Philosophical Investigations* and attended some lectures given by J. L. Austin, A. E. Duncan-Jones and Peter Strawson, among others. A not unrelated problem is to show clearly that this method is philosophically useful or significant. Not a few philosophers feel that indulging in "linguistic analysis" is an idle pastime – nay, that it is completely senseless. They do not see that anything is gained by a philosopher's "exhibiting" the uses or meanings of *ordinary* expressions, since anyone who knows a given language knows the meanings and other kinds of uses of expressions occurring in it. Or, if the function of the method is described, as it sometimes is, as the exhibition of the "rules of ordinary language," they retort that we all know these rules since we continually use them in ordinary discourse. A similar objection can be but significantly enough has not been raised respecting the usefulness of the philosopher's exhibiting the uses or meanings of technical expressions occurring in the natural sciences or in mathematics. For does not the natural scientist, or the mathematician, know what he is talking about when he employs his particular technical jargon?

Other questions or problems have already been dealt with to various extents. In chapter two I attempted to say what I mean by the term 'ordinary language' in speaking of the present method as partly concerned with the analysis of ordinary language. There I also distinguished, though only in a general way, between ordinary language and common sense beliefs: two things which are sometimes mistakenly identified with each other. A further clarification of this distinction will be attempted in chapter ten. It is clearly impossible, particularly within the scope of one chapter, to attempt to deal with all genuine problems or objections relating to the method. In addition to dealing with the problems or objections noted a little earlier, I shall therefore concentrate on a positive exposition and analysis of the method, and on its major philosophical applications. Actually, there is no better practical way of vindicating this method than to point out in detail the very considerable achievements it has to its credit; the valuable, in some areas even revolutionary, results it has given us in less than fifty years. I shall not attempt this here; but reference to some of these results will occasionally be made in the section that follows. Let me, however, remark parenthetically that the importance of the present method (apart from what I have said about it at the beginning of this chapter, in relation to concept-analysis) will become more fully appreciated if we recognize its relation to other philosophical methods of analysis and its far-reaching implications for philosophy as a whole. The chapters that follow should help to make this appreciation possible.

There are, to my mind, at least six major philosophical uses of "exhibition analysis":

(1) The first major use of the method is its exhibition of various features of ordinary language, of varying degrees of generality and philosophical importance. In this use of the method the object of analysis is a given ordinary language; and the results of the correct analysis are empirical facts respecting the nature of that language. The main point here is that this study of language is philosophical in character, not the sort which the linguist or grammarian is interested in. That is, the inquiry would constitute part of the Philosophy of Language; in the same way as the philosophical study of science constitutes the Philosophy of Science, and the philosophical study of art, Aesthetics and the Philosophy of Art. Its claim to being a philosophical inquiry partly lies in its aiming at a better understanding of ordinary language as an object of inquiry in its own right, as an empirical object. This includes the attempt to understand the *reasons* why ordinary language possesses the features it does possess; which, if pursued far enough, carries the inquiry outside or beyond language itself to man, the inventor and user of language, and to the world in which he lives. The attempt to relate language to the wider, non-linguistic matrix within which it arises – to human cultures and societies, human history, ultimately the nature of the world as a whole – is, as I conceive it, an important part of the Philosophy of Language. I say this particularly because this aspect of the

study of language has been neglected by many practitioners of philosophical analysis, especially the Oxford Analysts.

The methods that may be employed for the discovery of the precise relation of language to man and the world will be discussed in chapter ten.

I said that the attempt to understand why a given ordinary language possesses the general features it does, if pursued far enough, will take us to extra-linguistic phenomena. This is not to say, however, that it is impossible to discover any linguistic explanations of these features. But any such explanations that may be arrived at will themselves require explanation – a process which, sooner or later, carries us beyond language itself. The proper method for the discovery of linguistic explanations of less general linguistic phenomena is again our present method; and the present application of it illustrates one important form which the tracing of interrelations may take with its help. Here I might mention some general features that contemporary analytical philosophers think they discern in ordinary language, and which (assuming that they are genuine features of it), are in need of linguistic and/or empirical explanation. Among these are the "marginal indeterminacy" or some ordinary expressions (Max Black) or the "open texture" of empirical concepts (F. Waismann); the "stratification" of ordinary language (Waismann); the "defeasibility" of empirical concepts (Hart). Others are the vagueness of some ordinary expressions; and the (alleged) fact that the referents of many ordinary class names do not possess any determinate or relatively determinate characteristics in common, but only various criss-crossing "family resemblances" (Wittgenstein). A quite general feature of ordinary language that has also been pointed out by the present author in several of his published papers is "Standard" and "Non-Standard" Conditions regulating the correct application of various expressions. One kind of standard or normal condition arises in relation to the names of man-made artifacts or man-devised activities or processes, which involve the notion of *use* or *function* in their ordinary applications. Examples are 'table,' 'chair,' 'plane,' 'house,' 'cooking' and 'painting.' In their case, the standard conditions are those environmental and other conditions that are necessary for the full actual realization of the particular use or function involved in any given case. Thus the standard conditions relative to knives are those conditions which are necessary for the proper use of a knife *qua* knife; i.e., for cutting food, etc. A second, related kind of standard condition obtains in relation to art-names; i.e., names which involve the notion of a certain *aim* or *purpose* (or certain aims or purposes) in their ordinary applications. These conditions are necessary for an intact or complete work of art's being able to realize its aims as a work of art. They therefore constitute the perceptual, psychological and other conditions that are necessary for the enjoyment (and some are necessary for the full enjoyment) of an intact or complete work of art. In general, standard or normal conditions are those (kinds of) environmental and other (e.g. subjective) factors that are necessary for the (other factors are necessary for the full) causal operation or use of a given artifact or man-devised process or activity, as an instance of a certain kind; as called by a given general name. The corresponding non-standard conditions, on the other hand, are those that impede or completely prevent the causal operation of a given man-devised activity, a man-made artifact, and so on, *qua* this or that kind of activity, object, etc.

There are other sorts of standard conditions which "exhibition analysis" reveals; for example, the physical or other factors that constitute, or determine, what we call normal sense-perception; or those factors that constitute conditions of the possibility of a moral, as opposed to a non-moral act; or those factors which constitute conditions of a free as opposed to a compelled act; and so on and so forth.

Other general features of ordinary language or a part of it probably await discovery through careful employment of "exhibition analysis."

The use of "exhibition analysis" in order to *explain*, up to a point, the nature and working of ordinary languages, should be strongly emphasized. For there has been a very widespread tendency among those advocating and practising "linguistic analysis" to shy away from all attempts at explanation; to be satisfied with a description of observed features or aspects of ordinary language. Recently there have been encouraging signs of dissatisfaction with this restriction,[1] due, it appears, to a growing awareness that mere description barely scratches the surface of language; that it cannot satisfy the probing, inquiring intellect.[2]

[1] Cf. W. B. Gallie, "Art As An Essentially Contested Concept," *The Philosophical Quarterly* vol. 6, No. 23 (April, 1956), p. 101 and *passim*; and Strawson: "... Fully to understand our conceptual equipment, it is not enough to know, to be able to say, how it works. We want to know also *why* it works as it does. To ask this is to ask to be shown how the nature of our thinking is rooted in the nature of the world and in our own natures." *The Revolution In Philosophy* (London, 1957), p. 107. Strawson does not, however, distinguish linguistic explanation, explanation within a language, and extra-linguistic explanation. In speaking of explanation, he seems to have only the latter in mind.

[2] For some attempts to explain as well as to describe, using the method of "exhibition analysis," see my "Common Names and 'Family Resemblances,'" and "Art-Names and

(2) A second important use of the method, related to the first, is the discovery and analysis of the ordinary uses of particular verbal expressions which have been traditionally regarded as philosophically significant or important. I mean such expressions as 'know' and 'knowledge,' 'space,' 'time,' 'quality,' 'relation,' 'matter,' 'mind,' 'God,' 'good,' 'bad,' 'beautiful,' 'ugly,' 'free,' 'not free,' 'immortal,' 'mortal,' 'exist,' 'non-existent,' and a host of other expressions.

The discovery and analysis of the uses of such expressions is useful in another way. For it enables us to discover the ordinary criteria-features – whether determinate or relatively determinate characteristics, "family resemblances," or some other types of features – which something must possess in order that a given expression, in one of its ordinary meanings or senses, may properly apply to it. Once we have discovered the criteria-features involved in the paradigm or non-marginal instances of its application, we can, if we wish, frame an explicit *definition* of the expression as applied in paradigm, non-marginal situations. And it is a commonplace that, since Socrates, the attempt to frame real definitions of philosophically significant expressions has been one of the major tasks of philosophy. We shall say something more about the analysis of individual expressions later on. Let us merely note now that the more general features of ordinary language, discussed under (1), are discovered through the analysis of the usages of individual expressions. For instance, we discover the existence and nature of vagueness by noting and analysing, with the help of the present method, the usages of individual vague expressions. Similarly with "marginal indeterminacy," "family resemblances," etc. Wittgenstein's analysis of the ordinary usage of 'game' is a well-known illustration of this in the case of the notion of "family resemblances."

(3) A third major use of our method, which should be distinguished from (1) and (2) but especially from (1), is the elaboration of the "informal logic" of ordinary language. By this I mean such things as the discovery of the ordinary uses of the different so-called logical constants, and the nature of implication, contradiction, entailment, presupposition ane other kinds of possible logical relations between statements as they arise in ordinary pieces of reasoning. One of the most systematic

Aesthetic Judgments" (particularly the last part of the paper, where an attempt is made to go beyond the purely descriptive analysis of 'good' in aesthetic judgments offered by Helen Knight in her "The Use of 'Good' In Aesthetic Judgment" (*Aesthetics And Language* (Oxford, 1954), edited by William Elton). See also my "Works of Art and Physical Reality," *Ratio*, vol. II, No. 2 (January, 1960), pp. 148–161, for an attempt to explain why feelings and emotions are not included as an element in what we ordinarily call a "work of art."

accounts of these matters to date, as far as I know, is P. F. Strawson's *Introduction to Logical Theory*. Such an enterprise, as Strawson points out in outlining the aims of that book, will also "bring out points of contrast and of contact between the behaviour of words in ordinary speech and the behaviour of symbols in a formal logical system. . . ." [1] It will also help to "make clear . . . the nature of formal logic itself." [1] Thus exhibition analysis can contribute to logical theory (to the foundations or philosophy of logic, if you like) as well as to logic proper, formal and "informal." And part of its contribution to the latter will be the recognition, which the inquiries of Strawson and others have amply shown, of the significant fact that ordinary language does not constitute a neat, formal system.

(4) The fourth major use of "exhibition analysis," as I envision it, is the systematization of the categories of thought embedded in our everyday language and thinking.

This inquiry may be regarded as the subject-matter of metaphysics in one common sense of this expression. In some respects, this sense is not very different from one sense of 'metaphysics' which Kant distinguished in his *Critique of Pure Reason*; in which sense that work itself may be looked upon as a metaphysical treatise.[2] The major difference is that Kant did not think of the categories he drew up as being in any sense relative to ordinary language. It should be emphasized that an essential part of the present inquiry consists in laying bare, by means of "exhibition analysis" itself, the logical interrelations of the categories of human thought embedded in our everyday language and thinking. It is not enough merely to bring out the separate categories in isolation from one another. Kant's "deduction of the categories" in the *Critique of Pure Reason* is an imperfect and limited illustration of this "synoptic" endeavor: imperfect because, for one thing, he did not effect his systematization through an analysis of the ordinary language of knowledge, perception, understanding and so on.

The investigation outlined here, to the extent to which it involves the use of "exhibition analysis," should be distinguished from the three

[1] *Ibid.*, Preface.

[2] See *ibid.*, "The Architectonic of Pure Reason," pp. 508–509 in the J. M. D. Meiklejohn translation, 1930. Kant also distinguished a sense of 'metaphysics' in which the *Critique* is only part of a system of metaphysics. For a very recent, and as far as I know the only recent, attempt to present a systematic account of the categories of our thought as embedded in ordinary language, see P. F. Strawson, *Individuals: An Essay in Descriptive Metaphysics* (London, 1959). Strawson labels the inquiry he engages in in that work as "descriptive metaphysics," and defines its aim as the description of the "actual structure of our thought about the world . . . ," or the laying bare of the "most general features of our conceptual structure. . . ." (Introduction, p. 9)

uses of the method discussed under (1)–(3) above. At the same time its relationship to these, especially to (2), should be noted. For the analysis of ordinary categorial expressions may be regarded as part of the "exhibition analysis" of the uses of ordinary expressions we discussed there. It is here presented as a separate use of the method mainly in order to emphasize the special importance of the analysis and systematization of categorial expressions. For as we pointed out, it aims at a much more general view of language – or rather, of the conceptual framework embodied in language – than would result from an exhibition of the uses of individual philosophically-important expressions, or even of clusters of such expressions. This is even true in relation to our third major use of "exhibition analysis": the tracing of the "informal logic" of ordinary language. For though the actual or possible logical "moves" that are permissible in ordinary language depend, at least in part, on the categorial structure of the language, the tracing of the "informal logic" of ordinary language is neither identical with nor of the same degree of generality as the tracing of the categorial structure of language.

The foregoing four major uses of "exhibition analysis" are all concerned with the mapping of different elements or parts of ordinary language; though some also deal with the technical languages of the sciences, mathematics and formal logic. This mapping of ordinary language, we may note, helps us to employ more intelligently or effectively than otherwise a given ordinary language as a framework for ordering and communicating our philosophical, as well as our everyday, knowledge. Expressed in terms of concepts, many of the expressions and combinations of expressions occurring in any given ordinary language, inasmuch as they express concepts and thoughts, provide us with a conceptual framework in terms of which our philosophical, as well as our everyday thinking may be ordered, expressed and communicated. The conceptual frameworks provided by different ordinary languages may differ in structure or in conceptual content. Some may have a richer, a more refined or more sophisticated conceptual apparatus, capable of expressing finer shades of meaning or other subtle distinctions. For instance – to take an exotic example – I am informed that Eskimo is quite a subtle language, though its conceptual range is very limited: there are, I am told, no Eskimo words for "magazine," "wheel," or "car," or similar objects. The logical mapping of different languages enables us to pick out the language which best serves our philosophical purposes. The fitness of different ordinary languages to provide us with conceptual frameworks for the ordering and expression of philosophical knowledge (and/or scientific knowledge if and to the extent to which this may be desired or is necessary) partly depends on the degree of their development, sophistication or sensitivity. It also depends on the particular concepts or ideas that the philosopher has at his disposal at any given time; and on how precise, exact and accurate he wishes to be. That is, the utility of a given ordinary conceptual framework depends in part on the specific philosophical purpose it is intended to serve. If exactness, precision and conceptual subtlety are sought, a language like classical Greek or modern German may be the best choice; if what is sought is variety and range, then the best choice may be modern German or English.

Let us remember, however, that as regards human beings (about the gods we are ignorant), there is no conception – at least no proper analysis, ordering, expression and hence communication of thought – without or independent of *some* language that provides us with our *initial* conceptual equipment. Philosophical thinking, however much it may subsequently diverge from ordinary ways of thinking and expression, cannot but begin with some already-present ordinary language. To the extent to which it conforms to that language, it will be utilizing the latter's conceptual framework. But even if it departs from it, the nature and extent of the departure, hence the character of the new framework itself, will be unintelligible except in the light of the language from which it has departed.

A second point to remember is that the frameworks provided by different ordinary languages do not completely stand apart. They are translatable into one another to a greater or lesser extent depending on their structure, degree of development and extensiveness. I say "to a greater or lesser extent" because a given language may contain expressions or ways of speaking to which nothing corresponds in some other language or languages. I have already mentioned Eskimo in connection with the first. A good illustration of the second is given by F. Waismann. Waismann states that the question "What is a number?" is unaskable in Chinese. According to him, Frege was obsessed with the question "What is a number?" because of the fact that in English (or German) we speak of such things as "the number five." In Chinese, unlike English, 'five' is used only as a numeral in such utterances as 'five men,' 'five applies,' and the like. [1] Another example mentioned by

[1] "How I See Philosophy," *Contemporary British Philosophy* (London, 1956), edited by H. D. Lewis, p. 468.

Waismann is the distinction between "actor" and "action" – together with all its implications – in Indo-European languages.[1]

All this notwithstanding, it remains that the conceptual frameworks provided by English, Greek, Chinese or any other ordinary language are far from being *completely* language-bound. The conceptual framework provided by English is not an English conceptual framework; ideas expressed in Chinese are not themselves Chinese. More exactly or precisely, it does not make sense to speak of a conceptual framework or of individual ideas as English, Chinese, German, and so on. To speak in this way (whether affirmatively or negatively) is to commit a logical category-violation. The limitations imposed on their intertranslatability by differences in extensiveness, precision or subtlety can, theoretically speaking, be overcome. Only structural differences, I think, stubbornly stand in the way of complete intertranslatability, and prevent us from having a framework that is completely language-neutral.

(5) "Exhibition analysis" is the indispensable logical prolegomenon to philosophical "extra-linguistic analysis." It is the indispensable prolegomenon to the discovery, among other things, of the general features (if any) of limited parts or aspects of the world, or the pervasive features (if any) of the world as a whole, which scientific inquiry has so far ignored; or which has traditionally been regarded as a part of "doing philosophy." Since the exact nature and scope of this "extra-linguistic" philosophical analysis, as well as the precise manner in which "exhibition analysis" prepares the stage for it, will be outlined in chapter ten, I shall not say anything further about it here.

(6) The sixth and last important use of our method consists in the application of the kinds of analysis outlined in (1)–(3) above to traditional philosophical problems or "puzzles," to use a word that is fashionable at present. "Exhibition analysis," as understood in relation to (1)–(3) above is concerned, as I said before, with the study of language both as an end in itself and as a means to the better understanding of man himself, the inventor and user of language. The present use of "exhibition analysis" is also a means to the understanding of sonething other than language itself. But in its present use, the analysis of the different features or aspects of language outlined in (1)–(3) aims

[1] *Ibid.* The above should be distinguished from the idiomatic peculiarities of different languages that are not preserved in verbatim translations. But what the particular idioms *express* – more generally, the linguistic uses they have – can, at least theoretically, be rendered in other languages either as they stand or by the introduction of new expressions or turns of phrase.

at the rectification of error, the "dissolving" of philosophical "problems," "puzzles," "paradoxes" and "rival theories." It is corrective or therapeutic.

The student of philosophy, even the non-philosophical layman, is generally aware that the history of philosophy is chock full of erroneous views and doctrines, half-truths and startling exaggerations, paradoxes and even absurdities. (To mention only a few examples: the various classical conceptions of material and mental substances; the "views" of materialism, subjective, critical and objective idealism; Berkeley's identification or confusion of concepts and images; Kant's things-in-themselves; extreme scepticism; sensationalism; extreme rationalism (Cartesian-type or Hegelian-type); and so on.) This awareness is by no means a monopoly of linguistic analysts; nor have they been the first to point out or to attempt to correct these errors. The relative novelty of their idea partly lies in their claim that these errors are a result of a "misuse" or "abuse" of ordinary language: or of a particular technical language – depending on where the misused expressions occur. The precise nature of such "abuses" or "misuses" of language does not concern us here; something will be said about them in a later chapter. What does concern us is the fact that where philosophical errors *do* arise from "abuse" or "misuse" of language, the proper method for their diagnosis and rectification lies in a careful analysis of the particular language, or the ordinary uses of the particular expressions involved. Yet we must not suppose that philosophical errors are always a result of linguistic, and the corresponding conceptual, distortion; or that all the errors which philosophers have actually made or now make are due to this cause, or to this cause alone. At any rate, we can only discover whether these things themselves are true through an analysis of traditional philosophical concepts and views, and by comparing the concepts and corresponding expressions as employed there with the concepts and expressions as they occur in the relevant ordinary or technical language. For this purpose, "exhibition analysis"[1] has to be utilized.

In this connection I wish to emphasize that the correction of philosophical errors, the "dissolving" of philosophical "puzzles," is only *one* of the major tasks (even) of philosophical analysis. I say this because of the prevailing tendency among Linguistic Analysts to exaggerate this, therapeutic function of philosophical analysis and philosophy

[1] For an account of an indirect, negative method of uncovering misuses of language, see chapter eight.

as a whole. This tendency has become so strong that, in the hands of some of these philosophers, all or practically all philosophical *questions* have become transformed into philosophical "problems" or "puzzles." Consequently, they tend to regard any attempt to analyse the uses of expressions and the content of concepts which have been traditionally regarded as philosophically significant, simply in order to arrive at a better understanding of them, as sheer waste of time, or as completely misguided. This appears to be implicit, for instance in Wittgenstein's dicta that philosophical problems are not solved but dissolved, and that "the result of philosophy is not a number of "philosophical propositions". ..." The over-emphasis on the pragmatic function of philosophical analysis, the belief that the need for philosophical analysis arises only if and when ordinary language "has broken down," "has gone on a holiday"; that a question is a "borrowed question" unless it has given rise to a confusion, is strongly to be deplored.[1]

It is encouraging, however, that this is not the position of all Linguistic Analysts; also, that even when a philosopher professes to hold such a view, his actual practice is not always so narrowly confined. As Strawson rightly says: "This [the correction of distortion] is one of the tasks confronting the critical philosopher; and is worthy of a first mention, because so much of philosophy begins with paradox and the resolution of paradox. But it would itself be a paradox to represent the whole task of philosophy as the correction of philosophical mistakes." [2]

It is sincerely to be hoped that some day all the traditional philosophical "problems," "puzzles" or "paradoxes" we have will have been solved or dissolved. But it would be the height of irony if the only goal of philosophy were to eliminate itself. (Not that I seriously believe that the time will actually come when the philosopher will be left with no philosophical errors to correct!)

The critic of "exhibition analysis," even if his doubts about the utility of this method have been slightly dulled, will probably retain his doubts respecting what I said under (2) above. In particular, he may still be sceptical about the utility, or even meaningfulness, of analysing the uses of individual expressions in order that one may reach what I, together with many contemporary philosophers, claim to be a better understanding of them. As a matter of fact, it is mainly this aspect or

[1] To mention only two examples chosen at random: the striking current preoccupation with the concept of time in relation to the "puzzles" and "paradoxes" in McTaggart's view that time is unreal; and the preoccupation with the notion of universals only as involving a "problem" to be "dissolved."

[2] *The Revolution In Philosophy*, p. 106.

use of "exhibition analysis" that is usually attacked. It is to this that the critic specifically refers when (as I said before) he so often says that there is no point in "exhibition analysis" since anyone who knows a given ordinary language knows perfectly well the meanings or other kinds of uses of many of the expressions in it. For he knows how to employ these expressions correctly in actual discourse and understands what others convey by means of these expressions when they employ them. I shall now attempt to show how this last point, though certainly true, does not make "exhibition analysis," even as regards the particular purpose in hand, pointless or superfluous.

Now I think that even our critic will not deny that there are *some* ordinary expressions in whose case "exhibition analysis" is not pointless or superfluous. I mean in the case of (i) vague ordinary expressions, expressions that do not have generally accepted, relatively stable ordinary uses; that are not governed by definite linguistic rules. In their case, a survey of how different people employ them in actual contexts would help reveal the precise nature and extent of their vagueness. Also, as is shown by the existence of frequent misunderstanding in ordinary discussions and failure in communication, we are often not aware of the vagueness of certain expressions we frequently use. (I am leaving aside the deliberate exploitation of vagueness by sophistically-minded lawyers and politicians to the perennial detriment of men). A clear recognition of their vagueness is not possible without some, though not necessarily a systematic or detailed, analysis of their fluctuating usage.

All this notwithstanding, we must guard against the common error of regarding most or all of our ordinary expressions or most or all of our ordinary concepts as vague.[1] If most or all ordinary expressions or ordinary concepts are vague, it will be logical to think, as many who hold that ordinary language is vague do, that philosophical analysis – here "exhibition analysis" – is concerned with the clarification of the meanings of these vague expressions or of the concepts which these expressions convey.[2] But as I said before, it is not the case that all or even most ordinary expressions, or ordinary concepts, are vague in the *ordinary* meaning of 'vague expression' or 'vague idea' (notion, concept).

[1] Cf. Bertrand Russell, "Vagueness," *Australasian Journal of Philosophy*, I (1923); 88, and Max Black, "Vagueness," *Language And Philosophy* (Ithaca, New York, 1949), to mention only two thinkers who hold this view. See also next footnote.

[2] For two good illustrations of this view, at least as regards ethical expressions and concepts, see G. C. Field, "The Place of Definition in Ethics," and C. L. Stevenson, "The Emotive Meaning of Ethical Terms," in *Readings in Ethical Theory* (New York, 1952), edited by Wilfrid Sellars and John Hospers. See also chapter seven of the present work.

A vast number of ordinary expressions (and the corresponding concepts) are perfectly precise in their ordinary applications, in one common ordinary meaning of 'precise.' [1] Indeed, so relatively few are vague expressions in ordinary language, except in the field of practical politics, that it is not easy to find more than a few dozen examples of them outside that language "game." The latter, however, is full of vague expressions, and seems positively to thrive on them (also on ambiguity). Such political terms as 'liberal,'' 'conservative,' 'independent,' 'progressive,' 'reactionary,' 'nationalist,' 'internationalist,' 'Democrat,' 'Republican,' 'left,' 'center,' 'right' (also 'leftist,' 'rightist'), 'fellow-traveller,' 'neutralism' and 'positive neutralism,' 'non-alignment' and 'socialism' are good examples. Even 'communist' and 'democrat' are apparently becoming increasingly vaguer every day, as they are bandied about by people of all sorts of political colors or hues, in the four corners of the earth. Analysis of the way in which different individuals – or different nations – employ these expressions is certainly conducive to a better understanding of what these people, or nations, mean or imply by using them, if not also to better international understanding. If all this is true, we cannot justify the " exhibition analysis" of ordinary expressions on the ground that it helps or enables us to clarify or sharpen vague expressions or vague concepts; except in respect to the relatively small number of genuinely vague expressions. As to whether "exhibition analysis" necessarily involves or leads to a modification of ordinary meanings or ordinary concepts, that is a different question, and will be dealt with in the next chapter. (ii) In respect to expressions that involve marginal indeterminacy in their ordinary applications (be they vague or non-vague expressions), the presence of the indeterminacy, and its precise nature and extent, will be clearly recognized only through some analysis of their ordinary uses. A debate as to whether some object is properly to be labelled as "X" or "not-X," which, in some of the philosophically interesting cases can only be settled by a decision, has often been mistaken for a disagreement about non-linguistic facts pure and simple. Examples are the current debate whether or not euthanasia is to be regarded as morally right; whether electronic "brains" think; whether certain very esoteric kinds of modern artifacts are works of art. Also, failure to recognize this fact has sometimes given rise to the surreptitious extension, or restriction,

[1] For a discussion and defence of this point, and for an analysis of the ordinary concept of vagueness, see my "Vagueness," *Philosophical Quarterly*, vol. 12, No. 47 (April, 1962), pp. 138–152.

of the meanings of expressions involving marginal indeterminacy; without the philosopher effecting this change being aware of what he has done.

All this may be granted by our critic. Yet the crucial question remains in respect to expressions that are neither vague nor involve marginal indeterminacy. And in the case of expressions that do involve marginal indeterminacy, the question remains with regard to those applications of the expressions which *are* governed by well-defined rules.

With regard to these cases, as well as in the cases discussed above, we can reply to the critic in the manner in which Moore replied to him. We might reply that though we all know the meaning, and other kinds of uses, of a given form of words (e.g., "This is a hand") we are unable, without reflection, to *say* what that form of words means. "To know how to use a form of words correctly is one thing; to be able to say how we use it is quite another." [1]

Yet this explanation, though of great importance, is only the first step in the attempt to justify the present use of the method. For one thing, we have to discover the sense of 'know' in which we "know the meaning of 'X'" and the sense in which we are, at the same time, unable to say what is 'X's' meaning. Secondly, as Paul Henle rightly points out, "It is by no means apparent that one can always know how to use a word without being able to say how it is used." [2] Surely the inability to say how a given word is used is not due to any inability on our part to find the appropriate words in which to express our knowledge of its use. Nor is it due to our intellectual limitations. Nor is it due, necessarily, to the complexity of the meaning to be exhibited or described; though this is certainly one important reason, particularly in respect to many of the expressions in which philosophers are commonly interested. But if so, why does the knowledge of 'X's' meaning not automatically enable us, at least in some cases, to say what the expression does mean?

Here it is important to mention that the analysis of the meanings or other kinds of uses of an expression 'A' (or the analysis of the corresponding concept *A*), to be possible at all, requires a previous "pre-analytical" knowledge of the meaning of some other expressions B, C, D, etc. Unless the meanings of some words are known without analysis, the analysis cannot even begin. And to say that the meanings of some ex-

[1] G. J. Warnock, *English Philosophy since 1900*, p. 25.

[2] "Do We Discover Our Uses of Words?" *The Journal Of Philosophy*, vol. LIV, No. 32 (November 7, 1957), p. 750.

pressions have to be known without analysis, that they should be "pre-analytically known," so to speak, is to say that we should know how to apply these expressions correctly in everyday contexts.[1] This does not mean that for analysis to be possible, certain expressions have to be regarded as intrinsically *unanalysable*. Those expressions whose meanings or other kinds of uses are taken, for the purposes of a given analysis, as already ("pre-analytically") known, can themselves become the object of another analysis; and so on. But at pain of infinite regress in any given instance of analysis, we have to stop somewhere. We have to stop at expressions whose meanings are known, or are regarded as known, for the purposes of that analysis. This applies to Moore's form of analysis, though Moore thought otherwise, as well as to "exhibition analysis." For the essential feature of concept analysis *à la* Moore is that the analysandum be regarded as composed of certain "simpler" conceptual elements. Whether these elements are themselves "simple" (unanalysable) or "complex" is immaterial for the particular analysis or the particular stage of it involved. It is true, of course, that if they themselves are unanalysable in some sense of 'unanalysable,' the particular process of analysis perforce terminates with them!

In contrast to the expressions in terms of which a given analysis is to be expressed, it is logically unnecessary that the meaning of the expression to be analysed be known in the pre-analytical sense of 'known,' at the outset of the analysis. It is true that in most, if not in all, actual philosophical analyses the meaning to be analysed is known, in the above sense, to the philosopher doing the analysis. But it is perfectly possible to start with an expression whose ordinary meaning is not pre-analytically known, and to discover its pre-analytical meaning by observing how different people employ it in actual contexts (i.e., by means of "exhibition analysis" itself). Another, and frequently more

[1] This "pre-analytical" knowledge cannot be properly described as *intuitive* knowledge of the meanings of certain expressions involved in a given analysis. Besides its misleading traditional associations, 'intuition' does not correctly describe what we are talking about. The knowledge that is presupposed in semantic analysis is, as we have said, knowledge of how to use certain expressions correctly. This knowledge is not intuitive in any accepted sense of this term, but is acquired in the process of learning a language which contains the given expressions. The correctness or incorrectness of what one has learned is always open to checking, is in actual fact checked, by reference to other people's knowledge of how these expressions are properly used and, in cases of doubt, by reference to standard dictionaries. For I agree with H. D. Aiken that contemporary appeals to "intuition," whether by philosophical analysts or others, are the "contemporary semantical hangover of the discredited rational intuitionism of the seventeenth century, with all its antique gear of 'clear and distinct ideas,' its 'self-evident truths,' and its dogmatic appeal to the 'light of reason.'" ("Evaluation and Obligation: Two Functions of Judgments in the Language of Conduct," *Readings in Ethical Theory*, p. 519). But I do not agree that appeal to our "sense of language" comes to the same thing; though, as I have already pointed out, the "sense of language" is not very reliable.

practicable way of discovering the pre-analytical meaning of an expression, would be to look up the expression in a good dictionary and note its meaning or meanings. The dictionary would supply us with this information, if, in the particular case, it happens to give us a synonym; i.e., a "proper verbal definition" of the expression in hand. Very often, the dictionary also gives us a real connotative definition; that is, provides us with the expression's *post*-analytic meaning. Sometimes a dictionary provides us with both types of definition, with an expression's pre-analytic and post-analytic meaning. Let me add in this connection that a philosopher would help his readers to follow a given analysis he is offering if he starts off with a "proper verbal definition" of the expression whose meaning he wished to analyse. This is especially useful if the expression is rather unfamiliar, is not in current use.

The key to the answer to our original question, which also supplies the *raison d'être* of "exhibition analysis" (as also, *mutatis mutandis*, of the Moorean form of analysis) is this. In order that we may be able to state in a philosophically-useful form what an expression means, we must know what it means in a sense of 'know' different from the sense in which we may know its meaning by the very fact that we can use it correctly. At the same time – and this is important – *someone's*, not necessarily the analyser's knowledge of the expression's meaning in the latter sense of 'know' is absolutely essential for our being able to acquire a knowledge of the expression's meaning in the former sense. Without such knowledge we cannot start at all; the expression's meaning cannot be analysed. This is another, a more precise, way of saying that actual language – in the case of ordinary meanings and concepts, ordinary language – is the logical starting-point of philosophical inquiry as a whole.[1]

With this, we can state *one* major way in which "post-analytical" knowledge of an expression's (ordinary) meaning may differ from "pre-analytical" knowledge of it, and so define one major task of the "exhibition analysis" of the meanings of individual ordinary expressions. Stated briefly, it is this: that "pre-analytical" knowledge is knowledge of an expression's meaning or uses *implicitly*, in use; whereas "post-analytical" knowledge – the knowledge we seek as analytical philosophers – is knowledge of an expression's meaning *explicitly*. This includes explicit knowledge of the circumstances under which it would be correct to apply or to withhold the expression, and of the precise

[1] G. C. Field, *op. cit.*, expresses this point well in regard to ethical inquiry; though in terms of ideas or concepts rather than of the corresponding linguistic expressions.

differences between the expression's meaning and the meaning of other, related expressions. Where an expression involves marginal indeterminacy, it also includes a knowledge of the circumstances under which the expression cannot, without qualification, be either correctly applied or correctly withheld from application.

We now turn to a discussion of these points.

Ordinary expressions, or, more precisely, expressions used in ordinary, non-philosophical or non-scientific discourse, are determined or "defined" in and by actual use: by the ways in which they are employed in actual contexts. Another way of saying this is that their meanings are determined by the way in which they are employed by people speaking or writing the language in which they occur. Ordinarily, they are not explicitly defined; as, for instance, they are defined in a dictionary that gives a connotative or some other type of real definition of them. Since ordinary expressions are of various types, the layman's knowledge of their meaning in the present sense is itself of different sorts.

(1) Some ordinary expressions are referring expressions in the sense in which I have been employing this term. In the case of any such expression 'X,' the ordinary man knows its meaning in the sense that he can apply it correctly to certain objects, events, qualities, etc. when he encounters them; these things being parts of its denotatum in one particular sense or meaning of it. A knowledge of 'X's' meaning in this sense could be acquired ostensively; and whether or not this is the way in which any particular person comes to know its meaning, it appears to be the way in which every human being learns the meanings of *some* referring expressions. If this is not granted, the process of learning a language becomes inexplicable. For instance, the name of at least one sensible quality is learned ostensively. But no person who learns the meanings of a given referring expression in that way is ever directly acquainted with all the actual and possible parts of the expression's denotatum or denotata; or knows with certainty to what new objects he may encounter the expression properly applies. This is true even if the expression does not involve any marginal indeterminacy. If it does, it will also be true that objects may be encountered to which one cannot apply or withhold the expression *without qualification*, except by a linguistic decision.

It is readily seen that where a knowledge of the applications of a class-name is ostensively acquired – where one has, so to speak, an extensional knowledge of the expression's application – one *may* lack an "intensional" knowledge of the expression's applications. That is, one may be ignorant of what is comprised in the corresponding *concept*, what are the "defining or criteria features" of the things it names. In every case where a person has only an "extensional" knowledge of the meaning of some referring expression, "exhibition analysis" can provide him with the "intensional" knowledge of its meaning that he lacks. A person who has ostensively learned the application of a referring expression may then, through experience, acquire an "intensional" knowledge of its meaning. But this reflection would involve precisely the kind of analysis we are talking about; except that, in the case of the non-philosophical layman, the analysis (in the relatively rare cases where it arises), is often only vaguely conscious, unsystematic, and generally arises only under the stress of practical exigency. I do not mean that the layman actually studies how different people use the given expression; he does, rather, what even analytical philosophers (including the present author) have hitherto been doing: reflecting on how *he* uses, or how he has been using the expression on different occasions.

Let us note further that many of the concepts with which philosophical analysis and philosophy as a whole have been traditionally concerned, are abstract concepts. Or, stated in linguistic terms, many of the class names in whose meanings or other kinds of uses philosophers have been interested, are names of abstractions. Examples are such expressions as 'beauty,' 'ugliness,' 'goodness,' 'badness,' 'rightness,' 'wrongness,' 'rationality,' 'knowledge,' 'change,' 'freedom.' It is obvious that we do not have a knowledge of the meanings of these expressions in the sense of being able to point out or refer to "beauty" or "goodness" ostensively, as we can point out a table or a chair. Rather, we know the applications of these expressions in the sense of knowing how to refer correctly to particular beautiful things, good men and good ends, rational actions, and so on. Insofar as this is the case, our pre-analytical knowledge of the meanings of these names (as also of some non-abstract class names, some names of sensible things) does not usually include an explicit abstract knowledge of the "defining features" of their denotata. We do not, prior to some analysis, know abstractly what makes beautiful things beautiful, what makes right actions right, what makes rational actions rational. And if we are challenged to justify our calling a given thing right or good or beautiful by some other means than appeal to linguistic convention or somebody else's analysis, we find that we are frequently unable to do so without reflection. Even then, we are frequently unable to give more than a fragmentary and controversial justification of our use of the expression, after laborious reflection (witness philosophical controversies respecting the correct analysis of this or that ordinary concept). In such cases, in other words, we are perhaps unable to give more than a part of the "defining features" of the things properly named by the expression.

In order to avoid misunderstanding, let me hasten to add that when I speak of "exhibition analysis" as providing us with knowledge of "defining features," I am not suggesting that that knowledge is always, or often, expressible in one neat brief connotative *definition* of the corresponding expression. Also, where that knowledge can be so expressed, the definitions we succeed in constructing often involve many elements, or necessitate many distinctions and qualifications. These things make us hesitate to call them definitions, in the sense of handy summaries of one's findings.[1]

What is even more basic, the notion of "defining features" or "connotation" leaves out the conditions, which may be very complex or varied, under which alone certain expressions and *or their negatives* can be properly applied to things possessing the requisite "defining features." At the same time the inclusion of these conditions in the results of an analysis is necessary if the analysis, in the present types of cases, is to be adequate or complete. For instance, "being free to choose," in some ordinary sense or senses of this phrase, cannot properly constitute a "defining feature" of a "reasonable person," since for an agent to be ordinarily regarded *either* as a "reasonable person" *or* as an "unreasonable person" on the basis of the acts he performs, he has to act "freely," "without compulsion." [2]

Similarly with a (morally) "good man" *and* a (morally) "bad man." Yet an adequate understanding of the concepts *reasonable person* and *unreasonable person, good man* and *bad man*, requires the recognition of the role played by the concept of freedom of choice.

Besides the preceding type of condition, there is a type of condition we referred to earlier as Standard Conditions. This type of condition, though it does not form part of the connotation or the defining features of any type of class name, is implicitly involved in the correct applications of certain class names. Let us call one of these class names 'X.' The

[1] The truth of this is seen if, for instance, one attempts to construct definitions of the different senses of 'rational' I have discussed in my "What is rationality?" (*Theoria*, vol. XXIV, 3; 1958), pp. 17 – 187, on the basis of my analysis there. The same applies to Ryle's analysis of various senses of 'feeling,' or O. K. Bouwsma's analysis of 'expression' and 'express' (both in *Aesthetics And Language*), to mention only two analyses taken at random.

[1] See my "What is rationality?" pp. 180 – 181.

presence of the particular Standard Conditions relative to 'X' is *not necessary* for 'X' to be correctly applicable to a given object *A* that possesses the requisite defining features. The expression 'not-X,' however, cannot be properly applied to *A* unless it lacks these defining features *under the relevant Standard Conditions*. Examples of expressions of type 'X' here are all names of artifacts and man-devised activities or processes, such as 'pen,' 'table,' 'house,' 'knife,' 'plane,' 'carpentry,' 'teaching.' [1]

Finally, the concepts *defining feature* and *connotation* are tied with class names. In respect to types of expressions that cannot function as class names, these notions cannot be utilized.

For the foregoing reasons, and because other types of conditions than those we mentioned above may be involved in the analysis of the meanings of other classes of ordinary expressions, we shall say the following about "exhibition analysis": That it can give us (at least in regard to referring expressions) an abstract or general, explicit and systematic knowledge of the various contexts in which a given expression can, or cannot, be properly used. If there are marginal cases, it can also tell us in what contexts the expression cannot be applied, or withheld, without qualification. In some, though probably only in relatively uncomplicated cases, what may be deemed an essential part of the results may be expressed in one or more connotative definitions of the expressions.

(2) In contrast to (1) above, a person may know the meaning of an ordinary expression in the sense that he may be able to specify *some* of the contexts in which it *can* be correctly used; in addition to knowing how to employ it correctly in actual contexts. Indeed, there are expressions – what particular ones they happen to be in a given person's case is a variable matter – whose meanings we learn precisely in terms of some of these contexts. Moreover, some of these expressions are such that their correct employment *cannot be learned* except through a specification, hence a knowledge, of some of these contexts. This is most obviously true in respect to (a) expressions that name imaginary things, such as 'centaur,' 'fairy,' or 'mermaid'; and (b) (i) expressions that cannot function as names at all (e.g., adverbs, conjunctions, interjections), or (ii) expressions which, if they can be properly said to name anything at all, name complex activities, processes, occurrences or other states of affairs that lack a single, unified nature (e.g., participles such as 'knowing,' 'learning,' 'painting,' 'composing,' 'loving'). In the

[1] See p. 99.

case of expressions of type (a), pre-analytical knowledge of the contexts in which they apply includes some knowledge of their ordinary criteria features. Take for instance the words 'centaur' and 'satyr.' If the uses of these words are learned in the context of Greek mythology, by one's reading, say, some stories involving centaurs and satyrs, the description of these imaginary creatures in these stories will provide the learner with a knowledge of some of the characteristics which something must have in order to be called a centaur or a satyr without qualification. Note, however, that a person may know the meaning of an expression in the sense under consideration even when it is a referring expression. Here one may "know the meaning" of the expression both extensionally and intensionally. As a matter of fact, if one knows the criteria features of a referring expression, he will be able to point out or refer correctly to parts of its denotatum, to some of the objects to which it refers. On the other hand, if one knows the denotatum of a referring expression – in general, if one knows the expression's meaning in the sense discussed under (1) – one may acquire a knowledge of its comprehension ("objective intension") by observing and reflecting on the common characteristics or the resemblances which parts of the denotatum exhibit. Thus if one can identify certain objects ordinarily called works of art, he can acquire a knowledge of those common characteristics or those resemblances which these objects, these works of art, exhibit. But, and this is important, a person cannot acquire a knowledge of a thing's criteria features or a word's ordinary, conventional connotation – in general, acquire a knowledge of its meaning in the sense being discussed – in that way; he cannot know what common characteristics and/or resemblances are comprised by, or are even included, in it. This would be true even if it is, or were, possible for him to observe *all actual* objects referred to by that word (e.g., *per impossibile,* all works of art, in our earlier example). Only by observing and reflecting on the ways in which he and others actually use the expression in ordinary discourse can he acquire that knowledge. For to know a thing's criteria features or a word's conventional connotation is to know to what *possible* as well as to what actual things the word is applicable. And this, clearly, cannot be provided merely by the observation or conceptual analysis of some or all of the actual things to which the word refers. I mention this point here because a lack of clear awareness, or the ignoring, of the distinction between a word's connotation and its comprehension in the present sense – between a thing's criteria features and other features it has or may happen to have – underlies many of the confusions in traditional epistemology, ethics, aesthetics and other branches of philosophy.

It is worth noting that the pre-analytical knowledge of the conditions under which a given expression correctly applies, admits of degrees. This is true even where a knowledge of an expression's correct usage involves or includes an explicit, abstract knowledge of some of these conditions. For the conditions that must be known need not be all, or even the majority of, the conditions under which the expression is applicable.

Further, a child's knowledge of the conditions under which a given word is normally applied is fragmentary and vague [1] compared to an adult's knowledge of them; even though it may be perfectly able to employ the word correctly in simple situations. On the other hand, an ordinary adult's knowledge of these conditions is frequently fragmentary and vague compared to a linguist's or a grammarian's knowledge. Paul Henle therefore errs, I think, when he says that "a person would hardly be said to know how to use the term "father" unless he could decide on logical grounds the truth of the sentences, 'A father is a parent,' 'A father is a male,' and 'All male parents are fathers.'" [2] This may be true of the linguist and the ordinary adult; but it is not true of many young children, who know – in a perfectly straightforward ordinary sense – how to use the word 'father' in relation to their own fathers and the fathers of some of their friends or playmates. Another thing. It would not be correct to say that knowledge of (some of) the conditions under which a given word applies, in the sense of 'knowledge' under discussion, always involves knowing (some of) the *rules* of its use; if by this is meant one's being able to *formulate* them. This is again easily seen in the case of the child that knows how to use the word 'father,' and whose knowledge includes some (vague) knowledge of the word's intension. Its inability to formulate *some* of the appropriate rules governing the word's usage may be partly due to its ignorance of *any* of the rules governing its usage. Even an adult who has the child's

[1] We should guard against confusing the possession of a vague knowledge of these matters with an expression's being a vague expression. One may have a vague knowledge of the nature of the contexts in which a word 'X' applies, even if 'X' is a perfectly non-vague word in the ordinary meaning of 'non-vague word.' A good example is our ordinary vague knowledge of the nature of the contexts in which 'know' itself and its cognates apply. The neglect of this distinction is partly responsible, I think, for the view of some contemporary philosophers that analysis is, or has to be, the clarification of the meanings of vague expressions; the clarification of vague concepts. It also tempts one to regard all, or most, *ordinary* expressions and concepts as vague expressions or concepts. Except for actually vague ordinary expressions, "exhibition analysis" gives us that clear meaning or that clear concept which the ordinary usage of the corresponding expression actually involves.

[2] "Do We Discover Our Uses Of Words?" *The Journal Of Philosophy,* vol. LIV, No. 23 (November 7, 1957), p. 750.

knowledge of the applications of the word 'father' may be at a loss to formulate these rules; at least prior to reflection on the word's actual usage. The reflection itself is at least part of the process of "exhibition analysis," which, described in terms of the notion of rules of use, may be said to aim at a clear and systematic formulation of the rules of use of an expression whose meaning or some other type of use is to be analysed.

The upshot of the entire discussion in this section is that the knowledge we aim at securing, and which "exhibition analysis" does secure, is an explicit, abstract, clear and systematic understanding of the kinds of conditions under (or the contexts in) which a given expression is applicable; a clear formulation of the rules of its use. This constitutes knowledge which we do not ordinarily possess. For our pre-analytic knowledge is, generally speaking, fragmentary, vague, not fully explicit, not clearly or systematically formulated.

The reader can readily see from the discussion under (1) and (2) above the senses in which it may be meaningful to say that our knowledge of an expression's uses can be widened or deepened, when we already know these uses in an ordinary sense of this phrase. He can also see how it makes sense to tell someone that this or that is *not* what the expression means, or that this or that is all that it means, though he thinks otherwise. To give only one – but an extreme – example, the view that value judgments *merely* express certain feelings or attitudes, and do not assert anything, *though we ordinarily think that they do assert something*, is a perfectly sensible conception. (Whether or not it is a sound view is another question.) [1] This is *not* the same as saying that we do not know how to *use* value terms in sentences. But one must guard against the abuse of such an approach to (some) philosophical questions. For it is easy to abuse it; to impose all kinds of fictitious interpretations on an expression's meaning or other types of uses. Unless our pre-analytical knowledge of an expression's uses is taken seriously, we cannot hope to reach anywhere; and the result can only be confusion or futile controversy. It is impossible to extract anything from the meaning of an expression, that is not already contained in it: *in the sense of what is revealed, through analysis, to be involved or implied in its actual applications in discourse.* This is not always the same as, or merely, what *I* or *you* "mean by it"; what I or you "have in mind"

[1] Such a state of affairs, if true, would be quite surprising, however. It would be surprising that only relatively few men, i.e., some philosophers, should arrive at this knowledge, although millions of intelligent people constantly make value judgments in everyday life.

when we use it. The latter is individual pre-analytical knowledge: and we saw that it is not the whole story.[1]

To end this chapter, we shall now pass to a few additional points that arise in connection with the notion of "exhibition analysis," or the actual employment of that method.

The first point is a further clarification of the notion that one of the aims of "exhibition analysis" as such is to arrive at a clear and systematic understanding of the everyday uses of various ordinary expressions. Here let us note that the notions of correctness and incorrectness cannot be meaningfully applied to actual *uses* of expressions; any more than we can apply them to an expression's ordinary meaning(s), or to the concept(s) conveyed by the expression. (It makes no sense to speak of an "incorrect meaning of a word or phrase." We sometimes say that a person is employing a word incorrectly, i.e., not in its "correct meaning." But this is another way of saying that he is not applying it in the (or a) meaning it actually has. A word either has or does not have a certain meaning; the notions of correctness and incorrectness are inapplicable to its meaning itself. Similarly, a word expresses or does not express a certain concept; the concept expressed by the word – or any other concept for that matter – cannot be spoken of as correct or incorrect.) A particular instance of "exhibition analysis" is successful if it provides us with one or more of the actual uses of a given expression; it is unsuccessful if it fails to provide us with it or with them. In the latter case what may be arrived at is not an "incorrect use" of the expression, but something that is mistakenly regarded as a use of it. The distinction of "correct" and "incorrect" properly applies not to actual uses but to actual usage. The success or failure of a given instance of "exhibition analysis" depends on whether or not what is analysed is *correct usage*. For, as I have pointed out before, following the Oxford Analysts, it is the analysis of an expression's actual (correct) usage that reveals its actual uses. It follows that a philosopher who looks for the actual uses of an expression may

[1] Our discussion of the nature of, or what is involved in, "exhibition analysis" has a direct bearing on and enables us correctly to evaluate such arguments as Moore's Open Question Argument. I mention this argument in particular since it can readily be generalized to bear upon all areas of philosophical analysis. Moore's reasoning, because of the element of truth it contains, threatens to throw doubt on practically any analysis one cares to make – particularly on any explicit definitions at which one may arrive as a result of analysis – if one does not know that it is only partly true. These remarks are parenthetical, however; and I shall not attempt to elaborate them. I shall also not attempt to deal with Moore's argument or any generalized form of it.

be sometimes misled into taking an actual incorrect usage for a correct one. Another error arises if one is misled by superficial resemblances between the correct usage of the expression he is interested in and the correct usage of other expressions that may or may not be related to it in meaning or in other kinds of uses. (Usually, the danger is greater if the meanings or other uses are related.) In any case, and whatever the particular source of error, it is useful for the philosopher to recognize incorrect, as well as correct, *usage*. Knowledge of incorrect usage is, nevertheless, only of negative value. In the long run, what is of primary importance is the knowledge of the actual *uses* of ordinary expressions. One way of discovering this consists in finding out empirically how we learn the applications of ordinary expressions – in general, how we learn a given language. This technique, used extensively by Wittgenstein in his *Philosophical Investigations*, is of considerable value; as shown by the results reached there by its means. We also had a glimpse of its usefulness in our analysis of the nature of "exhibition analysis"; and we shall have further occasion to speak about it in chapter nine. But it has its dangers and limitations. For one thing, the ways in which different persons actually learn the applications of a given expression may be more or less various than the uses themselves; there being no necessary or unique one-one correspondence – at least in many cases – between a given use and a given way of learning how to apply the corresponding expression or expressions. For instance, there are different ways of teaching the ordinary use of the word 'centaur.' One common way consists in showing the learner drawings of centaurs, accompanied by the appropriate explanations; for example, by the statement that these creatures do not actually exist. Another way would be to let the learner read stories describing centaurs and their imaginary activities (e.g. in Greek Mythology). A third and quick way would be to point out the meaning of the word in a dictionary.

One should be careful, in employing the present technique – in those cases where the learner is taught the meaning of an expression by appeal to common, everyday situations or to common objects – not to overemphasise the *most current, everyday, mainly practical* employment of language; minimizing or completely ignoring the relatively restricted employment of language for the expression of scientific or philosophical ideas. Further, even with regard to the ordinary uses of a given expression, the applications which the learner is taught should not be exclusively drawn from one area of life; even if it provides us with the most common situations in which the expression is employed. For example, one would get a misleading picture of the uses of such words as 'belief,' 'faith,' and 'trust' if one is only taught their everyday non-religious uses: if the exemplary material employed to teach their uses is drawn exclusively from such non-religious contexts as believing what a friend says, trusting one's wife or husband, having faith in the skill of a plane's pilot; and so on. In order that one may have a picture of *all* the current actual uses of a given expression, the applications of the expression should be learned in relation to all the "language games" in which it plays a part. What is more, its uses in one "language game" should not be overemphasized at the expense of its uses in other "languages games"; nor should one get, or be given, the impression that its uses in one particular "language game" are somehow the only legitimate, proper, or paradigm uses. Thus in the case of the words 'belief,' 'faith' and 'trust,' it will not do at all to regard their non-religious uses (say) as the only proper or legitimate uses.

Finally, it should not be assumed, without a painstaking investigation of the matter, that ordinary language is fully adequate as it stands for the expression of philosophical or scientific ideas; on the ground that it is adequate for the transactions of everyday life.

The second major technique for the discovery of the uses of expressions, which is the one I have chiefly spoken about, is the empirical survey of how people actually apply an expression we are interested in. In many cases, a *majority* usage can be taken as providing us with an actual use of that expression. This is not belied, let us notice, by the fact that there are a number of expressions in English, say, whose most current usage is *not* correct usage as defined by standard grammar books. A common-place example is the prevalent use of 'me' instead of 'I' in such sentences as "John is taller than me" and "Who, me?" Here the difference between correct and incorrect usage is a purely grammatical one, and does not involve a logical, conceptual difference. Since it is quite possible that in some cases grammatical differences of the kind under consideration do involve logical differences, differences respecting use, majority usage should be taken only as a general guide to the ordinary use of expressions. In any case, only an examination of actual usage can reveal the exceptions.

In practice, we frequently encounter other difficulties in the attempt to discover the actual uses of expressions. These difficulties are due to the fact that ordinary discourse is studded with idiomatic expressions peculiar to the particular language, or even to a particular dialect of it. Figurative expressions and elliptical sentences also abound in ordinary discourse. Here, as elsewhere, the analytical philosopher should attempt to find out the uses of particular expressions by careful examination of as many as possible of the concrete contexts in which they are applied. For here the danger lies in one's imposing a purely personal interpretation, or of one's covertly introducing a new application, hence a new use, while ostensible describing the expression's actual uses. This danger is present when a philosopher tells us that such and such is what we *really* mean by a given expression, even though we may think otherwise. Or when the philosopher implies that the application or the use he is ostensibly trying to describe is somehow hidden from the general view; but that he has special access to it. It is perhaps these dangers, among others, that lead H. D. Aiken to regard the arguments employed by analysts in defense of what he regards as their theories (in the field of Ethics at least), as "so many unconscious expressions of and appeals to individual attitudes and sentiments." [1] Yet I think he is being extravagant when he says: "I think it is not at all extravagant to say that in ethics the chances of confusing analysis with expression or persuasion are so pervasive, and their removal so well-nigh impossible, that the very significance of the arguments themselves remain at the least an open question." [2]

In speaking about majority usage and the discovery of the actual uses of expressions, we must guard against another danger. We must not confuse majority usage with what the majority *believe* about this or that factual matter; or even with what they believe are the actual uses of the expressions they employ. I have already spoken about the difference between common-sense beliefs and ordinary language (see chapter two); and what I said there also goes for other beliefs. The difference between discovering an expression's actual uses by seeing how the majority of people apply the expression, and what these people say are the actual uses, is perhaps not as obvious. Nevertheless, it is there. The latter is an expression of opinion – usually not very considered and careful at that – based, at best, on a cursory or hasty reflection on the way in which they and/or others apply the expression. It is therefore, at best, based on an imperfect utilization of "exhibition analysis," and, as such, carries far less weight than the careful and systematic "exhibition analysis" of the trained philosophical analyst.

In the preceding remarks, and in my earlier discussion in chapter two,

[1] "Evalution and Obligation: Two Functions Of Judgments in the Language of Conduct," in *Readings in Ethical Theory*, p. 159.

[2] *Ibid.*

I have explicitly asserted, or implied, that semantic analysis – here "exhibition analysis" – when properly conducted, involves an empirical survey of the everyday usages of ordinary expressions. The word 'usage' is crucial here. "Exhibition analysis" can make an empirical study of ordinary usage; and through a *logical* analysis of this empirically discoverable usage, it can reveal the actual ordinary uses of the expressions concerned. As far as this is concerned, we can say that the ordinary uses of expressions are discoverable through an empirical survey of ordinary usage. But this does not explicitly provide us with the ordinary uses of the particular expressions, which are implied or involved in these usages. Genetically speaking, a given expression acquires certain uses by the expression's being actually applied in certain ways; i.e., by actual usage. And the uses it acquires are determined in nature by its actual usages. This is why an analysis of the latter reveals the former. But a mere inventory of actual usages does not tell us what the expression's uses are. In many cases, we may find upon analysing these usages that some of them form one cluster or group, others a different cluster or group, and so on. Each of these clusters will involve one meaning or one sense of the expression. Or to state the matter differently, we will not find that *every single usage* ($usage_1$) we come across uniquely determines one *use* of the expression; though any one usage belonging to one group implies or involves a particular use. Thus, to take a simple example, observation of the ordinary usages of the word 'sentence' reveals that this word is sometimes applied (1) to such utterances as "This table is brown," "Peter is taller than John," "The weather is fine to-day," "The velocity of a body is equal to the distance it covers in unit time"; and so on. (All these sentences are what grammarians call indicative sentences.) Similarly, this word is sometimes applied (2) to such utterances as "Is Mary at home?" "Do you have a cold?" and so on. Again, the word is employed to refer to such utterances as (3) "Open the door!" "Do not kill," and "Please give me some money." And so on. Here *each* of the utterances mentioned under (1) provides us with *one* $usage_1$; while *all* the utterances mentioned under it together provide us with *one sort of usage* ($usage_2$) of 'sentence.' Similarly each of the utterances mentioned under (2) provides us with one $usage_1$, distinct from the $usages_1$ provided by the other utterances under it, and from those provided by each of the utterances mentioned under (1). At the same time, all the utterances mentioned under (2) together provide us with one $usage_2$, distinct from the $usage_2$ provided by the utterances mentioned under (1). And so on. Each of these $usages_2$ (but not each usage$_1$) determines, hence provides us with one *use* of the word, in our employment of this term here and elsewhere in this book.

Whether, in this particular case, each of these uses corresponds to one *sense* of 'sentence' is a question into which we need not enter. It is clear, however, that all three uses we have listed together correspond to one meaning of 'sentence,' not to three separate meanings; they all belong to what we might call one "family of uses" of the word. A different meaning of 'sentence,' which may or may not correspond to another "family of uses" of this word, is provided by the applications of 'sentence' in such utterances as: "The judge sentenced the criminal to life imprisonment"; "He received a very light sentence."

From what we have just said it is clear that the word 'usage$_1$,' in our employment of it, refers to "type" in Charles Peirce's "token/type" distinction: what corresponds to "token" in that dichotomy is what I shall call "usage$_0$." On the other hand, 'usage$_2$' in our employment of it refers to a fairly general *kind* of application of an expression. To illustrate what has now become a trichotomy, let us take the following example: we have two distinct usages$_0$ (two occasions of the application) of the word 'table' when, at two different times, I say: "Use this table for writing." Similarly, we have two distinct usages$_0$ of the sentence as a whole, in the two cases. But we have one and the same usage$_1$ of 'table,' and of "Use this table for writing," in both cases. However, we have a different usage$_2$ when we say: "Use my logarithmic table," on whatever occasion it may be made.

It will be observed that usage$_0$ corresponds to P. F. Strawson's sense (c) of 'use,' where "a use of a sentence" = "an (one) occasion of the uttering or writing of a sentence"; while usage$_2$ corresponds – and this is not surprising at all – to his sense (a), where "'use' (of a particular word, phrase, sentence) = (roughly) 'rules for using.' But usage$_1$ does not correspond to Strawson's sense (b) of 'use.' [1] For in this employment of 'use,' an expression may have the *same* use even when it is employed in two different senses or meaning; while this is not the case with respect to our own employment of usage$_1$. We might also add that what we might call a "family of usages$_2$" would correspond to what we called a "family of uses" in *our* employment of 'use' in this book, which is the same as Strawson's sense (a) of the word above. Thus, to revert to an earlier example, the different usages$_2$ of 'sentence' in the utterances mentioned under (1)–(3) above together constitute a family of

[1] "On Referring," *Essays In Conceptual Analysis*, p. 28 footnote 1. See my discussion in chapter three, pp. 25ff.

usages$_2$ distinct from the family of usages$_2$ to which its usage in the utterance "He was given a light sentence" belongs.

"Exhibition analysis," we said, uncovers, distinguishes and analyses the different uses of a given expression; it can also uncover and distinguish the various "families of uses," if any, obtaining in relation to the expression. But it does not, or need not stop here. For though there may be no such things as "families of families of uses" of one and the same ordinary expression – whether or not such clusters occur can only be discovered through "exhibition analysis" itself – the uses of different ordinary expressions can and do form parts of such larger groups. These, depending on their size and importance, constitute different "language games" or parts of a language game in Wittgenstein's or some similar use of this expression. Thus statements expressing ordinary moral imperatives provide us with a good example of a family of families of uses of expressions; and together with moral judgments or evaluations they form a part or the whole of that larger body of expressions, that language game, which we call the language of morals. At the same time, by tracing the similarities and the differences, and the relations between moral and non-moral imperatives, and between judgments of moral value and (say) judgments of aesthetic value, "exhibition analysis" brings out some of the important logical strands that bind the language of morals as a whole to the rest of ordinary language.

In the light of the above discussion we can see the truth, but also the ambiguity, in Arthur Pap's statement that "... the expression "ordinary language" suggests that semantic analysis of the sort practiced by analytic philosophers is an empirical study of contingent speech habits; which it clearly is not if the result of the analysis is a proposition that is translatable into other languages, and so is not about a particular language at all." [1] Because the results of analysis are what we have been describing, and because sometimes, as Pap holds, they are or can be put in the form of a proposition or a set of propositions, "exhibition analysis" is not merely "an empirical study of contingent linguistic habits." Such an empirical study is only the first, though a necessary stage of "exhibition analysis."

Let us note that the uses that a proper analysis of correct ordinary usage reveals are the uses that the particular expressions actually have in some language. These uses are what they are because the ordinary usages of the people speaking that language are, as a matter of fact,

[1] *Semantics And Necessary Truth* (New Haven, 1958), p. 397. Italics in original. See also pp. 181 and 271–2 of the same work.

what they are. For this reason we can say, if we like, that there is a factual or contingent element in the actual uses of ordinary expressions. This is not to say that these uses are conventional. Ordinary usages are conventional; but it does not make sense (it is not merely false) to say that the uses which these usages imply or involve are themselves conventional. If the $usages_2$ of a given expression change, its uses will change; but they may or may not change if some of their $usages_1$ change. We have a good example of the former in the change which has occurred in the usage and use of such words as 'fond,' 'charity' and 'mistress,' since Elizabethan times. In the case of each of them, a change in $usage_2$ has resulted in a change in their uses or meaning. On the other hand, as we saw earlier, some $usages_1$ of the word 'me' have changed in colloquial English and American insofar as it is now frequently applied in place of 'I' (in e.g. "Who, me?") without a corresponding change in its uses.

The addition of a new usage to a word's customary usages sometimes gives rise to a new use of that word. A clear example is Shakespeare's employment of 'incarnadine' as a verb (in *Macbeth*): a word that had hitherto been applied only as an adjective. This addition resulted in a new use of the word; i.e., in the sense of "to dye crimson."

Throughout this chapter and elsewhere in this book, we have been speaking about *actual* uses of expressions. We should now note that an actual use is one among an indefinite number of *possible* uses. A possible use is one which an expression can or may have, whether or not it actually has it. It is a use which we can conceive or apprehend even if no expressions that we ourselves know, or no expressions in a given language (or any actual language at all?), do or may actually have. It is a use that can be implied by an expression or by different expressions *if* it is, or they are, applied in certain ways. As such, it is independent of the fact that it is, or is not, implied in an actual usage.

Paul Henle has recently expressed the view that we decide our own use of verbal expressions; that we do not formulate them inductively as we do when we formulate other people's uses of expressions; though philosophers have reasons for the decisions they make and do not make them arbitrarily.[1] Now if a decision is here involved at all, it will be a decision respecting our $usage_1$ or $usage_2$ (in the latter case, it will also involve $usage_1$) or our uses (or the meanings) of an expression. In the light of our earlier remarks, it is seen that a decision regarding

[1] "Do We Discover Our Uses Of Words?" *Journal Of Philosophy*, vol. LIV, No. 23 (November 7, 1957), pp. 750, 755–756, 757.

usage$_1$ may or may not affect the uses of the expression we employ; depending on whether only some, or all, of the usages$_1$ of the expression are involved. On the other hand, a decision regarding a usage$_2$ will necessarily affect some use of the expression; while a decision regarding a use of the expression will be, indirectly, a decision about some usage$_2$ of it. For it is the latter (and hence usages$_1$) that concretly reflects the expression's uses or any changes effected in them.

The formulation of the uses involved in *my* present or past usage is arrived at through a logical analysis of that usage. As such, it certainly constitutes a discovery of some kind and is not, or does not involve, a decision. Also, my past usage at least – say the usage I adopted when I first learned how to apply a given expression – is not adopted by a decision on my part; it is learned from others. As for my future usage at any given moment, my decision whether or not to continue to employ the expression as I have been hitherto employing it (if I make a decision at all) is sometimes made before I launch on my analysis. My inquiry as an analytical philosopher would then consist, first, in recalling what I had decided upon and, second, in analysing it. Normally, we do not make decisions whenever we continue to employ an expression in the way or ways in which we have been hitherto employing it. We do so more or less unconsciously. And only infrequently, I think, do we make some decision when we begin to apply an expression in a *new* way; except perhaps if we are linguists or philosophers. Very often the change occurs, when it does occur, accidentally; or under the unconscious influence of a different usage we come across in books or in the press, in other people's conversation, and so on. In these cases my analysis of my usage of a given expression requires that I recall how I have been, and how at present I am employing the expression; and the analysis proper consists in discovering the implied uses. If now I predict how I shall employ the expression in the future, supposing that I am interested in making such a prediction, I have to do so on the basis of my recollection of my past and present employment of it, and my knowledge of the present and possible future factors that might influence my usage. My prediction will only be probable; it may well be falsified by my subsequent usage. In any case, it will be a prediction in a straight-forward sense and will not involve any decision.

The upshot of all this is that the uses of ordinary expressions are not, *generally speaking*, idiosyncratic, shifting, non-objective. They are governed by conventional rules which are implicit in the notion of a correct or proper usage. However – and this is why I used the qualifying phrase "generally speaking" – there are some ordinary expressions – words which we label "vague" ("very vague," etc.) – whose usages$_2$, hence uses, are fluid and shifting. With respect to these, but only these expressions, Henle's view that we decide our own use of verbal expressions is true. But as far as I can see, they constitute a relatively small fraction of the expressions occurring in any ordinary language with which I am acquainted, such as English. Oh the other hand, even with respect to verbal expressions whose usage is well-bounded by rules (i.e., non-vague expressions), there is scope for decision in respect to what we have referred to as marginal or borderline cases of their application. In contrast to vague expressions, however, decision here has relatively limited scope; except where a philosopher decides to alter a given usage$_1$ or given usages$_2$ of an expression as a whole, for various logical or empirical reasons. But these things will become clearer in chapters seven and ten, where we shall have a good deal to say about attempts at the reconstruction of ordinary language.

CHAPTER SEVEN

SEMANTIC ANALYSIS III
ANALYSIS AND RECONSTRUCTION

In chapters five and six I attempted a somewhat detailed exposition and analysis of two forms of semantic analysis. It was assumed there that in the case of neither form of analysis, the concepts, meanings or other kinds of uses analysed are in any way affected by the process of analysis itself. The first question we want to ask in the present chapter is whether this assumption or presumption *is* as a matter of fact true; or whether our two forms of semantic analysis – particularly "exhibition analysis," on which, in a certain respect, the other form of analysis itself rests – *necessarily* involve a modification of the analysandum.

One familiar form of the view that philosophical analysis alters the analysandum is found in the writings of the Absolute Idealists. These thinkers hold that analysis *distorts* or *falsifies* what is analysed; and in the case of some of them, this is a result of their view that the universe is an organic unity composed of internally-related parts. Bergson, on different grounds, holds a similar but somewhat less extreme view of analysis. But both of these views, and their logical underpinnings, have been so thoroughly and convincingly refuted that I shall not say anything more about them here.[1]

A more interesting and, to my mind, a more important form of the view that analysis alters the analysandum is found in some current philosophical writings. In this form of the view, it is held that analysis really consists in *replacing* the meaning or the concept analysed by another meaning or concept which may or may not preserve something of the original analysandum. Also, it is held that the alleged replacement is *desirable* because the analysandum is regarded as somehow defective.

[1] For a detailed criticism of the doctrine of internal relations and the Organic Theory of Reality see my *The Coherence Theory of Truth: A Critical Evaluation* (Beirut, 1961), Chapter III.

The analysis, if successful, will consist in the improvement on or refinement – and not merely in the redefinition – of the original concept or meaning; since it will provide us with a concept or meaning that is free from its defects. A case in point is S. Körner's view that analysis really consists in replacing a given concept which has undesirable metaphysical implications by another concept which does not.[1] Körner refers to the procedure involved as "replacement analysis." An alleged example of "replacement analysis" is Russell's analysis of existential propositions.

The first thing to note is that "replacement analysis" is not really a form of analysis [2]; for the simple reason that the modification of any concept or meaning, or its replacement by another concept or meaning, does not constitute either the whole or a part of what we mean by 'analysis' in ordinary discourse. It also does not correspond to any philosophical (extended or modified) meaning of 'analysis' which approximates in any degree to the ordinary meaning. For we cannot gainsay the fact that the ordinary meaning of that word essentially involves the idea of *discovering* what the analysandum *is*, and what it implies. The redefinition of the analysandum is not a part of the ordinary meaning of 'analysis.' It appears, therefore, that Körner himself practises "replacement analysis" in thinking and speaking of the designated procedure as analysis! He does not give us an analysis of the ordinary concept of analysis; or even a mere extension of it. He really substitutes (probably unwittingly) a new concept for the ordinary concept, and for our two philosophical concepts of it. Moreover, "replacement analysis" itself logically *presupposes* "semantic analysis" in our first or our second form of it. Stated in terms of our second form of analysis ("exhibition analysis"), which is the more basic and comprehensive of the two forms of analysis, "replacement analysis" logically presupposes the discovery and the conceptual analysis of the actual uses of expressions (or the corresponding concepts) involved or implied in the correct usage of the relevant expressions. Without these, it is logically impossible to determine (a) whether or not the given use (or concept) *is* defective; and, if it is defective, (b) in what way it is so. It is only where a disease is known to be present, and a correct diagnosis of it is made, that the proper remedy can be administered. Thus, for

[1] "Some Types of Philosophical Thinking," *British Philosophy in the Mid-Century* (London, 1957), edited by C. A. Mace, p. 121.

[2] Though I myself regarded it as such, following Körner, in my "On Three Forms of Philosophical Analysis," *Proceedings of the 12th International Congress of Philosophy*, Venice and Padua, vol. V, 1958, pp. 263–269.

example, Nelson Goodman rightly starts off, in a recent paper entitled "About," [1] with an attempt to show, by means of exhibition analysis – actually, by means of a *reductio* argument – that some of the ordinary uses of 'about' lead to paradox. It is only then that he turns to the task of formalizing the concept of "aboutness," by modifying the expression's ordinary uses. In a similar vein, C. L. Stevenson, in "The Emotive Meaning of Ethical Terms," [2] briefly states – though he does not attempt to show – that the question "Is X good?" is ambiguous and confused, before he sets out to offer a substituted question which he believes is clearer and more adequate than the original question.

If this is true, it also follows that the employment of our two forms of analysis does *not* necessarily involve or include "replacement analysis." For, whether or not the latter is a form of analysis (and I have indicated that it is not), what it logically *presupposes* cannot involve or include it as a part. Further, we cannot meaningfully extend the concept of semantic analysis to include "replacement analysis." For the latter does not contain any elements that are also contained in the ordinary, or even in our philosophical, concepts of analysis. A more important reason is that the extension of the concept of, say, exhibition analysis to include "replacement analysis" would be illegitimate except if the latter always follows the former (preferably in a logical sense of 'follow'). And this, as we shall now attempt to show, is not the case.

Let us note at the outset that whatever the outcome of our present inquiry, it cannot support the general view exemplified by Körner. For that view apparently regards the analysis of ordinary concepts or of meanings as consisting wholly and solely in – and not merely as including or involving – "replacement analysis," while our discussion of semantic analysis so far, if true, show that view to be erroneous. Second, two different views should be here distinguished: The view that holds that "replacement analysis" is desirable but not logically unavoidable in analysis; and the different view that it is logically *inescapable*, wherever semantic analysis is practised, whether or not it is also desirable. Perhaps it is the latter that Körner holds. In any case, it is that view whose validity we have set out to determine.

My view is that "semantic analysis" (e.g., "exhibition analysis") does not inescapably involve the redefinition of the analysandum in respect to any type of ordinary expression. A redefinition of the analysandum can only occur if we go, or attempt to go, a step beyond analysis; but

[1] *Mind*, vol. LXX, No. 277 (January, 1961), pp. 1–24.
[2] *Readings in Ethical Theory*, pp. 415–429.

nothing compels us to do so. It may, indeed, be sometimes desirable; but that does not make it inescapable. On the contrary, it may be desirable precisely because it is *not* inescapable.

I shall now attempt to support my view by considering the relevant kinds of expressions. I shall begin with those kinds of expressions which, *prima facie*, appear to support the opposite view most strongly.

(1) It might be thought, first of all, that the semantic analysis of *vague* ordinary expressions necessarily involves their redefinition. This is, however, quite false; though it may well be that the redefinition of vague expressions is desirable for philosophical purposes.

As I have stated before, a vague expression, in the ordinary sense of this term, is an expression that, among other things, lacks a (relatively) fixed ordinary usage. It is employed differently by different persons; or it is not governed by any stable, generally-accepted rules. Many, perhaps most, vague ordinary expressions are not extremely or "hopelessly vague." An examination of the usage of these expressions will reveal a certain common "core of meaning," so to speak, varying in extent with different expressions, together with different degrees of unfixity of meaning. Examples of such moderately vague ordinary expressions are, I think, 'intellectual,' 'genius,' 'originality' and the cognate 'original,' 'creative,' 'religious,' 'mystical,' and 'nationalism.'

As I stated in another place, the discovery of whether a given expression utilized by philosophy is vague, and if so, the nature and extent of its vagueness, is one of the possible tasks of "semantic analysis" ("exhibition analysis"). But the discovery of these things does not include or involve the attempt to overcome or diminish the expression's vagueness through the modification of its usage one way or another. The latter requires the prior discovery of the vagueness, its precise nature in the particular case, and its extent.

(2) The same situation logically obtains, *mutatis mutandis*, in respect to expressions that involve "marginal indeterminacy" in their ordinary employment, whether or not they are also vague expressions. The attempt to diminish or completely eliminate the "marginal indeterminacy" of any such expression is not involved in, but rather presupposes, an analysis of the conventional applications of that expression. For example, before we can properly feel the need for, advocate, or attempt the restriction or the broadening of the present concept of art (in the purely classificatory, descriptive sense of 'art') we must know (a) to what things 'art' ordinarily applies and to what things it definitely does not apply; and (b) to what things its correct applicability or inappli-

cability is indeterminate in the light of actual ordinary usage at the time. Hence any attempt to give an *unqualified* intensional definition of an expression that suffers from marginal indeterminacy is bound to fail unless its usage is deliberately restricted or broadened. This is true even where the proposed definiens contains words that themselves involve marginal indeterminacy. The framing of intensional definitions is, however, not a part but a by-product of semantic analysis. Moreover, it will be remembered from chapter three that the framing of intensional definitions is not always even possible. Similar considerations apply to attempted definitions of vague expressions. But here the restriction of the ordinary usage is frequently insufficient, and sometimes is completely useless, for the elimination of the existing vagueness (unless a "common core" of meaning obtains, and the new usage is limited to it). Thus the present vague uses of 'genius' can perhaps be eliminated by our limiting the word's applications to, say, a person with an IQ of 135 or above.

One implication of the preceding is worth making explicit. Correct semantic analysis as such does not, and cannot, resolve or diminish any marginal indeterminacy or any vagueness in the expressions whose uses are discovered and analysed. In this I find myself in complete agreement with Alice Ambrose [1]; though she mistakenly, to my mind – along with many other contemporary philosophers – equates marginal indeterminacy and vagueness.

The attempt to attain a clear understanding of ordinary concepts, which is an essential part of semantic analysis, does not consist in or necessarily involve the elimination or diminution of vagueness or of open texture; even where the concepts analysed *are* vague or open textured. (What a clear understanding positively consists in, here as in all other cases of semantic analysis, I have already indicated in the preceding chapter.) The elimination or diminution of vagueness or of open texture may however be desirable for the unhampered and smooth philosophical *employment* of these concepts; for the clear expression and communication of the results of philosophical inquiry.

(3) What I have said will be true, only more obviously so, in respect to any philosophically-important ordinary expressions that are not

[1] "The Problem of Linguistic Inadequacy," *Philosophical Analysis* (Ithaca, New York, 1950), edited by Max Black, pp. 15–37. I am referring in particular to her discussion on pp. 26ff. But the analysis of a general idea, though it cannot consist in or include "the removal of vagueness, or even the diminution of it" (*Ibid.*, p. 26), is a logically necessary first step, and so is an invaluable help, in any attempt to diminish or remove vagueness or marginal indeterminacy.

vague and/or do not involve marginal indeterminacy in their ordinary applications. For what redefinition can be necessarily involved in their case if analysis does not, by its very nature, distort or alter the analysandum? Suppose that some of these expressions, though non-vague and not involving borderline cases, express concepts or have meanings that are self-inconsistent; or that, as Körner contends, imply unwanted or undesirable metaphysical beliefs. Or suppose that they suffer from other defects. In what conceivable way can the analysis of the concepts or meanings concerned consist in or involve the elimination of the particular defect? If analysis *qua* analysis does not include or involve the elimination of vagueness or marginal indeterminacy, it also cannot, it seems to me, involve or include the elimination of the foregoing, or other, defects. But once more, the correct analysis of the defective concepts is an indispensable first step in the attempt to remedy these defects.

In the foregoing discussion I have attempted to show that semantic analysis–at least the two forms of it that we have so far discussed–does not (in a logical sense) necessarily involve or include, and does not necessarily lead to, a redefinition of the analysandum. From the former it follows, *a fortiori*, that semantic analysis does not consist in "replacement analysis." This remains true even if Körner is, or were, right that "replacement analysis" is the form of analysis actually practised by contemporary analytical philosophers.

Our next task is to discover the different kinds of logical situations, if any, in which it is desirable for philosophers to modify ordinary language for *philosophical purposes*. But a warning is necessary. We cannot, without a careful comparison of science and philosophy, validly argue, as some philosophers do,[1] that redefinition is *permissible* in philosophy since it is permissible in science. For this reason I shall not myself use any analogies or disanalogies to science in our attempt to deal with the present question. Most of what I have to say about philosophy *vis-à-vis* science in respect to redefinition will be stated in another place. In line with this, I shall also not say anything here about the desirability or undesirability of the philosopher's redefinition of ordinary expressions in the light of the empirical facts he does, or may, utilize. That again will be dealt with later. At present we are interested

[1] Cf. for instance Paul W. Kurtz, "Has Mr. Flew Abandoned 'The Logic of Ordinary Use?'" *Philosophical Studies*, vol. IX, Nos. 5–6 (October–December, 1958), p. 76. See also Yehoshua Bar-Hillel, "Analysis of 'Correct Language,'" *Mind*, N. S. vol. LV, No. 220 (October, 1946), in which the author calls for the utilization of constructed language-systems in philosophy analogously to the employment of constructed forms in science.

in determining the desirability or undesirability of semantic reconstruction only insofar as it arises in relation to semantic analysis.

The question of the redefinition of ordinary expressions in philosophy arises, it is essential to note, in relation to the philosopher's attempt to express and so to communicate the results of his inquiries. Concerning semantic analysis, it arises in relation to his attempt to express and communicate the results of particular analyses. So, stated precisely, our general question is whether (any given) ordinary language is capable, as it stands, of adequately expressing, hence communicating, the results of philosophical inquiry. In its more restricted present form, our question is whether ordinary language is capable of adequately expressing and communicating the results of semantic analysis. A clear awareness of the precise nature of our question will save us a great deal of trouble and confusion.

Semantic analysis in philosophy, as we have envisioned it, may arise in relation to various technical languages such as that of physics (to the extent in which it is technical), as well as in relation to ordinary language. As far as the former is concerned, it arises in relation to Philosophy of Science, Aesthetics and Philosophy of Art, Philosophy of Religion and Philosophy of Mathematics. It also arises in the analysis of the technical terminology (if any) of a given philosopher; whether in his writings on the foregoing branches of philosophy or in metaphysics, epistemology or ethics. In relation to ordinary language, semantic analysis includes the analysis of the non-technical utterances of philosophers. We thus get a double question. I shall attempt to answer both questions together as much as possible. What is left out in relation to technical languages I shall supply to some extent in chapter ten.

The answer to our question, to my mind, is quite simple. Redefinition of ordinary language *is* permissible and desirable where there is a good reason for doing so. Since there can be different kinds or sorts of redefinition, the matter can be expressed more precisely by saying that, in any given case, the kinds of redefinition that are permissible and desirable are those for which there are good reasons in that particular case. Even in this form, our prescriptive rule may appear to be platitudinous if not tautologous. The crucial point, and one which tends to generate much heat, is what reasons are "good reasons" – or what kinds of redefinition, under what conditions, *are* permissible and desirable.

The following list does not pretend to be exhaustive; though it seems to me to give the major forms of redefinition that are persmissible and desirable *whenever there are good reasons for effecting them:*

(a) The restriction of an ordinary concept;

(i) Without eliminating any "openness" in the concept, if present;

(ii) By eliminating the "openness" of an open-textured concept;

(iii) By eliminating the "openness" of an open-textured concept and restricting the concept in other ways;

(b) The broadening of an ordinary concept;

(c) The broadening and the restricting of an ordinary concept, in different respects or directions;

(d) The elimination of vagueness;

(e) The elimination of inconsistencies in an ordinary concept.

I shall now consider these forms of redefinition separately, in order to discover, in each case, the major kinds of situations in which it is permissible and desirable. I should point out at the outset, however, that perhaps in the overwhelming majority of cases where past philosophers effected any of these or other forms of redefinition, they were perfectly unaware that they were doing so. This is true whether the particular redefinitions effected were permissible and desirable, or not permissible and undesirable.

(a) The restriction of ordinary concepts is a familiar procedure in traditional philosophy; and in many of its famous instances it has brought untold harm to it. It is enough to mention the widespread restriction of the notion of knowledge to "*certain*" knowledge, and the relegation of probable knowledge to the limbo of "belief" or "opinion." What we have here is not a mere distinction drawn between the concepts of probable and "certain" knowledge, but the downright exclusion of the former from the concept of knowledge. A similar restriction occurs when some philosophers or poets "conceive" of happiness as a kind of rarefied, quasi-mystical experience that is practically, if not altogether, unattainable in our "imperfect" world. Some, but less extreme, restriction is also implied by the famous saying: "Call no man happy until he is dead." Here the element of relative permanence involved in the ordinary notion of happiness is exaggerated to span one's entire life; with the consequence that some states of affairs ordinarily referred to as "happiness" cease to qualify as such.

Our two examples illustrate what seem to me to be illegitimate restrictions of ordinary concepts. They do not give us greater clarity but only lead to confusion; and no greater preciseness is gained. This has been amply shown in the history of philosophy in regard to the concept of knowledge.

The restrictions effected might have been legitimate and desirable for philosophical purposes if they had eliminated any openness in the two ordinary concepts. For the elimination of openness *may* result in a concept that is more precise or better fitted for the cognitive, noetic, non-practical purposes of philosophy. This is *not* to say that open-textured ordinary concepts are not precise enough or not perfectly adequate for the everyday purposes of life, which involve the communication of ideas as well as action. (It is enough to reflect on how we employ such simple everyday concepts as *table* and *chair, in the different meanings or senses of* 'table' and 'chair' respectively, to see the truth of this.) There is no contradiction in holding that a given ordinary concept is perfectly adequate for ordinary purposes but is not perfectly adequate for philosophy. Let us note that the elimination of "openness" will be desirable, in practice, only in respect to concepts that are in philosophical currency; and even then it will be requisite and useful only in relation to the borderline cases. Most of these borderline cases arise relatively rarely in ordinary life, and so do not materially affect or impede ordinary communication. Their rarity is, in general, one main reason why these borderline cases *are*, and tend to *remain*, borderline cases. (There are a number of notable exceptions to these things, however. For example, in the case of art, the rarity of borderline cases – if borderline cases there are really rare – is certainly not the only, or even the main, reason for this phenomenon. The openness of the concept of art is mainly due to, and reflects, an extremely important feature of the activity we call creating a work of art. I mean the fact that a work of art, by the very meaning of this expression, is *expected* to be an original creation.) But – and this is a striking and significant fact – a considerable number, perhaps many, of the ordinary concepts that are the stock-in-trade of philosophical analysis and philosophical discussion, appear to be open-textured. Examples, chosen at random, are: 'life,' 'living,' 'inanimate,' 'intelligent,' 'thinks,' 'consciousness,' 'conscious,' 'mind,' 'imagines' and 'imagination.' What is more, a good deal of philosophical discussion and controversy concern the borderline cases, directly or indirectly. Note for instance the current debate in philosophical circles as to whether electronic "brains" (note the use of the word) think; or the debate as to whether or not euthanasia is morally right ("Is euthanasia murder?" – Note the "openness" of the concept *murder*). These debates may be usefully terminated by the restriction of the relevant concepts through the elimination of "openness." As to what particular concepts may require such redefinition, this can only be discovered in practice by a painstaking and piecemeal analysis of individual philosophically-significant concepts.

The restriction of ordinary concepts in other ways than the elimination of any "openness" in them is legitimate and desirable at least in two major types of case; i.e., where an ordinary concept is (1) vague, and/or (2) internally inconsistent. The question here is not Under what conditions is it legitimate to restrict a vague or an inconsistent concept? With the exception of some philosophers who identify vagueness with marginal indeterminacy,[1] it is commonly agreed that vagueness, as well as inconsistency, is an *un*desirable quality and ought to be removed. The real question is in what ways, and to what extent, the restriction of such concepts can eliminate their vagueness and/or inconsistency.

That some ordinary expressions are vague in their ordinary uses is I think unquestionable. Some of these vague words may originally have been quite precise but may have lost their precision through their being used in non-ordinary, such as philosophical, senses. There are also expressions that are vague in their philosophical employment, whether or not they are also vague in their ordinary employment, if any.

To the shame of philosophers, it is difficult to find vague ordinary expressions that have really been improved in their hands. The words 'substance,' 'free' and 'not free,' 'compelled,' 'determined,' 'responsible,' 'reasonable' (also 'rational,' 'irrational,'), 'idea' are, it seems to me, perfectly, or almost perfectly non-vague in their ordinary uses. Yet as any student of philosophy knows, the philosophical uses of these words are (or at least have been until recently) hopelessly confused and sometimes even mutually exclusive.[2] On the other hand, the words 'liberal,' 'liberalism,' 'conservative,' 'internationalism,' 'nationalism' and other political terms; 'believer,' 'unbeliever,' 'fundamentalist,' 'immoral,' and other religious or ethical terms, are examples of words that are more or less vague in their ordinary employment and often also vague (sometimes even vaguer) in their philosophical employment.

In the first type of case distinguished above, the vagueness of a philosophical expression can be remedied by our *going back* to its

[1] For example Max Black and Alice Ambrose Lazerowitz, to mention only two such philosophers.

[2] Many if not all of the above expressions and others like them have two or more ordinary senses or meanings. This does not, however, make them vague or otherwise imprecise. For an expression to be *ambiguous* in a given context, it must of necessity have two of more senses or meanings to begin with. But it is plainly false that expressions that have two or more senses or meanings are always used ambiguously in ordinary discourse. Also, ambiguity and vagueness are two different things.

ordinary uses and conforming to them. If these ordinary uses involve marginal indeterminacy, we should strive to conform to the expression's more or less clear-cut, standard ordinary applications. The expression's philosophical employment can then be limited to these. A good example would be the word 'idea.'

If an expression is vague in its ordinary employment, the preceding cannot be profitably done in order to remedy any vagueness from which it may be suffering in its philosophical employment. Or if an ordinary expression is vague, it cannot, as it stands, be profitably employed in philosophy or even in ordinary discourse. To be profitably employed, it has first to be redefined. This brings us to the question as to the extent to which the restriction of its ordinary and/or philosophical uses can serve this purpose.

The answer appears to be that the restriction of the uses of a vague expression can satisfactorily serve this purpose if the expression is not, as we ordinarily say, "hopelessly vague"; that is, if it possesses a range of applications common to the majority, or a large minority, of its actual applications by different users. The desired result can then be achieved by confining its future usage to this common range of applications.[1] This is possible whether the "defining features" constituting this latter are determinate or relatively determinate characteristics, or only certain "family resemblances." If the expression is "hopelessly vague," it will be necessary to substitute an entirely, or almost entirely new (non-vague) concept for the old one conveyed by it. In such cases, it is advisable to use a new but related ordinary word in place of the old expression; or at least to qualify the old expression by an epithet. In some cases it may be advisable to coin a new expression.

As regards inconsistency, the claim is frequently made in contemporary writings that ordinary language *as a whole* is inconsistent. This I have not found to be borne out at least by the very limited analyses of ordinary concepts I have hitherto undertaken. Further, it would be quite surprising if ordinary language as a whole were inconsistent, in view of our undoubted ability to use ordinary language smoothly and effectively in the vast majority of everyday situations. Yet I do not wish to assert that the uses of *no* ordinary expressions are inconsistent. It may well be true that the uses of some (but by no means the majority of) ordinary expressions are inconsistent. The Theory of Types, for instance, is widely believed to have eliminated certain inconsistencies

[1] This can be done, for instance, in the case of 'happiness' or 'happy'; though it is not what philosophers have usually done. (See the section on open-texture.)

in ordinary language. Yet this, even if true, is a far cry from saying that the uses of all or most ordinary expressions are inconsistent.[1]

But, in a sense, all this is immaterial for our present discussion. As will be remembered, our question is to what extent, if at all, can redefinition by restriction remove inconsistency in ordinary language, *if it is or were present.* The factual question as to what particular expressions have inconsistent uses, and the number of these expressions, is quite a different matter. Our question can also arise in relation to any non-ordinary – say philosophical – uses of expressions that may be inconsistent.

I can think of two possible ways in which inconsistency can be removed by redefinition. The first consists in the replacement of the concept in hand by an *entirely* new one. This, to my mind, is permissible or desirable only where the concept is very complex and suffers from pervasive or subtle inconsistencies, or inconsistencies that are otherwise hard to locate. The second way of eliminating inconsistency consists in the restriction of the inconsistent concept, not its complete replacement by another concept. In its milder and usually more desirable form, this means the elimination of one term of the conflicting pair of elements in the concept; leaving the other part, now freed from inconsistency, in the now-restricted concept. Thus if the concept's logical content be represented by elements (characteristics) *a*, *b*, *c*, *d*, *e*, and *c* and *e* are mutually exclusive, consistency can be achieved by eliminating either *c* or *e* from the concept. In its more drastic form, both *c* and *e* are eliminated from the concept. In the main, the former alone is desirable; since the redefined concept remains as close as is possible to the original concept.

Our prescriptive rule can be readily reformulated in terms of meanings or other kinds of uses of expressions. But this will not be done here.

A different type of situation is frequently encountered in traditional philosophy. Seizing upon one particular part of the meaning of an expression as *the* essential part, a philosopher often tends to minimize or completely ignore the rest of its meaning, without being aware that he

[1] Cf. "Ordinary language is limited; it is frequently inconsistent with itself." Paul Kurtz, *op. cit.*, p. 76. Kurtz does not say in what way he thinks the latter is true, and does not offer any evidence in support of it. For, clearly, the burden of proof lies on anyone who maintains that ordinary language is inconsistent.

For a somewhat detailed criticism of the general view that ordinary language is intrinsically inadequate or defective, as well as for corroboration of other points made in the present chapter, see Alice Ambrose, *op. cit.*, *passim.*

is doing so. In the latter case the overemphasis on the cherished part results in the elimination of part of the expression's meaning.

The desire to bring into relief a given part of an expression's meaning regarded as important is perfectly legitimate if the emphasized part *is* important in some way. It is not legitimate to *over*emphasize this one part – or, what is worse, actually to exclude other parts of the expression's meaning. For these, whether important or unimportant, are likewise part of the meaning. The situation becomes still worse when these changes are effected in ignorance of their real nature: when the philosopher covertly restricts the meaning of the expression, but supposes that he is merely giving us the results of a semantic analysis of it (e.g. in the form of a reported definition). But nothing positive is gained even where the redefinition is intentional and the philosopher expressly tells us what he has done and why he has done it. The original meaning is not improved. Moreover, the desired emphasis can very well be made without one's resorting to such a drastic measure as the restriction of the expression's meaning. The philosopher is free to *tell* us how important is the part of the meaning he favors, without tampering with the ordinary meaning.

A possible example of what I have been saying, drawn from Aesthetics, is Clive Bell's "theory" that Art is "significant form." [1] As Beryl Lake shows, "adopting his [Bell's] view clearly amounts to deciding not to call anything which we do not also call 'significant form,' 'work of art.'" [2] She also maintains the Croce's view of Art as "intuition" or "intuitive knowledge" involves a similar restriction.[3] This, if true, would constitute a second example of the kind of restriction we are talking about. But it does nor really seem to me to be the case, except if 'intuition' is taken to denote an idea or a set of ideas evoked (as we say) by a work of art. It would not be true if it is taken to denote an emotional experience evoked by a work. For as an analysis of the ordinary uses of 'work of art' shows, ideas but *not* feelings or emotions (emotional experience) are ordinarily regarded as a possible part or aspect of works of art.[4] If 'intuition' is understood in the sense of 'emotional experience,' Croce's "view" (really his covert stipulated

[1] For a somewhat detailed attempt to show that Bell's "view" is, in effect, a *restriction* of the meaning of 'work of art' to "significant form," see Beryl Lake, "A Study Of The Irrefutability Of Two Aesthetic Theories," *Aesthetics And Language* (Basil Blackwell, 1954), pp. 107–113. I am assuming for the sake of illustration that 'significant form' does mean something, and that its meaning is part of the ordinary meaning of 'work of art.'

[2] *Ibid.*, p. 110.

[3] *Ibid.*, pp. 100–107, *passim.*

[4] See my "Works of Art and Physical Reality," *Ratio*, vol. II, 1959, pp. 148–161.

definition) would be tantamount to a complete redefinition: to the complete *replacement* of the ordinary concept of 'work of art' by a different concept. (A work of art, under what I have elsewhere called Standard Conditions, does evoke, by the very meaning of 'work of art,' an aesthetic (emotional) experience.)[1]

The expression 'work of art,' which we have used to illustrate restriction of meaning, is a referring expression. The same type of restriction involved can occur, however, in respect to non-referring expressions; namely, in respect to expressions that name fictitious entities (e.g., 'centaur'), and expressions that do not function as names at all (e.g., 'existence').

We now pass to the redefinition of concepts through the extension of the ordinary meanings of the expressions conveying them.

The extension of the meanings of expressions does not raise any significant problems except with regard to ordinary expressions. One – a broader – philosophical use of a non-ordinary expression is as good as another – narrower – philosophical use of it. True, confusion may result from the stretching of the current meaning of a philosophical expression; but this can be avoided if the philosopher effecting the extension makes clear what he is doing, and in what way he is extending the old meaning.

It might be asked whether the same does not really apply in respect to *ordinary* expressions; whether it is not permissible for a philosopher to stretch the ordinary meaning of an expression, so long as he makes it clear that he is doing so, and indicates the respect in which he is doing it. The answer, to my mind, is No. In order to see why this is so, we must consider the kinds of situations in which the meaning of an ordinary expression can be legitimately extended.

Our rule, here as elsewhere, is the following: an extension of the meaning of an expression is *not* permissible, therefore, *a fortiori*, is undesirable, unless there is a real need for it. At the same time, it is my belief that indiscriminate or whole-sale extension of the meanings of ordinary expressions is not *needed*, hence is not desirable. At any rate, the desirability of extending the meaning of any given expressions one may wish to redefine has to be individually demonstrated.

That there are situations in which the philosophical extension of the ordinary meanings of expressions is permissible and desirable I fully concede. For instance, as we shall see in chapter ten, scientific or other

[3] See my "Art-Names and Aesthetic Judgments," *passim*. For other common examples of restriction of meaning of the present sort, see the section on extension of meaning.

empirical discoveries sometimes make such a procedure desirable. What interests us here is whether purely logical or conceptual considerations ever make it desirable, in relation to semantic analysis.

It is clear that internal inconsistencies in concepts cannot be eliminated through redefinition by extension. They cannot provide us, therefore, with any good reasons for the redefinition of expressions by extension. Marginal indeterminacy, on the other hand, can be eliminated by extending the meaning of the expression that involves it; provided that a *sharp* boundary line is now drawn, by express stipulation, between the meaning as extended and the meaning of its new, restricted negative. Indeed, any *restriction* of an expression's meaning by stipulation, whenever it includes the drawing of a sharp boundary line around the new meaning, so to speak, logically or necessarily entails a corresponding extension of the meaning of its negative. Stated otherwise, whenever we eliminate the marginal indeterminacy of an expression 'X' through a restriction of its meaning, we *ipso facto* and automatically eliminate the corresponding marginal indeterminacy of 'not-X' through an automatic *extension* of its meaning. Or, when 'X' becomes *more determinate*, in the sense of not involving marginal indeterminacy,[1] 'not-X' likewise becomes more determinate in the same sense of 'determinate.'

The same is true, *mutatis mutandis*, in respect to vagueness. Whenever the meaning of a vague expression is restricted, a corresponding extension occurs in its negative. Hence whenever vagueness is eliminable through restriction of a vague expression's meaning, the corresponding extension of its negative's meaning is, *ipso facto*, permissible and desirable.

If the meaning of an expression is in any degree indeterminate in other ways (if any) than through vagueness or marginal indeterminacy, and if this can be remedied by some restriction of the expression's meaning, the corresponding extension of the meaning of its negative is again perfectly in order.[2]

So far we have talked about the extension of the meaning of an

[1] The qualification is necessary, since the indeterminateness of the meaning of expressions may be of different kinds. One kind of such indeterminateness, distinct from marginal indeterminacy, is vagueness.

[2] I should perhaps add that in respect to marginal indeterminacy or any other type of indeterminateness of the meaning of expressions except vagueness, if any, the meaning of an expression is not really determinate or indeterminate simpliciter: it is rather "sufficiently" or "not sufficiently" determinate in this or that particular context. It is for this reason that I said before that expressions involving marginal indeterminacy in their meanings are indeterminate *only* in relation to borderline cases – i.e., in terms of the present analysis, only when we attempt to employ them in relation to certain, but not all, objects or situations.

expression if and when it is inconsistent or vague, or involves marginal indeterminacy; where the extension is intended to eliminate this inconsistency, vagueness or marginal indeterminacy. There are, however, other sorts of extension of meaning.

In the first place, the meaning of an expression 'X' may be extended because it is felt that there is a great similarity, discovered through semantic analysis, between it and the meaning of another expression 'Y': a similarity so great as to justify the extension of 'X's' meaning to include 'Y's' meaning. 'Y' is then eliminated from the particular philosopher's technical vocabulary; or, if it did not originally form part of it, it is not added to it at all.

A second form of "assimilation" consists in adding to the meaning of an expression 'X' a given *part* of the meaning of a second expression 'Y' so that 'Y's' meaning is narrowed down. In the present type of case the added element of meaning will not fall within the indeterminate penumbra of 'X's' meaning (even where it possesses such a penumbra). It will be a definitely *new* element added to it. This procedure is compatible with two logical alternatives: (i) the new element of meaning is henceforth excluded from 'Y's' ordinary meaning; or (ii) it is retained in 'Y's' meaning as well.

It is possible of course to extend the meaning of a given expression, in different directions, in both of the foregoing ways. Also, in the case of the second form of extension of meaning, it is possible to "assimilate" two or more new elements of meaning from a number of different expressions.

The first type of "assimilation" does not seem to me to be permissible or useful except where the "donor-expression" is hopelessly vague or hopelessly inconsistent. (This is only a more extreme form of a type of extension we spoke about earlier, and which we found to be justified in certain specified types of cases.) The second type of "assimilation" is useless, hence is not desirable, where the "donor-expression" is vague or inconsistent.

As to whether good reasons could be discovered elsewhere, this will become clearer as we proceed.

We have described the present types of extension of meaning as involving the *assimilation of the whole or a part of the meaning of another expression*. In respect to some expressions, this way of characterizing the present form of redefinition is unnecessary and too restrictive. We can get a more general type of extension of meaning if we broaden this characterization in the following manner. The meaning of an ordinary expression will be said to be extended if it is made to apply to objects (including situations, events, and so on) to which it does not ordinarily apply; whether or not this extension involves the assimilation of the meaning, or part of the meaning, of other expressions. As formulated in the present broader form the present general kind of extension is amply illustrated by the history of philosophy, and is therefore of particular interest to us. In some cases the situation is unambiguous. The use of the term 'right' (in the ethical sense) synonymously with 'rational' – for example, in consequence of a "view" claiming that right acts are the same as rational acts (Cf. Plato and Aristotle) – is a case in point. For in point of fact right acts are, logically speaking, only a sub-class of rational acts. All morally right acts are also rational acts; but the term 'rational' applies to non-moral as well as to moral behavior. There are certain states of affairs or actions that are rational but non-moral; hence neither right nor wrong. Similarly with 'wrong' and 'irrational.' [1]

Other clear examples are (what is in effect) the materialist's extension of the uses of the words 'matter,' 'material' and 'physical'; and the idealist's extension of the uses of the words 'mind' and 'mental' (also 'idea' and 'ideal'). A special instance of the former is the "view" of some traditional materialists that thought is a form of motion. Both materialists and idealists regard the extension of meaning they effect (whenever they are aware that they are effecting an extension of meaning) as dictated by empirical facts. But (assuming that they are empirical) numerous criticisms have amply shown that these "views" are simply false. In other words, the redefinitions these philosophers effect are not justified on empirical grounds. Further, there do not seem to be any logical, semantic grounds for effecting the proposed extensions. As for our first example, the extension of the ordinary uses of 'right' to render it synonymous with 'rational,' rests, in the last analysis, on a lack of clear awareness of the *differences* between their ordinary uses.

The examples we have so far chosen illustrate the extension of the meaning of an ordinary word with a view to making it applicable to objects to which it *definitely* does *not* apply. There are other actual historical cases of extension of meaning which are not as clear-cut as these. As we saw in relation to our discussion of redefinition by restriction, the meaning of an expression may be restricted in such a way as to make the expression definitely *in*applicable to *borderline* cases.

[1] See my "What is rationality?" *Theoria*, vol. XXIV, 3; 1958. The above can also be used to illustrate the restriction of the meaning of an expression such that it is no longer applied to certain things to which it originally applied: i.e., if we limit the applications of '*rational*' to moral situations.

Similarly, and in an opposite move, the meaning of an expression may be extended in order to make the expression applicable, without qualification, to borderline cases. Such situations logically arise because the possibility of our encountering borderline cases means the absence of a hard-and-fast dividing line between objects in whose case the unqualified applicability or inapplicability of the particular expression is indeterminate, and objects in whose case the unqualified inapplicability of the expression is definite. That is, it is theoretically possible to encounter objects such that we cannot know with assurance whether to regard them as definitely X's or definitely not-X's, or only as possibly X's and possibly not-X's, without qualification.

All this is of more than purely logical or theoretical interest. For one of the traditional questions of philosophers is whether this or that object has such and such a nature or "essence." For instance, whether perceived objects are really mental; or whether the universe as a whole exhibits some overall order or purpose. Stated in linguistic terms, philosophers assert, deny or inquire about the applicability or inapplicability of various expressions to objects other than and often quite different (in some cases entirely or almost entirely different) from those to which they ordinarily apply. Where the new objects are *very* different in character from those to which a given expression ordinarily applies, we can safely say that the expression is inapplicable to them; and it would remain so, unless its ordinary meaning is appropriately extended. Thus thought is very different from motion; and to speak of it as a form of motion is to misuse language, to extend illegitimately the ordinary meaning of 'motion.' But what about the theist's application of such expressions as 'effect,' 'purposive,' 'orderly' to the universe as a whole (as for instance in some of the traditional arguments for God's existence); or the application of such expressions as 'cause' (also 'unmoved mover'), 'good' '(all) powerful,' '(all) knowing' and purposive' to presumed supernatural beings? Suppose we apply the words 'effect' and 'orderly' to the universe as a whole: would we be extending the ordinary meanings of these words to (i) a borderline case, or (ii) to a case to which these words, in their ordinary meaning, are definitely inapplicable; or would we be (iii) merely applying them to a new member of the class of objects to which these words *are* ordinarily applicable? And suppose that in the present example we are able to rule our (iii): on what grounds can we decide between (i) and (ii)? I submit that in some cases, if not also here, there is nothing on the basis of which a definite decision can be made.

In the case of an expression involving marginal indeterminacy it is legitimate, it seems to me, to extend the meaning of the expression so as to make it definitely applicable to the borderline cases, if the philosopher is aiming at greater precision. However, as I pointed out before, this is easier said than actually done; since we sometimes cannot tell whether a given object is or is not a borderline case.

In respect to a particular object o to which a given expression 'A' is definitely inapplicable, an extension of 'A's' meaning to render it applicable to o is permissible if the resemblance between o and the objects to which 'A' ordinarily applies is greater than the dissimilarities between them. Or, where this does not obtain, if there exists some similarity between the features of o and those of A that is deemed important for some philosophical reason or other; and it is desired to bring this similarity into relief. In practice, the permissibility and desirability of the extension will frequently be an open question; and controversy, pro and con, will rage among philosophers – unless philosophers agree on methods of measuring degrees of similarity and dissimilarity. But I see no practicable way in which such agreement can be achieved, except perhaps in relatively few cases; since some or all of the features involved in relation to philosophical questions of the present sort are often non-quantitative in nature. The only relatively practicable alternative is for philosophers to reach agreement piecemeal on particular expressions. This will often be a long, arduous and, sometimes, very discouraging procedure, philosophical debates (and Congresses too) being what they are. Otherwise, philosophers will be forced to wait (though only in respect to some expressions) until law courts, politicians, religious leaders or governments make the decision whether to extend the meaning of this or that expression. Philosophers (supposing that they agree) can then thankfully use any such redefined expressions in their writings, in their new, extended meanings. I shall give two recent historical examples with which I am acquainted, in which an extension of meaning has been effected through court or government action. The first is the extension of the meaning of 'traitor' to include the giving of aid by the head of a State to an enemy invader (in the trial of Marshall Pétain); the second is the extension of the meaning of 'hero' (with corresponding restriction of the meaning of 'traitor') to include any attempts to overthrow a totalitarian or otherwise tyrannical ruler during wartime by a citizen of that country serving in the armed forces (in the recent rulings in West Germany regarding the Stauffenberg case; respecting the abortive attempt made on Hitler's life in 1944).

The philosopher who advocates redefinition by extension can point to one (to my mind the only) advantage of doing so: the introduction of a certain degree of logical tidiness and elegance into our thinking; the comparative simplification of the vast complexity of the "logical grammar" of ordinary language. One of the traditional tasks of philosophy has been the logically-related systematization of our thought in terms of general concepts; and extensions of meaning may help to reduce the number of general concepts required for this.[1] This will in turn make it easier for us to see the forest and not merely the individual trees, so to speak. The disadvantage is that this process introduces a certain artificiality or unreality into our thought; a simplicity that is too good to be true. As long as this process of simplification by extension does not distort the picture almost beyond recognition (as it *does* in the system of a Hegel or of a Bradley), and as long as we are fully aware that we are introducing an artificial simplicity, no serious harm will be done. Indeed, I am at present inclined to think that some over-simplification and artificiality may be practically inescapable, *in practice*, in any philosophical inquiry that goes in any degree beyond piecemeal description of the logical content of individual concepts, the piecemeal exhibition of meanings or other kinds of uses of expressions; in any attempt to pinpoint similarities and differences. This seems to be especially true if one wishes to lay different emphases on this or that similarity, on this or that difference. The semantic analysis of concepts, meanings and the like, in all its different forms, can, *in practice*, be likened to the making of a map: to borrow a well-known analogy of Gilbert Ryle's. The map is useful in making us see our way about; but its usefulness is forfeited if we mistake the map for the mapped area; if we regard every feature on the map as corresponding to some feature of the mapped terrain.

There is another important point – and a second danger incidental to the extension of ordinary meanings or concepts. The extension of a given concept logically results in the relative emptying of the concept; and the greater the extension, the emptier will be the resulting concept. This means that there is always a danger of emptying a concept too much – to such an extent that it becomes vacuous or almost vacuous, hence useless – in the attempt to make it applicable to an increasing number of entities. This is the case, for instance, with Thales's "Water"

[1] The above applies only in a very limited way, if at all, to extremely general concepts (categories); except where the extension of meaning is limited to borderline cases. For more drastic extension may lead to type violation. (See chapter eight.)

and the Objective Idealist's "Absolute." In such extreme cases, essential distinctions or differences are lost in the philosopher's insatiable and self-defeating quest for unity. On the other hand, if we attempt to preserve these distinctions or differences in our very general concepts, we run the danger of making them internally inconsistent.

We now come to a type of modification or ordinary language which, like redefinition by extension, consists in the application of an expression to objects to which it does not ordinarily apply; or (in some cases), to objects in respect to which its applicability or inapplicability is not fully determined by the rules of language. The difference is that the "extension" is achieved by the addition of a new sense or meaning to the expression's original senses or meanings. As an example of this type of "extension" – though philosophers who employ it generally do not regard it as any form of modification of language – I might mention the extension of the ordinary meaning of 'time' by the creation of a distinction within the ordinary concept of time. This occurs, for instance, if the philosopher regards (calls) the duration of the self's psychic states as "(metaphysical) *time*." A second example is the use of the words 'express' and 'expression' by aestheticians who subscribe to the Expression Theory of Art, to signify roughly (a) the artist's (alleged) "embodying" of his emotional experiences in the works of art he creates, and (usually also) (b) the *communication* of these (alleged) experiences to those who contemplate the works. A third example, I think, is the traditional philosopher's use of the expression 'free' and 'determined,' and related expressions, in the perennial controversy regarding "freedom of the will." (I also strongly suspect that the use of the word 'universals' in the Platonic sense constitutes a further example.) This type of modification of language, it will be noted, is similar in some ways to the drawing of distinctions within an ordinary concept that does not, so to speak, latently contain them.

Is such an "extension" of meaning ever permissible? My answer is Yes in the following types of cases: (1) where the new objects to be denoted by the expression in question equally resemble and differ from the objects denoted by any *one* of the expression's ordinary senses; or (2) where the new objects bear a *greater* resemblance than non-resemblance to the same.[1] It is clear that the "extension" is not permissible if there are no resemblances at all or only negligible, superficial resemblances, between the proposed and the actual denotata.

[1] I have already noted the practical difficulties involved in the attempt to apply these criteria to actual expressions. So I shall not say anything about them here.

A difficulty arises if the resemblance between an expression's proposed and actual denotata, though not superficial or negligible, is considerably less than the differences present. The former would then constitute a special sub-class of borderline cases; and, in my opinion, no general prescriptive rule can be laid down in regard to them. Individual cases must be judged on their own merit, in the light of the nature and importance of the particular purposes which the proposed "extension" is intended to serve. However, the "extension" is superfluous if the proposed denotata are already denoted by other expressions.[1] Above all, "extensions" in the present type of case are *not* permissible if they make the proposed new sense or meaning inconsistent with any of the old senses or meanings of the expression. Finally – and this is precisely why the present cases are doubtful ones – the extension is permissible only if the new sense or meaning is not so poor in logical content as to be almost vacuous [2] (i.e., too broad to exclude objects other than those expressly proposed for inclusion).

Let me add that these three provisos also apply, though only to a lesser extent, to (1) and (2) above.

We do not need to say anything about the redefinition of an ordinary expression by the simultaneous extension and restriction of its meaning in different respects; the conversion of a vague expression into a non-vague one; and the elimination of inconsistencies in an inconsistent ordinary expression. All three have already been taken care of in our earlier discussion of redefinition of ordinary meanings by restriction and extension respectively.

There is one final type of modification of the uses of expressions that we have not mentioned so far. I mean the modification, sometimes the complete change, of the emotive overtones of an emotive expression, without any accompanying change in the expression's ordinary meaning. (An example is the attempts of the Fascists in Italy and Germany to lend war an aura of moral goodness or nobility.) Clearly, this type of change is not a type of redefinition in the sense in which we have been concerned with it so far. As we have seen in chapter three, a word's emotive coloring (if and when such a coloring is present)

[1] As examples of "extention" of meaning which illustrate this, I might mention the traditional philosopher's use of the word 'is' and its derivatives in the sense of 'exists,' or in the sense of 'is real.' The first is exemplified in Descartes' "I think therefore I *am*"; the second in "Permanence *is*; change *is not*" (Parmenides) and "Change *is*; permanence *is not*" (Heraclitus). Similarly with the traditional philosopher's use of 'being,' 'non-being' and 'becoming.'"

[2] The notion of existence (subsistence) as applied to Platonic universals is almost certainly a case in point.

is not a part of its meaning; and emotive coloring is not a form of meaning at all. Yet it is an extremely important type of change that constantly occurs in actual life, particularly in different cultures or ages. The causes of this kind of change are usually many and complex; and some philosophers as well as many social and religious leaders have played, or have attempted to play, an active part in bringing about changes in the emotive coloring of particular expressions. What concerns us here is that in recent times this activity has, in many quarters, ceased to be regarded as one of the philosopher's proper tasks – a view fully shared by the present author. A philosopher is free, if he wishes, to attempt to modify the emotive coloring of ethical and other value terms. But in this present understanding of philosophy, the philosopher who does so will be acting in his capacity as a citizen of a given state, a member of a particular community or purely as a human being, as a social or religious reformer, an art critic, a humanitarian, and the like – not as a philosopher. The discovery of the kinds of situations in which it is permissible and desirable to effect changes in the emotive coloring of particular expressions is, to my mind, one of the important tasks of Ethics, Aesthetics and Theory of Value in general. It therefore constitutes one of the proper tasks of philosophy. The actual effecting of the changes, whenever they are permissible and desirable, is nonetheless not a philosophical task. A philosopher's analysis of the emotive uses of particular expressions may however influence other philosophers or non-philosophical laymen in their own employment of these expressions to evince certain attitudes or emotions or to influence others.

So far we have discussed the various possible kinds of redefinition of ordinary expressions, chiefly with a view to discovering the types of situations in which these are permissible and desirable. There we also maintained or implied that we can discover whether a given expression requires redefinition, and if so, the kind of required redefinition, by means of "exhibition analysis." The view has however been advanced that "The reform of common syntax (and of common semantics and pragmatics) cannot be accomplished by direct logical analysis alone. This task should be approached by construction of consistent language systems, by elaborating a "pure semiotic," which will supply the necessary terminology, etc.: shortly by the method of logical empiricism." [1] An appropriate reply to this, to my mind, has

[1] Yehoshua Bar-Hillel, "Analysis Of 'Correct' Language," *Mind*, vol. LV, No. 220 (October, 1946), p. 339.

already been given by Alice Ambrose in the essay referred to before [1]; and I shall not repeat it here. I only take exception to Ambrose's use of the words 'vague' and 'vagueness' in connection with ordinary language when what is meant, I think, is "marginal indeterminacy" or "open texture." (See earlier in this chapter.) We must however discuss a point of some importance which may seem to throw doubt on the very possibility of piecemeal modification of particular ordinary expressions, whenever such a modification is deemed desirable. For if the point I have in mind is borne out, a thoroughgoing and systematic modification of ordinary language would be necessary if *any* change in it at all is necessary. From this it would only be a step to the view that any "reform" of ordinary language can only be properly accomplished with the help of a constructed model.

The point I have in mind is that any change in the uses of any ordinary expression has some – sometimes far-reaching – repercussions on the ordinary uses of other ordinary expressions; that the redefinition of one expression perforce leads, by the inexorable demands of logical consistency, to the redefinition of other expressions. The simplest example is the restriction of the meaning of an expression as a result of the extension of the meaning of its opposite, or vice versa; at least in the case of pairs of expressions that do not involve marginal indeterminacy.

Frequently, the concomitant changes in meaning are not confined to the negative of a redefined expression. A cluster of expressions that are connected in meaning (not necessarily similar in meaning) are affected by the redefinition of any one of them. Or stated otherwise, a change in one concept affects a cluster of other concepts that are logically related to it. Or a "shift" in the meaning of one expression results in shifts in the meaning of related expressions. A familiar example is the change in the ordinary meaning of such words as 'belief' and 'opinion,' resulting from the traditional restriction of the ordinary meaning of 'knowledge' to absolutely incorrigible knowledge. In the case of some ontological categories, the changes in meaning are more embracing. Note for instance the drastic linguistic changes produced by the substitution of 'sense-datum' or 'sense-data' in every occurrence of 'physical,' 'sensible' or 'material object,' 'quality,' 'event' or 'state of affairs.' [2] Similarly with other phenomenalist "theories." Another

[1] *Op. cit.*, pp. 24–25.

[2] In this type of substitution or "translation" we have a good example of the attempt at a *complete replacement* of one meaning or one concept by another meaning or concept: at least

example is provided by the idealist's elimination of 'matter' and 'material' from his philosophical vocabulary and his dubbing everything in heaven or on earth 'idea,' 'mental' or 'mind,' as the case may be. The same is true, *mutatis mutandis*, of (what is in effect) the materialist's proposed modification of ordinary language.

The fact that logical consistency requires the progressive redefinition of some ordinary expressions as a result of redefinition of other ordinary expressions related to them, throws light on the nature of a considerable part of traditional philosophy; in particular, on traditional systems of metaphysics. It also, *pari passu*, throws light on the character of some of the devices employed by traditional philosophers to defend their "views" or to attack rival ones. Thus a traditional philosopher may start with the redefinition of one or a few philosophically-significant ordinary expressions, which he thinks is necessitated by the "nature of things." Whether or not the latter happens to be the case, we soon find that the philosopher is compelled, under the conscious or unconscious influence of the demands of logical consistency, or as a result of adverse criticism, to extend the process of redefinition to other expressions. Adverse criticism is particularly potent here; as such criticism, whatever else it may be, involves in effect the discovery of internal inconsistencies in the new uses of the redefined expressions, and/or inconsistencies between these uses as a whole and the rest of ordinary language. To guard his position against such attacks – indeed, to make it invulnerable to them – the philosopher is driven to a redefinition of related ordinary expressions in line with the redefinition he started with. This process will, ideally speaking, go on and on until the uses of all ordinary expressions that are in any way logically related to the modified ones have been themselves concomitantly and consistently modified. Once this point is reached, the "view" in hand will become absolutely irrefutable, impregnable.

If the process I have sketched is anything like the truth, it gives us one explanation of how and why some alleged explanatory hypotheses that are originally empirical in nature gradually become analytical, hence non-explanatory and non-experimental, empirically irrefutable. Such, for instance, would be the belief in God's existence, if it is true (as John Wisdom, say, holds) that this belief is now no longer a refutable, empirical belief. The crucial point, of course (on which Karl Popper and others have rightly insisted) is that a "view" such as the one in hand

if we interpret the Sense-datum Theory as providing us with (nothing but) an alternative language, not, or not also, a set of alleged empirical discoveries.

will become invulnerable precisely because it will now be completely analytical, non-empirical, and not because it is empirically true!

Lett me add, however, that we can logically arrive at *alternative* "languages" or "sub-languages" that are internally and externally consistent (i.e., consistent with the rest of ordinary language as well as with themselves), starting from *one* particular sort of redefinition of particular expressions. This is well illustrated by the differences between Subjective and Objective Idealism, on the one hand, and the (lesser) differences between the various systems of Objective Idealism on the other hand (e.g., the systems of Hegel, Royce and Bradley). What particular alternative "language" or "sub-language" we ultimately arrive at depends on the extent of the changes we effect in the uses of the expressions we redefine, and on how far we are prepared to extend this process of redefinition in one direction or another. Thus objective Idealism (e.g., in Hegel's, Bradley's or Royce's philosophy) seems to involve a greater and more extensive divergence from ordinary language than Subjective Idealism (e.g., in Berkeley's philosophy).

The foregoing discussion fits in well with what we shall say in the next chapter regarding the rôle of the *reductio ad absurdum argument* in philosophy. For the redefinition of the ordinary uses of expressions or of concepts, particularly of the magnitude of, say, Subjective and Objective Idealism, frequently results in violation of logical type. But more of this later.

The upshot of the preceding discussion is that the modification of the meaning of even one ordinary expression may logically necessitate changes in the meaning of other expressions. Whenever we propose a redefinition of some ordinary expression, therefore, we should be prepared to effect such concomitant changes in the ordinary meanings of some other expressions as may be logically required by the proposed change. If this is borne in mind, it would restrain any tendency to effect changes that are not absolutely necessary. It does not, however, preclude the effecting of any changes whatever in the meanings of ordinary expressions.

At the same time, and by the same token, our analysis does not logically entail or otherwise support the view that a wholesale, thoroughgoing redefinition of ordinary language is necessitated by just *any* change in it. Even changes in the most general epistemological or ontological categories, such as the categories of matter and mind, knowledge, truth and falsity, leave unaffected a large portion of ordinary language. It is clear that ordinary language as a whole would not be affected by the redefinition of any limited number of expressions occurring in it unless it constitutes a system in the formal logician's sense of this term; whereas (as Strawson and other linguistic analysts have shown) ordinary language is definitely not a system. It is, or can be, least of all regarded as a formal system by those who *advocate* the "reform" of ordinary language with the help of some formal system or other; or those who advocate its complete replacement by some constructed formal system. The advocates of neither position are therefore entitled to argue from the phenomenon we are considering to the necessity or desirability of constructing artificial "languages"!

It might be retorted that all this merely goes to show that if we are to modify ordinary language in order to convert it into a formal system, we have to go all the way: we have to effect a thoroughgoing and systematic change in it. And what better model could we hope to utilize than some already-constructed formal system?

The trouble with this argument is that it is premised on the false presumption that ordinary language can be so "reformed" as to become in the end a full-fledged formal system. Yet even if the presumption were true, the system we would get would simply not be ordinary language: it would be just one more formal system alongside the systems we have. The probable difference – admittedly an exceedingly important one – between it and the other formal systems would be its greater closeness to actual ordinary language; since, *ex hypothesi*, it would be arrived at by the progressive modification of the semantics and syntax of ordinary language.

It is important to note here that it is really impossible for philosophy to get away completely from ordinary language, even if the latter is intrinsically defective. Many of the concepts in which philosophy has been traditionally interested are ordinary concepts. In order to replace these concepts by allegedly more adequate concepts, we have to know exactly what the former are, in what respects they are defective, and hence in what specific respects the "ideal language" is to differ from ordinary language. Nay, we cannot know whether or not ordinary concepts are inadequate without a careful study of these concepts. In general, as Bar-Hillel himself states, "everyday-language ... is ultimately the only medium for constructing, interpreting, and comparing artificial language-systems, and therefore (and for many other reasons) absolutely indispensable." [1] Yet strangely enough, Bar-Hillel writes

[1] *Op. cit.*, p. 339.

on the same page that "the direct analytical approach seems to me a deplorable waste of time and energy ...." For all the foregoing can only be properly achieved through close attention to and careful analysis of ordinary language.

I mentioned before a second, more extreme position, held by some critics of ordinary language. I mean the position of those who advocate the replacement of ordinary language by some artificial, "ideal language." The advocates of this position, like those who propose to "reform" ordinary language, may be prepared to grant that a study of ordinary language is useful, even indispensable, for the construction or the better understanding of artificial language systems. Yet they will rightly insist that this does not, as such, invalidate their proposal to replace ordinary language in philosophy by some artificial language-system, *once the latter has been constructed*. To meet this proposal, we must go back to our earlier contention that the replacement of ordinary language by an artificial language-system is simply unnecessary; since ordinary language is not intrinsically defective. If this is true, the wholesale modification of ordinary language with a view to "reforming" it is not called for; *a fortiori*, its replacement by an artificial language-system is out of the question.

The foregoing discussion leads to an important point: it points to a possible *rapprochement* between the "ordinary language" and the "artificial language" approaches. The study of ordinary language, we said, is useful or even indispensable for the construction of artificial language-systems, and helps us to understand the latter's nature better. If it can now be shown that the construction of artificial language-systems is useful for a better understanding of ordinary languages, or serves any other philosophical purpose, it will have been shown – in general terms only, it is true – that instead of being mutually exclusive or incompatible, the two approaches are really complementary. And this indeed seems to me to be the case.[1]

In the first place, the careful and detailed comparison and contrast of ordinary languages and artificial language-systems sharpens our understanding of both. Also, and as a consequence, we will be better able to withstand the temptation to judge the one by standards and principles applicable to the other; to demand of the one that it be like the other; hence to avoid condemning the one for not doing, or not being able to do, what the other does.

[1] Cf. P. F. Strawson, "Construction And Analysis," *The Revolution In Philosophy* (London, 1957), pp. 104–105, and *passim*.

In the second place, artificial language-systems are of undoubted usefulness in the Philosophy of Science. The rigorous deductive systems of modern formal logic, and the deductive techniques utilized in the construction of these systems, have already thrown much light on particular scientific concepts and on the nature of science as a whole. And philosophers have been able to express their results with great rigor, preciseness and exactness, thanks to them. This promises to continue with even greater success as these methods are applied with greater care and with sharper logical tools both to new and old concepts.[1]

It is quite possible that this approach and the techniques it utilizes will also be found to be fruitful in other branches of philosophy; when employed systematically and exhaustively. One possible area of application is Ethics; where the construction of so-called deontic logical systems has been under way for some time now. In what ways and to what extent the formalization of ethical, aesthetic, epistemological or other types of concepts will be *philosophically* fruitful will become clearer with the passage of time. The essential thing, it seems to me, is to view different approaches to philosophy with an open mind; with a mind ready to learn from any approach that appears promising to the unjaundiced eye of reason. We should be tolerant of alternative approaches to philosophical inquiry, free from parochial and partisan narrowness and prejudices. For only by the toleration of differences can progress be hoped for in philosophy. Indeed, philosophy will be in danger of stagnation or even degeneration if the possibility of discovering new methods is not envisioned; or if the door is not left open for their discovery and utilization. These remarks also apply to all that I have hitherto maintained, and all that I shall later maintain, about possible or actual methods of philosophical analysis.

Finally, what I have just said should not obscure what seems to me to be the patent fact that semantic analysis has its rightful tasks which it, and it alone, can fully carry out. I am alluding to the tasks of semantic analysis that I spoke about in chapter six. Some contribution in respect to these may possibly be made through the construction of logical systems; but this contribution can only be a partial and secondary one.

Our discussion in the present chapter would be incomplete without a consideration of a form of semantic analysis which, though clearly distinguishable from "replacement analysis," is easily confused with

[1] There are, it can be shown, very good reasons for the success of the methods of logistic in the Philosophy of Science: the language and concepts of modern *science* being what they are. But these reasons do not concern us here.

it.[1] At the same time, the method I have in mind (and to which I shall refer as Semantic Analysis III), is important in its own right and has played a significant part in much of contemporary philosophy. No discussion of the major forms of philosophical analysis can therefore afford to neglect it.

The present method is a *bona fide* method of analysis, as "replacement analysis" is not, and is historically associated with Bertrand Russell. It has also been widely adopted; for example, by A. J. Ayer and other logical positivists or logical empiricists. As described by Ayer, the method consists of a logical device whereby the philosopher arrives at a definition of a symbol *in use*. The sentence arrived at with the help of this device, the definiens, is logically equivalent to, though it is not synonymous with, the sentence in which the symbol (expression) to be defined, the definiendum, occurs. Thus the definite description 'The author of *Waverley*' in the sentence "The author of *Waverley* is Scotch" (Example A) is defined in use in the sentence "One person, and one person only, wrote *Waverley*, and that person was Scotch." [2] Another example of definition in use Ayer gives is the translation of "A cat is a mammal" into "The class of mammals contains the class of cats" [3] (Example B). This translation provides us with a definition in use of the word 'is' in the original sentence.

I think it is clear in what sense the present method is a method of (logical) analysis. A correct definition in use of the definiendum is a gain in understanding of the latter's uses or meaning. In every such case the definiendum's meaning or a part of it is indicated, though not by means of a lexical definition. The definiendum's meaning is not modified or replaced by another meaning, unlike "replacement analysis." In this last respect the method is similar to the method of analysis discussed in chapter five – indeed, to all other methods of philosophical analysis. The basic difference between it and the method discussed in chapter five is that here the definiens is not synonymous with the definiendum, or even with the sentence in which that expression occurs. Because of this, the definition we get is different in kind from the connotative or other forms of real definition provided by successful analysis of the form discussed in chapter five.

[1] Körner, for instance, does not distinguish the two. As I stated earlier, he regards Russell's treatment of existential propositions in his Theory of Descriptions as an instance of "replacement analysis." Whereas, as I shall try to show, the Theory of Descriptions involves the use of a different – our present – method.

[2] *Language, Truth & Logic* (London, 1936), p. 69.

[3] *Ibid.*, p. 72.

In the case of Example B, the meaning or use of 'is' in it is explicated in terms of the class concepts *mammals* and *cats*, and the concept of logical inclusion; that is, by employing concepts not identical with any concept that one may suppose is expressed by the definiendum. There is here, as also in example A, no "resolution" of the concept of a complex whole into the concepts of the "simpler" elements of which the complex is composed, as in the classic example of a horse being divisible into legs, head, neck, etc. related in a certain way. Rather, the analysis uncovers a relation of inclusion of a class (that of cats) in a relatively proximate genus (the class of mammals). It is interesting that this type of "division," if we wish to call it that, is the type of "division" we find in Moore's *other* classic examples of analysis; the analysis of the concept *brother* in terms of the concepts *male* and *sibling* in the sentence "A brother is a male sibling." The latter utilizes the relation of logical inclusion between the class of siblings and the class of brothers, since the latter is a sub-class of the former. But apart from the fact that it also utilizes the differentia "maleness," thereby giving us a definition *per genus et differentiam*, while no differentiae are utilized in our example B, the analysis there is of a different sort from the analysis of *horse* in Moore's other example; though Moore himself does not seem to see this in his accounts of the nature of analysis as he allegedly practises it.[1]

The situation is still different with the definition in use of definite descriptions, the classic example of the use of the present method. According to Russell, the definition is use of a definite description, such as 'The author of *Waverley*,' is an application of his principle that whenever possible, logical constructions out of known entities should replace

[1] I might mention here parenthetically that Moore likewise fails to see that in the case of his analysis of the concept *hand* as involved in the statement "This is a hand" (coupled with pointing to a hand) in terms of what he calls sense data, we have yet another sort of "division." For the sense-data of a hand are not, according to Moore, parts of the hand or even of its surface: the relation between the hand and these sense-data is that of "source" to something arising from that "source" ("The Status of Sense Data," *Philosophical Studies*, p. 192). If we understand the relation "being a source of" in a causal sense, which Moore's extremely spare remarks about the notion of "source of" give credence to, though not if we think of the physical hand as the whole cause of the sense data of it which we directly apprehend (see *Ibid.*, p. 192), we see that analysis as envisioned by Moore himself leaves no room for this sort of analysis. But causal analysis is certainly a common, important and perfectly legitimate activity and, if properly conducted, provides us with explicit definitions or parts of definitions of the verbal expressions expressing the analysandum (the concept of the phenomenon that is the effect, or of the object that is the patient). These definitions or parts of definitions may not, in many cases, give us the whole or part of what people ordinarily have in mind in using the relevant definienda. But they would provide us at least with the kind of explicit definitions that scientists frequently give us, without, in the present cases, necessarily modifying the meaning of the definiendum as it is understood and employed in ordinary discourse (if it is an expression occurring in ordinary language to begin with).

inferences to unknown entities.[1] Russell points out that the uses of this principle are various, and the Theory of Descriptions, which is illustrated by the definition in use of any given definite description, is only one of its uses. When a proposition in which the words "the-so-and-so" occur is fully analysed, these words disappear.[2]

This method of analysis has the undoubted advantage over the form envisioned by Moore, and even our version of that method, in being free of the restrictions imposed on the latter two by the synonymity condition and its implications. The definition in use of certain verbal expressions by appeal to the concepts of modern logic, such as those of the calculus of classes, as in Example B, is a perfectly proper and useful procedure in philosophy. Yet, regarded merely as a means of arriving at definitions in use, it is not needed except where explicit lexical definitions or ostensive definitions are very difficult if not impossible to come by.

The definition in use of definite descriptions is equally cogent and useful. It enables us, as Russell has pointed out, to understand clearly the meaning of such sentences as "The present king of France does not exist," and to avoid confusions regarding the use of the words 'exist' and 'does not exist.' Russell maintains that an important consequence of the theory of descriptions is that it is meaningless to say "A exists" unless "A" is or stands for a phrase of the form "the so-and-so." [3]

I shall not inquire whether the foregoing and other conclusions that Russell derives from the Theory of Descriptions are really logical consequences of it. I shall not even inquire whether the Theory of Descriptions itself is a logical application of, and whether it necessarily presupposes Russell's "principle of construction"; and whether the latter is a cogent principle. These questions fall outside the scope of the present discussion. But whatever the answer to them, it is undoubtedly true that the method of "translation" which the Theory of Descriptions gives us does help to clarify the meaning or uses of definite descriptions. Let me emphasize, however, that the method does *not* show that the ordinary uses of definite descriptions or verbs like 'is' are in any way defective. But it does uncover, as Russell and Ayer have stated, the errors of some philosophers in misconstruing the meanings, or implications of the meanings, of these and other expressions; and it provides

[1] "Logical Atomism," in *Contemporary British Philosophy*, First Series (New York, 1926), edited by J. H. Muirhead, p. 363. See also pp. 364–365.

[2] *Ibid.*, pp. 364–365.

[3] *Ibid.*, p. 365. For other, related consequences of the theory according to Russell, see *History of Western Philosophy*, Sixth Printing (New York, [1945]), pp. 83ff.

us with a precise way of eliminating or avoiding these errors. On the basis of our empirical knowledge of the world, and of our knowledge of the correct ordinary meanings of definite descriptions and the expressions 'exist' and 'does not exist,' it enables us to avoid the error of attributing some sort of metaphysical reality to such things as golden mountains, or of thinking that a phrase such as "the present king of France" does refer to some queer sort of metaphysical entity. But the theory of descriptions itself, as such, does not and cannot *show* the non-existence of any alleged entity. Our ability to eliminate a definite description or any other verbal expression from a given sentence without affecting the truth-value of statements formed from it, cannot conjure anything existent out of reality. The existence of the author of *Waverley* and the non-existence of golden mountains have to be already known *in order* that a proper "translation" of those definite descriptions in accordance with the Theory of Descriptions may be effected. Stated differently, the correct definition in use of a definite description requires that it be eliminated from a sentence that would form *true* statements when actually affirmed. The choice of the requisite sentence is therefore logically prior to, and cannot be decided by, the method of "translation" itself.

It remains, nonetheless, that the translation removes the temptation to posit the existence of new kinds of entities, in some peculiar, non-ordinary (and probably dubious) sense of 'exist,' through a misconstruing of the "logical grammar" of definite descriptions and such words as 'exist' and 'does not exist.' Insofar as it does so, it is a specific application of the Law of Parsimony of which, as Russell points out, his "principle of construction" is one general form.

CHAPTER EIGHT

DEDUCTIVE INFERENCE AND ANALYSIS

In the preceding chapter we saw how a philosopher can utilize the results of exhibition analysis and other forms of semantic analysis that we have discussed, in the attempt to answer particular philosophical questions and to resolve – or dissolve – philosophical "puzzles." We saw that one major way in which the latter may be achieved consists in the construction of deductive arguments logically grounded on the results of accomplished analyses. There is, however, a second, more direct use of deductive arguments in relation to semantic analysis, with which we shall concern ourselves in the present chapter. Certain deductive arguments themselves can, in some cases, *reveal* or *uncover* some aspects of the logical grammar (or what Gilbert Ryle calls the logical powers) of one or more of the propositions constituting the premises of such arguments. Since the logical grammar of a proposition is logically a product of the logical powers of the concepts that compose it, as logically related in the particular propositions – or better, the logical grammar of concepts consists in the logical grammar of the propositions into which they enter as logical constituents[1] – the deductive arguments we have in mind reveal the logical grammar of the concepts which form the propositions serving as their premises.

The present use of deductive argument arises in respect to (some of) what I shall refer to as "direct arguments," and also in respect to what I shall correspondingly refer to as "indirect arguments." By 'indirect argument' I refer to the traditional *reductio ad absurdum*, or to the so-called Indirect (Chain) Argument, which is logically equivalent to the *reductio* argument. While by 'direct argument' I refer to such deductive arguments as the syllogism and the conditional argument, among others. I am not here concerned to give, or to attempt, a general definition or characterization of direct, or indirect, arguments. Our

[1] See below, p. 174.

discussion of types of direct argument, and our discussion of the *reductio* or Indirect Argument should make the distinction between the two sorts of argument clearer. For our present purposes, it is enough to state here that a direct argument is a type of deductive argument in which the valid consequences drawn are logically consistent with all the premises. On the other hand, an indirect argument is a type of argument in which valid consequences are drawn that are logically inconsistent with one or more of the premises, showing that at least one of the premises is either false, nonsensical or absurd, or self-contradictory but not absurd.

We shall begin with a consideration of direct arguments; after which we shall pass to indirect arguments.

I

I mentioned earlier that the syllogism is one major type of argument I have in mind in speaking of direct arguments. Traditionally, philosophers have employed the syllogism to deduce true propositions (conclusions) from other propositions (premises) believed or assumed to be true. This, as far as I can see, is rightly the only philosophical use to which syllogisms can be put whenever *both premises* in the argument are *synthetic, empirical propositions*. The deduction of a valid conclusion from the premises will implicitly utilize or logically rest upon the logical grammar (the logical powers) of the premises, and therefore of the constituent concepts. But it will not itself reveal, or help reveal, anything new about the logical grammar of the premises and hence about their constituent concepts. That is, it will not tell us anything about them that we do not already know by the mere fact that we know or believe that the premises are true (and hence, also that they are linguistically correct or well-formed) propositions. This is true of chains of syllogisms as well as of individual arguments.

In contrast to this, the valid conclusion of a syllogism both of whose premises are analytically (or logically) true propositions, may give us new information about the logical grammar of these premises and their constituents; while a chain – especially a relatively extended chain – of such syllogisms will almost certainly reveal something we did not know, or were not aware of before, about the logical grammar of some or all of the premises and their constituents. I use the word 'may' in connection with individual syllogisms because, in their case, the relevant information which the valid conclusion gives us about the premises will invariably be trivial or commonplace. It will be something we already know; and thus the construction of syllogisms for that purpose will be completely unnecessary. The syllogism

All lonely men are men
All men are mortal
∴ All lonely men are mortal

(assuming that the second premise is analytically true in ordinary language), obviously does not tell us anything we did not know about the logical grammar of 'lonely' and 'mortal.' We already know that the class of lonely men is included in the class of mortal things; and that the sentence 'All lonely men are mortal' is a correct, self-consistent sentence; etc. At the same time, the difficulty of constructing long chains of syllogisms – chains in which the conclusion of the first syllogism becomes the major or the minor premise of the next syllogism in the chain – with nothing but analytically true propositions as premises, makes the use of the present sort of syllogism next to worthless as a practical device of exhibition analysis. This difficulty does not, however, arise with respect to any form of argument in which a valid conclusion is, or a number of valid conclusions are drawn from a relatively large number of premises (at least three or four), all of which are analytically true.

Deductive inference becomes a device of considerable utility in exhibition analysis in the case of the deductive systems of the various traditional Rationalist philosophers, to the extent to which portions of their systems, or their systems as a whole, are validly deduced from their avowed premises.

Consider, for example, Spinoza's philosophy as expounded in the *Ethic*. In that work, Spinoza's philosophy is a remarkably coherent deductive system in which the innumerable "theorems" and "corollaries" are – often validly – drawn from the definitions and the "axioms" or "postulates" given at the beginning of the book's five parts. Although these "axioms" are regarded by Spinoza as self-evident truths about reality, they can be more correctly regarded as propositions that are analytically true in, or relatively to, Spinoza's system. That is, they can be properly regarded as definitions of some of the basic (metaphysical) expressions that Spinoza uses as his technical philosophical vocabulary in the *Ethic*, or as logical consequences of his explicit definitions in that work. The following "axiom," occurring at the beginning of Part I, is an example of the former: "A true idea must agree with that of which it is the idea" (Axiom VI); while the following "axioms" appear to be examples of the latter: "From a given determinate cause an effect necessarily follows; and, on the other hand, if no determinate cause be given, it is impossible that an effect can follow" (Axiom III); "The knowledge of an effect depends upon and involves the knowledge of the cause" (Axiom IV). On the other hand, "The essence of that thing which can be conceived as not existing does not involve existence" (Axiom VII) can be regarded in either of two ways: (a) as a definition of the expression 'Essence of a thing which (i.e., the essence) does not involve existence'; in which case 'An essence which can be conceived as not existing' will be the definiens; or (b) as a logical consequence of a definition of 'Essence of a thing which does not involve existence.' At the same time, Axioms I and II, *viz.* "Everything which is, is either in itself or in another," and "That which cannot be conceived through another must be conceived through itself," respectively, can be regarded either as definitions or as direct applications of the law of contradiction. The latter itself is analytically true in ordinary language and also (in effect) in Spinoza's system; it can therefore be regarded as a partial definition of a 'thing' ('object,' 'quality,' etc.) in accordance with the ordinary use of this expression, or a logical consequence of such a definition.

The upshot is that these "axioms" are essentially similar to the propositions which Spinoza calls "definitions," such as "By cause of itself, I understand that, whose essence involves existence; or that, whose nature cannot be conceived unless existing" (Def. I). For these definitions give us the meaning of key expressions as Spinoza applies them in his system. If this is true, the "propositions" and "corollaries" which Spinoza draws from the definitions and "axioms" – such as the propositions about Substance, Attributes, Modes, God or Nature in Book I of the *Ethic*; e.g. Props. V, VI, VII, X, XI, XII, etc. – wherever they are validly inferred from these premises, can be regarded as so many instances of the exhibition analysis of the propositions constituting the latter. By the same token, they can be regarded as instances of exhibition analysis of the concepts of God, Substance, Attribute, Nature, infinity, power, unity and plurality, etc. which occur in these "propositions" and "corollaries." Stated in other words, these conclusions exhibit the *logical interrelations* between the various Spinozistic concepts; giving us a wealth of information about the logical grammar of these concepts as they are framed and utilized by the philosopher. For the logical interrelations between different logically-related concepts are, as we have pointed out in chapter six, an integral part of their uses or logical grammar. For a concept has certain logical relations to other concepts by virtue of its content; or stated in terms of verbal expressions, different but related expressions possess certain semantic relationships by virtue of their meaning or uses in the particular language, sub-language, or (in the case of traditional philosophical systems) the system in which they occur. We can thus consider a deductive *system* such as the present one, as a whole, as one vast and highly complex "map" or "chart" of the logical grammar or uses of the interrelated concepts. By the same token, it provides us with a "map" or "chart" of the logical grammar of the interrelated analytical propositions that constitute its "topographical" features. Correspondingly, the sum total of all the "propositions" and "corrolaries" in it can be regarded as the logical products, or results, of one complex series of exhibition analyses.

I said that the semantic (or logical) relations between different verbal expressions obtain by virtue of the meanings of these verbal expressions. The reason I did not say that these relations are a part of the meanings of these expressions themselves is that that would strain the ordinary meaning of 'meaning' too much. For, in relation to Spinoza's or any other similar system, we would ordinarily say that the meanings of the key expressions that occur in them are given in (and only in) the definitions (and, to my mind, some or all of the "axioms") of the system. Everything else would be a logical consequence of the meanings these expressions have there. The system as a whole, or even the individual "theorems" and "corollaries" in it, would not be ordinarily said to be a definition or definitions, an explication or explications of the meaning of these expressions. We can, however, properly regard these "theorems" and "corollaries" as providing us with the various *uses*, or different aspects of the uses, of these key expressions in the particular system. But in doing so, we would be implying a basic distinction or difference between 'meaning' in its ordinary meaning, and 'use.' The – a – meaning of an expression will then not be (roughly or exactly) identical with the – a – use of the expression in the relevant sense,[1] but only with a *part* of it. This is as it should be; for in the sense in which we have been speaking of the uses of expressions in relation to semantic analysis, it is perfectly proper to say that a person may know the meaning of an expression but may not know its use or uses (corresponding to that meaning) completely, fully. Thus, to return to Spinoza, we may know

[1] See chapter three, pp. 25 ff.

the meaning of 'Substance'; *viz.* "something which can be conceived in and through itself," but certainly not know that "Substance" is one; i.e., that it would be self-contradictory, in the light of the way Spinoza employs 'substance,' 'conceived in and through itself,' 'one,' etc. to say that there can be two or more Substances. What is more important, we may know the meaning of 'Substance' as set forth in the various "axioms" and definitions in the system, and yet not know many of the things that are analytically true about Substance which the "theorems" give us. This is precisely why we said before that exhibition analysis, or any other form of semantic analysis, is concerned to give us an *analysis* of the *meaning* of a particular analysandum, not the meaning itself. This is also precisely why and how the valid conclusions of deductive arguments of the present sort can be properly regarded as revealing new things about the uses of expressions: it is because of this that we acquire new understanding or insight into the uses of expressions and concepts we employ in discourse; that we get an advance in clarity. Otherwise, such deductive inference cannot be utilized as a device of exhibition analysis, which is intended to give us a better or clearer understanding of the "logic" of our expressions and concepts, and in that sense to constitute a "discovery" of something "new."

The foregoing is true of the systems of Leibniz, Hegel, F. H. Bradley and other system-builders in the History of Philosophy insofar as some or all of their major "views" are valid deductions from propositions that are analytically true relatively to their system: insofar as they are true by virtue of the way these philosophers define or apply the crucial expressions occurring in them. A very clear example of the use of the deductive method in philosophy is provided by Leibniz in his "First Truths" [1] and his "Necessary And Contingent Truths." [2] Thus in the first essay, Leibniz deduces some fourteen fundamental propositions about the nature of true propositions; the principle of sufficient reason; the principle of identity of indiscernibles; the relation between a "complete or perfect concept" of an individual substance; pre-established harmony between created monads; the relation between the body and the soul; space; time; motion; and so on, from the proposition that all true propositions are "identical propositions" (such as "A is A," "A is not non-A") or are logically reducible to identical propositions "by the help of definitions, or by the resolution of concepts

[1] In T. V. Smith and Marjorie Grene, editors, Selections: *From Descartes To Locke* (Chicago, The University of Chicago Press, 1957), pp. 300–301. Translated from *Opuscules et fragments inédits de Leibniz*, ed. Louis Couturat (Paris: Félix Alcan, 1903), pp. 518–523.

[2] *Ibid.*, pp. 306–312.

which constitutes proof *a priori*, independent of experience."[1] He defines 'identical proposition' in terms of "first truths," and the latter as "those which make a self-identical statement in themselves or deny the opposite statement by the very fact of its being opposite."

If we now take "All (non-identical) truths are reducible to identical truths by the help of definitions, etc." as itself a definition, or as true by virtue of a definition, this proposition (which is the premise underlying the whole series of deductions) can be properly regarded as analytically true by virtue of the way Leibniz uses the key words 'true' (and 'truth'), 'identical truth,' 'definition,' and so on. Indeed, we can regard this premise as a (stipulated) definition of 'true' (and of 'truth' in the same sense). We can take Leibniz as saying: "I shall use the expression 'true proposition' (or a 'truth') to mean a proposition that is itself an "identical proposition" or is reducible, with the help of definitions, etc., to identical propositions." If so, those of the fourteen conclusions, if any, which are validly inferred from this definition (which are so drawn does not concern us here, however), will provide us with a (partial) analysis of "identical propositions," "analytic propositions" (including tautologies), and the notion of truth (or true proposition) as Leibniz employs it in this and other works, such as "Necessary and Contingent Truths" and "The Principles of Nature and of Grace." They will provide us with some of the logical interrelations, in Leibniz's conceptual framework, between the concepts of truth (true propositions), "identical propositions," and a host of other Leibnizian concepts; for example, in the propositions (conclusions) "There are no purely extrinsic denominations" and "Every individual substance involves in its perfect concept the whole universe." Actually, the fourteen inferences we are talking about also give us some of the logical articulations, in relation to one another, of such Leibnizian concepts as substance, numerical and qualitative identity and diversity, space, time, cause, effect, universe, and a large number of other concepts. For in the course of the deduction as a whole, Leibniz implicitly or explicitly appeals to additional premises that are, or can, be likewise taken as analytically true relatively to his system, and/or in ordinary language. Thus consider Leibniz's deduction of the principle of identity of indiscernibles. He says –

Two individual things differing only in number cannot exist in nature. For surely it should be possible to produce a reason why they are different – which reason must be sought for from some difference in the things themselves.[2]

[1] *Ibid.*, p. 300.

[2] *Ibid.*, p. 301. Italics in original.

The premises from which this principle is deduced are (a) the principle of sufficient reason, which itself is deduced by Leibniz from his ultimate proposition about true propositions; and (b) the proposition that *number is not a quality* – more precisely, that a thing's being *one* thing is not a quality of it. And this is certainly analytically true in Leibniz's system as well as in ordinary language, by virtue of the way 'one,' 'number,' and 'quality' are normally employed. Otherwise, two things that are numerically different will necessarily be qualitatively different by the mere fact that they are numerically different, rendering the principle of identity of indiscernibles pointless or senseless. For in that case, two things A and B which are *numerically different* would satisfy this principle, they can be numerically distinct, even if and when they are qualitatively identical in respect to "other" qualities or properties they possess. Whereas the whole point of the principle is that this is impossible.

It is of some importance to note here that what we have been saying does not apply to – it is not illustrated by – the manner in which Descartes employed the "geometrical method." I mean his deduction of his own existence, the existence of God, and the existence of the external world in the "Meditations." For Descartes constantly utilized certain empirical, synthetic propositions, as well as analytically true propositions, as logical premises. Thus he appeals to the fact of his own doubting or thinking as a premise in proving the *Cogito*. For his *Cogito* is really a deduction from the following premises:

If anything doubts (or thinks), it exists;	(analytically true)
I doubt (or think);	(empirically true, in Descartes' case)
∴ I exist.	(empirically true, in Descartes' case)

This is, of course, not what Descartes himself thought he did in proving that he existed; and he definitely denies that "I think therefore I am" is, or involves, a deductive inference.

Similarly and more obviously, Descartes' proof of God's existence by means of the modified Ontological argument and the Cosmological argument employs an empirical premise or empirical premises. In both cases, as also in the case of his proof of the existence of an external world, the conclusion itself is empirical, synthetic, not analytic.

This leads us to another point of some importance. So far, I have spoken about the analytical use of "direct" deductive arguments in which *all* the premises are analytic propositions – though, as I said, this obtains mostly, if not only, where we have a chain of simple arguments (e.g. syllogisms) or a complex argument with a relatively large number of premises. We have not said whether the same applies to arguments in which some of the premises are synthetic propositions. The deduction of "I exist" given above illustrates the fact that *some* such arguments cannot serve in the present capacity. It illustrates the fact that at least *some* conditional arguments in which one premise is singular or particular cannot be employed in the manner under consideration. I mean conditional arguments which actually result in a synthetic, empirical conclusion. The same is true of syllogisms in which the conclusion is synthetic. Let us note, however, that a syllogism may have an analytically true proposition as a conclusion, even when *one* of its premises is synthetic. (Whether the same is possible with respect to conditional arguments, I do not know.) But whenever the conclusion of a syllogism, or the conclusion of a conditional argument, is analytically true, the argument can, theoretically speaking, serve in the present capacity. However, as I pointed out in relation to individual syllogisms, the conclusions of such simple arguments will inevitably be so trite from the standpoint of exhibition analysis as to be worthless in actual practice. This drawback, once again, is remedied if relatively long chains of arguments – especially arguments of different types, such as conditional arguments, syllogisms, etc. – are employed.

It will be noted that in our discussion so far we have not mentioned immediate inference. The reason is clear: immediate inference merely gives us *equivalent* propositions. If you like, they merely state in other words what we already now. They reveal nothing at all or nothing of significance about the logical powers of the equivalent propositions; and therefore about the logical grammar of the concepts occurring in them.

In the foregoing examples from Spinoza and Leibniz, many or all of the key expressions (whose logic is to some extent revealed by the deductions we noted) are given by these particular philosophers a special, non-ordinary meaning. To see this it is enough to consider, for example, how Spinoza or how Leibniz employs the word 'substance'; or how Spinoza employs the word 'God.' In the case of these and like expressions, the particular deductions reveal a part of their logical grammar *qua* technical philosophical expressions with a certain non-ordinary meaning. So long as these key expressions are or have been given meanings that are mutually consistent, the valid deductive conclusions which we illustrated in their case would be necessarily consistent with one another and with the premises in which these expressions occur. However, if we consider these expressions as *deviating*, and not merely as differing from ordinary language in their meaning; that is, if we consider them as *misusing* the particular expressions, our valid deductive inferences will serve to make clearer or more obvious to us the nature and extent of this deviation from, or the expressions' violation of, ordinary language. But (unlike "indirect" deductive arguments), they will not and cannot logically *demonstrate* the occurrence of a misuse of language; or enable us to know its extent or degree of gravity. Also, a scrutiny of the particular inferences may fail to reveal the presence of any such deviation from ordinary language.

On the other hand, these inferences may be quite unnecessary for this purpose simply because one may perceive that a deviation from, or a violation of ordinary language has occurred, merely by scrutinizing the premises of the arguments themselves. In short, a valid deductive inference can sometimes serve as a sort of magnifying glass, "enlarging" and thereby making more readily visible any deviations from ordinary language that may lurk in the argument's premises.

Valid "direct" deductive inference is also a useful device in the exhibition analysis of *formal concepts:* logical, scientific, mathematical or other. It can serve in the same capacity in relation to *systems of logic* and systems of pure mathematics. The set of theorems validly deduced or deducible from the postulates of the logical or mathematical system can be regarded as providing us with an exhibition analysis of the primitives that occur in the system's set of postulates. As is well known, the postulates of an uninterpreted logical system or of a modern pure mathematical system (as opposed to, say, traditional Euclidean geometry) consist of a set of propositional functions in which the "primitives" or "undefined terms" are variables defined *implicitly* by means of the relations between them stated in the set of postulates. Hence the theorems deduced or deducible from these postulates with the help of the particular rules of derivation employed in that system, will exhibit the logical powers [1] of these undefined terms in that system. A system of this kind as a whole can be regarded as one vast logical map or chart of the logical powers of these undefined terms in their numerous logical interrelations.

As examples of such systems and hence of the present use of deductive inference, it is sufficient to mention the system of Euclidean geometry

[1] There are, it can be readily seen, interesting differences between the "logical powers" of these terms, which stand for variables, and the logical powers of expressions that have a meaning in the ordinary way; which (say) stand for particular concepts ("constants"). But these differences do not concern us here.

as rigorously axiomatized by Hilbert; or the pure non-Euclidean system of Lobachevsky and Bolyai, or the system of Riemann. The system of ordinary arithmetic is another obvious example. The theorems of plane Euclidean geometry – insofar as, or assuming that they are rigorously deduced from the set of postulates in the system – bring out the logical content of the concepts of parallel lines, triangle, circle, polygon, and a host of other concepts, as explicitly delimited in the definition and the axioms of traditional Euclidean geometry; or as implicitly delimited in the axioms of modern Hilbertian geometry in which all the theorems are deducible from a set of twenty-one postulates, containing five primitive terms. Similarly with Veblen's deduction of the theorems of Euclidean geometry from a set of twelve postulates, which contain two undefined terms.

Our earlier remarks in this chapter respecting one important difference between meaning and "use" (in the relevant sense of the latter expression), and the implications consequent on this difference, are applicable here in respect to such systems as traditional Euclidean geometry. Thus the properties of any given geometrical figure are not normally said to be part of the meaning of that figure. For example, we cannot properly regard the proposition that the sum of the angles of a plane Euclidean triangle are equal to 180°, as part of the meaning of 'plane triangle.' What we normally say is that this property is a logical consequence of, follows logically from, the meaning of 'triangle' as (explicitly) defined in that system. Hence we cannot properly say that the proposition "The sum of the angles of a plane triangle is equal to 180°" provides us with a partial analysis of the meaning of 'plane triangle' in that system. But we can rightly say that it provides us with a very partial analysis of the use or logical grammar of 'plane triangle' in that system.

Similarly we cannot speak of the theorems of an uninterpreted logical or (pure) mathematical system as providing us with an analysis of the meaning of the primitive terms in it. But there is an additional reason here. Since these terms stand for variables, they themselves are not normally said to have any *specific* meaning; though they are not, for that reason, denied all meaning altogether. So the question whether or not the theorems can be said to provide us with an analysis of the meaning of these expressions does not really arise.

II

In Section I we outlined the use of certain "direct" deductive arguments and of deductive systems, including the axiomatic systems of pure mathemathics and logic, in revealing the logical grammar of certain propositions (hence of their constituent concepts) occurring in these arguments or systems. We now pass to a consideration of the similar role played by "indirect" deductive arguments: the *reductio ad absurdum* argument or Indirect Chain Argument. As in the case of "direct" deductive inferences that we have discussed, this type of inference can be employed to reveal particular aspects of parts of the uses or logical grammar of various philosophically-important expressions. However, unlike the relevant "direct" arguments, the *reductio* or Indirect Argument reveals the logical grammar of a given expression only negatively. It shows, to put the matter in general terms, the tenability or untenability – actually the untenability – of this or that philosophical "view" or proposition; and in the course of doing so, it shows the illegitimacy of certain ways of applying some expression(s) that occur(s) in the statement expressing the offending proposition.

The *reductio ad absurdum* argument is usually described in logical textbooks as a type of argument that is employed to prove the falsity of a particular proposition which is to be disproved (or whose contradictory is to be proved) through the deduction of contradictory consequences from it. It essentially argues from $p \supset (q\bar{q})$ to $\bar{p}$.[1] The demonstration of the falsity of a particular proposition – hence the truth of its contradictory – is certainly one major use of the *reductio* argument; but this use does not interest us here. We are interested in its use in demonstrating that certain statements are self-contradictory or are absurd (or, as Gilbert Ryle puts it, are nonsensical) because they entail logically incompatible consequences. In this way the *reductio* exhibits in a dramatic though only negative way something about the meaning and the general logical character of some – at least one – of the verbal expressions occurring in the sentence shown to be self-contradictory or absurd.

Gilbert Ryle, in the well-known essay already referred to (footnote 1)

[1] Gilbert Ryle, in "Philosophical Arguments" (Oxford, 1945), p. 6, distinguishes the "strong" *reductio* from the "weak" *reductio* argument. This distinction is immaterial for our present discussion; but I might mention that according to Ryle, the former (and more powerful) *reductio* argues from $p \supset (q\bar{q})$, or from $p \supset \bar{p}$, to the same conclusion, $\bar{p}$. Thus the *reductio* argument as we are discussing it in the present chapter corresponds to Ryle's "strong" form of the argument.

has forcefully stated what appears to be for him the essential function of the *reductio* in philosophy; namely, the diagnosis of logical paradoxes or philosophical problems; and the (partial) cure of these maladies by pointing out the "misreading of the logical powers [the "logical geography" as he also calls it, or the "logical grammar" as others refer to it] of propositions and ideas" resulting from the mis-employment of expressions. Stated in terms of concepts, the function of the *reductio*, on this understanding, is the discovery of errors due to one's operating with a concept as though it belongs to a certain logical type when in reality it belongs to a different logical type.[1]

The gist of the *reductio*'s role as envisioned by Ryle may perhaps be expressed by the following quotation from the work cited:

> The discovery of the logical type to which a puzzle-generating idea belongs is the discovery of the rules governing the valid arguments in which propositions embodying that idea (or any other idea of the same type) can enter as premisses or conclusions. It is also the discovery of the general reasons why fallacies result from misattributions of it to specific types. In general the former discovery is only approached through the several stages of the latter. The idea is (deliberately or blindly) hypothetically treated as homogeneous with one familiar model after another and its own logical structure emerges from the consecutive elimination of supposed logical properties by the absurdities resulting from the supposals.[2]

Ryle adds a little later that "to find or understand a rule it is necessary to appreciate not only what it enforces but also what it permits and what it forbids." [3] It is what a particular rule forbids and, therefore at least negatively, what it permits, that the *reductio* helps to discover. I might add that if contradiction helps us to discover the logical type to which a puzzle-generating concept belongs, the absence of contradiction can likewise be symptomatic and informative. A concept that does not generate contradictions in a given application positively reveals, by that very fact, that it is being properly employed; hence, also, that it would be properly employed if applied in other contexts of the same type. Obviously the logical force of freedom from contradiction can never be equal to the force of contradiction. Contradiction is an incontrovertible proof of logical misuse of concepts; whereas the absence of contradiction, however often and variously shown in respect to a particular idea, cannot completely remove the shadow of possible contradiction, hence the possibility of logical misuse, the next time the

[1] *Ibid.*, *passim.*
[2] *Ibid.*, p. 14.
[3] *Ibid.*

idea is utilized. Nor, of course, can one be certain that, where it is not detected, contradiction does not lurk unseen. Nonetheless, every use or an idea which, on scrutiny, appears not to generate contradictions, is (with probability) one proper application of the idea exhibited (one proper use of the term expressing the idea). It is an added understanding, a bit of knowledge gained – though not such as to be immune to revision.

In the present connection we must clearly distinguish two logically different types of cases: (1) expressions whose meanings are intrinsically, inherently self-contradictory; and (2) expressions that are perfectly self-consistent in their usual, normal, ordinary applications, but which *may* generate contradictions when misapplied or misused; as, for instance, if they are employed by some philosopher in a restricted, extended or otherwise peculiar sense or manner.[1] In the case of expressions falling under (1), a *reductio ad absurdum* is inevitable at every step of their employment. As for expressions falling under (2) – and these comprise all or practically all ordinary expressions (except those expressions, if any, whose ordinary meanings are self-contradictory) – any contradictions that their employment may generate arise only in their non-ordinary applications. Ryle, as the foregoing brief sketch of his view of the *reductio* should indicate, thinks only of (2) in his discussion. But cases of type (1) should not be ignored or neglected. For though it may be true that the ordinary meanings or senses of all ordinary expressions are self-consistent, so that no expressions falling under (2) may fall under (1), we should remember that there are a considerable number of expressions coined by traditional philosophers; and some of these may involve contradictions that are hidden from the philosopher's view. Also, of course, philosophers often use ordinary expressions in novel, philosophical senses. At any rate, even if no actual expressions employed by philosophers suffer from any contradictions, it is still theoretically possible that an expression of this kind (if not also an ordinary expression) may have a self-contradictory sense or meaning; and this suffices for the drawing of our distinction. If there be such expressions, a *reductio* will reveal the inconsistencies in them, and perhaps indicate exactly wherein this inconsistency lies; thus serving as an analysis – admittedly very partial or incomplete – of the meaning of the offending expressions.

[1] Here as elsewhere I prefer to state my points in terms of expressions rather than concepts (or ideas), for reasons which should now be clear. But they can be readily expressed, *mutatis mutandis*, in terms of the latter.

With these brief remarks about expressions of type (1) we pass to a somewhat detailed discussion of the philosophically more important – because the more prevalent and widerspread – misuse of ordinary expressions that are perfectly consistent in their ordinary employments. This discussion will at the same time throw further light on expressions of type (1); since the logical causes of contradiction may operate in respect to expressions of both types (1) and (2). For it is immaterial whether the meanings of the expressions involved are inherently self-contradictory or not.

In order to deal with our present question, we must return to the notion of categorial misuse or mis-application of (ordinary) expressions, which Ryle regards as the source of contradiction and of philosophical problems or puzzles. Ryle illustrates his thesis by taking the two statements "Numbers are eternal" and "Time began a million years ago." Both of these involve expressions of type (2).

About the statements in hand Ryle says:

> Both are linguistically regular statements but the latter sentence expresses no proposition. It tries to say what cannot be significantly said, viz. that there was a moment before anything else, which contains a patent contradiction. The former sentence is nonsensical if construed as expressing a proposition of one type but not if construed in another way. If it is construed as a terse way of saying that numbers are not temporal things or events or, better, that numerical expressions cannot enter into significant expressions as subjects to verbs with tenses, then what it says is true and important. But if it is construed, as childlike people have construed it, as saying that numbers, like tortoises, live a very long time – and in fact however old they get, they cannot die – then it could be shown to be absurd.[1]

Here the expressions 'number' and 'time' are shown to be categorially misused by showing that the sentences in which they are misused, in one or more (including all) of their interpretations, are self-contradictory or are nonsensical.

In these and in his other illustrations (e.g., his discussion of the "systematic ambiguity" of 'punctual,' 'exist,' and the like, *Ibid.*, pp. 15–16), Ryle does not attempt to show the relationship between the foregoing, logical misuses of expressions and errors resulting from another sort of misuse of ordinary expressions. I mean their use in *senses* or *meanings* which are different from their ordinary senses or meanings and are, in some respect or other, incompatible with them. Ryle does not mention or discuss this latter type of case as a possible source of contradiction; hence as providing the *reductio* with a second major philosophical use. Indeed, he speaks of the detection and

[1] *Ibid.*, p. 13.

rectification of categorial errors as *the* function of the *reductio*. Moreover, he does not think of this function of the *reductio* in connection with, as related to, philosophical analysis. Whereas we are here envisioning it in connection with, and as related to, semantic analysis; insofar as it helps to reveal the logical character of various concepts and, at least negatively, the meanings of the expressions conveying these concepts. It is now incumbent on us to show (a) the precise relation between the two types of error, and thereby to show (b) that the two *are* distinct types of error and not one and the same type of error variously called; and finally, to show (c) how the *reductio* can reveal misuses of expressions of a non-categorial, non-logical type.

First of all, both categorial errors and non-categorial violations of the ordinary meanings of expressions are species of improper employment of ordinary expressions. The question, however, is whether categorial errors are logically inseparable from violations of an expression's *meaning* or *meanings*. In order to answer this question, let us consider the sentences "Sunday is in bed" and "The writer of this paper never wrote a paper," which Ryle mentions in "Categories" [1] as examples of absurd sentences, as sentences which commit a categorial error. The *sense* in which Ryle is thinking of the offending expressions 'Sunday' and 'the writer of this paper,' the sense in which the sentences they figure in are absurd, is obvious. But Ryle neglects to inquire into the relation between the logical types of different expressions. (In the essay just referred to he prefers to speak of 'proposition-factors,' which, as defined by him, can be regarded as factors which bear the same logical relation to expressions, except sentences and clauses, as propositions bear to sentences or clauses.) [2] He therefore does not observe that 'Sunday' and 'the writer of this paper' can be given perfectly proper interpretations in the sentences in which they occur, giving rise to no category violations. These sentences are contradictory or are absurd in certain contexts, not just in any and all contexts – in any sense of 'Sunday' or 'the writer of this paper.' Thus 'Sunday' may be the name of a person or an animal (Cf. 'Friday' in *Robinson Crusoe:* "Friday is in bed" makes perfectly good sense in the pages of, or when

[1] *Logic And Language*, Second Series (Oxford, 1955), pp. 70 and 78.

[2] Ryle's definition is as follows: "... I use 'proposition-factor' ... to collect whatever is signified by an expression, simple or complex, which can be a complement to a gap-sign in some sentence-frame or other (or which can be a value of a variable in some propositional function or other)." (*Ibid.*, p. 77) This definition is not perfectly adequate, since propositions are expressed by statements, or sentences in use, and not by sentences as such. Thus a "*proposition*-factor" is, properly speaking, the complement of an expression *qua* factor of a sentence in use.

uttered in connection with, that novel). Similarly 'the writer of this paper' may, without violating ordinary usage, refer to (say) a person who dictated a paper to a secretary, or spoke it into a dictaphone. Let me add that some metaphors and other figures of speech, as well as many jokes (as Ryle points out) depend on type violations. Unfortunately for poets, though, not all type-violations can yield figures of speech. But it would be rash to assume that some far-fetched but not quite improper figurative meaning cannot be given to any expression or sentence, by some wildly ingenious or imaginative mind! ("Sunday is in bed," for instance, may be taken as an instance of Personification.)

It is not true, however, that the specific meaning of an expression logically determines the logical type to which it belongs, "Sunday is in bed" and our other examples notwithstanding. That the *specific* meaning of an expression does not determine its logical type – even in these examples – is seen by noting that there are ranges of expressions having no sense or meaning in common, which nonetheless belong to the same logical type. Examples, chosen at random, are 'horse,' 'ass,' 'cow,' 'monkey'; 'Peter,' 'John,' 'Mary'; 'red,' 'brown,' 'mauve.' On the other hand, synonymous expressions do belong to the same logical type in respect to the sense or senses in which they are synonymous. In our examples, 'Sunday' as the name of a day of the week, and as the name of a person, belongs to two different logical types. But this is not necessarily true in respect to other expressions. An expression which has different senses or meanings may – but also may not – belong to different logical types (sometimes, perhaps, to as many different types as it has senses or meanings). The question whether, *as a matter of fact*, all, or some, or none of the actual expressions in any language [1] belong to as many different types as they have senses or meanings, and to what particular types a particular expression belongs, does not concern us here. It seems to me that the answer to the question whether or not a given expression belongs to two different types in two (or more) meanings it ordinarily has, depends on how great or how small is the *difference* in the two meanings. We might state this by saying that an expression will belong to two different logical types in its employment in two different meanings, if these meanings are different in *kind*. But this is perhaps tantamount to saying that an expression will belong to different types *qua* employed in two different meanings it has, if it belongs to two different logical types! Whether this is so we shall have

[1] The particular language about whose constituent expressions we choose to speak is immaterial in discussions of logical type; as Ryle points out.

to find out as we proceed. For the moment, what emerges from our analysis is this: that whenever a type violation occurs, the specific meaning of the relevant expression will also be grossly violated. *Hence detection of type violation*, say *through a reductio, will also entail the detection of gross violation of the expression's meaning*. I say "gross violation" of meaning because the mere use of an expression in an illegitimate sense or meaning does not necessarily result in type violation. Thus 'horse,' if employed in the sense of 'monkey,' does not give rise to a type violation. For 'horse' and 'monkey' belong to the same type. The violation of meaning is an "intra-categorial," not an "inter-categorial" violation, so to speak. Whereas the employment of 'horse' in the sense of 'triangle' (say) would constitute a "*gross*" violation of the meaning of 'horse.' It would be an "inter-categorial," not an "intra-categorial," violation. If a type violation is of the latter kind, the sentence in which the misused expression occurs may be false in its employment in some contexts; but it will be perfectly regular, non-absurd.

I said that an expression consisting of a word or a phrase (but not a sentence or a clause) belongs to one logical type in one, and sometimes in more than one, sense or meaning. This means that it can be coupled, in that sense or in those senses, with an indefinite but finite number of other expressions to form non-absurd sentences; that it can be inserted in an indefinite number of sentence-frames, to borrow Ryle's phrase. As a matter of fact, there is an indefinite but finite number of expressions which can be inserted in all these same sentence-frames; and all these expressions will, it appears, belong to the same logical type. If this is true, then it would likewise be true that all the frames in which the expressions belonging to one logical type can be inserted without absurdity will themselves belong to the same logical type. For instance 'a triangle' and 'a rhombus' can be inserted, without absurdity, in such sentence-frames as '... is a three-sided figure' and '... can be circumscribed by a circle,' to take only two examples. This means, at the same time, that 'is a three-sided figure' and 'can be circumscribed by a circle' can be inserted without absurdity in the sentence-frames 'a triangle...' and 'a rhombus...' respectively. And in the same way as 'a triangle' and 'a rhombus' belong to one logical type, 'a three-sided figure' and 'something that can be circumscribed by a circle' belong to one logical type. Actually, in this particular example all four expressions belong to the same logical type. This is not the case with many other examples. For instance, in the sentences "Grass is green" and "Cypresses are tall" – in general, where the 'is' is not one of identity – the two predicate-expressions are only logically complementary to the two subject-expressions. The reason for this is logical and not merely syntactical, linguistic.[1] It does not depend merely on whether the gap-sign is at the beginning, in the middle (in the position of verbs and some adverbs in the case of English) or at the end of the sentence. The type differences remain even in an inflected language such as Latin, in which a given gap-sign, as a kind of gap-sign, can occupy practically any position in a sentence. Logical type is determined by the kind of use or function which expressions can properly have in sentences or clauses. The inflections (in inflected languages) and the "syntactically correct" positions (in non-inflected languages) are merely the linguistic reflection or representation of these functional (and hence type) differences. In order that a given string of expressions may form a correct sentence, it must conform to the syntactical rules of the particular language. But the resulting sentence could be absurd. A string of words which "*grossly* violates the rules of syntax will not be absurd but, instead, nonsensical or meaningless *as a whole*, though the words composing it, taken separately, will have meaning; unless they are so-called nonsense syllables such as 'brillig' and 'jabberwock'. An absurd sentence does not make sense, as we say: but "making sense" and "not making sense" admit of degrees; and a string of words which grossly violates the rules of syntax frequently "makes even less sense" than an absurd sentence. I say "frequently" and not "always" because absurdity itself admits of degrees. Thus I think we would ordinarily say that "Sunday is in bed" is less absurd than say, "Quadruplicity digests solemnity." In general and roughly, a sentence is ordinarily regarded as the more absurd in direct proportion to (a) the number of words it contains that violate logical type, and (b) the *extent* of the type

[1] It is essential to note that two or more expressions will be of the same logical type only if they can be alternative complements in all the *possible* sentence-frames in which any one of them can be a complement without absurdity. If we have an expression *A* which can be, without absurdity, a complement in sentence-frames a, b, c...n, then another expression *B* will belong to the same logical type only if it can be, without absurdity, a complement in all of the sentence-frames a, b, c...n. This is implied when Ryle rightly states that "Two proposition-factors are of different categories or types, if there are sentence-frames such that when the expressions for those factors are imported as alternative complements to the same gap-signs, the resultant sentences are significant in the one case and absurd in the other." (*Ibid.*, pp. 77–78). If this does not overstate the matter, Ryle puts the obverse far too weakly when he says that "It is...not quite correct to say...that two factors are of the same type if there is any case where both can fill the same gap.... Though nearly, it is not quite true to say that every gap-sign in its context in a determinate sentence-frame indicates the category of all its possible complements." (*Ibid.*, p. 78). The moral of all this is that type-differences can be quite easily and conclusively established; whereas the attempt to establish type-identities is a long and arduous task and can never, in practice, be realized with finality.

violation in each case. For it may be remarked, though we cannot go into this here, that there is a certain logical order between the different logical types corresponding to the grammatically different kinds of expressions occurring in a given language; and there are different extents to which an expression may go in departing from its proper type. To give a simple example, there is a greater logical kinship between the logical types to which 'man' and 'stone' respectively belong, than between the first of these types and the type to which '$\sqrt{2}$' belongs. It may perhaps be the case, nevertheless, that logical kinship consists of a family of relations of different sorts, dependent on different features of the related logical types. This seems likely since, as we have seen, a logical type A is logically "complementary" to another type B, if the sentence-factors falling under A are capable, without absurdity, of replacing a *given* gap-sign in a range of possible sentence-frames constituted by sentence-factors belonging to type B. Thus the type to which 'a triangle' belongs is a "complement" [1] to the type to which '... is a three-sided figure' belongs. The relation of complementarity between two logical types is of a different kind from the logical relation that holds between any one type and all other possible types. Two complementary types are logically closer – they possess a greater degree of "kinship" – than non-complementary types; just as (say) the types to which 'man' and 'stone' respectively belong are logically closer than the types to which 'man' and '$\sqrt{2}$' respectively belong. But the two are different kinds of "kinship." For the types to which 'man,' 'stone,' and '$\sqrt{2}$' respectively belong are non-complementary types. As a matter of fact, these types are not, in their nature, the kinds of types (and this indicates that there are *kinds* of types) that *can* enter into relations of complementarity with one another. These types are actually of the same kind; whereas only types of different kinds can enter into that relation. I need not add that a difference in kind of logical type between two types is not a sufficient condition for them to be related in that way.

But what exactly can one mean by saying that the type to which 'man' belongs is closer to the type to which 'stone' belongs than to the type to which '$\sqrt{2}$' belongs? The answer appears to be that there is a greater number of sentence-frames in which 'man' and 'stone' can alternately fill one and the same gap-sign without absurdity, than the

[1] I say 'a 'complement'" and not "the 'complement'" because more than one type can be complementary to another type. An example is the type to which any substantive belongs. Thus the type to which, say, 'Peter...' belongs is a complement of the type to which '... is fiar-haired' belongs as well as to the type to which '... is taller than (Mary)' belongs.

number of sentence-frames in which 'man' and '$\sqrt{2}$' can alternately fill one and the same gap-sign without absurdity.

This, if true, is difficult if not impossible to substantiate. But its truth or falsity may perhaps be determined by discovering what logical relations of implication, contradiction and the like obtain between statements that involve different sentence-frames ("sentence functions"). For as Ryle states, logical relations between statements (he says "propositions") reflect and in a sense are identical with differences in the logical types of the sentence-factors in them.[1]

The notion of the logical "kinship" of types outlined above faces certain serious difficulties. For though we can readily point out types which are quite remote from one another – which are at the opposite ends of the scale so to speak – it is very difficult if not impossible to assign relative "positions" to intermediate types; to those types that are *not* readily seen to be remote from one another. Perhaps even the notion of a *rough* ordering of types is artificial or arbitrary, nay fictitious, reflecting nothing in the types themselves. Also, it is quite possible that some or all logical types – at least those under which ordinary expressions fall – are open textured; analogous, and perhaps corresponding to the open texture of some ordinary concepts. If all this is true, it is also possible that the notion of open texture in respect to logical types is closely related to the notion of degrees of absurdity, and related to the difficulty, in many instances, of deciding with assurance whether a given sentence is or is not absurd. For it may be the case that the line between absurd and non-absurd sentences is not a sharp and clear-cut one.

So much for logical types. The next question we want to consider is whether the *reductio ad absurdum* argument can serve to uncover and exhibit *intra*- categorial violations; that is, violations of an expression's ordinary meaning or meanings that are not so drastic as to result in absurdity.

The answer to the question is in the affirmative. For though sentences which suffer from an intra-categorial violation will not be absurd (unlike sentences in which inter-categorial violations occur), *some* of these sentences will be self-contradictory; though this fact will only be apparent where the violation is a gross one – sometimes so apparent that it does not need to be demonstrated with the help of, say, a *reductio*

[1] The logical relations of a statement depend on the *types* of sentence-factors which constitute it. For the latter determine the (logical) syntactical relations between these factors; and these in turn determine the statement's logical form. Consequently, the types of sentence-factors involved determine the logical type to which the statement itself belongs.

argument. Thus suppose a philosopher misuses the ordinary notion of time, in such a way (say) as to attribute to time some characteristics of abstract space (as Bergson claims philosophers have been constantly doing): say by treating any given stretch of time as composed of a finite or infinite number of durationless time-points. These features that are attributed to time will now be incompatible with the features which time really possesses. In other words, the modified or new meaning of 'time' will conflict with its ordinary meaning,[1] resulting in contradictions. We could also mention McTaggart's view that time is unreal and "nothing does change." These examples are particularly interesting and instructive because the "views" they involve have been arrived at with the help of philosophical argument. Indeed, the arguments referred to are all – or can be cast into – *reductioes*. What their authors did not realize is the ironical fact that far from showing that (what they supposed was) the ordinary notion of time or motion is self-contradictory, the arguments demonstrate that the particular interpretations of time or motion involved were illegitimate. In other words, that the meaning attributed to the corresponding terms is not their actual meaning. The cause of contradiction lay not in any inconsistency or contradiction in the ordinary meanings of these terms, but in the philosopher's deviation from them. It should be noted that, strictly speaking, what the *reductio* shows in such cases, as also in cases where inter-type violations occur, is one of two things: either (i) that the philosopher using the *reductio* has actually started with the particular term (say 'time') in its ordinary meaning or meanings, and did *intend* to give an analysis of it, but actually misinterpreted or misanalyzed it; or (ii) that he actually *substituted* some other meaning for the ordinary meaning; that from the very start he modified or even completely changed the meaning of the term. In actual cases it is often difficult to determine which of the foregoing has occurred; and quite often the philosophers doing the one or the other are themselves far from aware of what they are doing. But whatever the actual situation may be in a given case, the *reductio* reveals the essential fact that in that particular context some term has been misused; that a change has occurred in its meaning. I am assuming throughout, it will be observed, that ordinary expressions, in their ordinary meanings, are self-consistent. Whether or not this is justified we have already discussed in the previous chapter.

[1] And I might add: it will also conflict with the ordinary meanings of *other* ordinary expressions.

At any rate, if the meaning of an ordinary expression *is* inconsistent, it will thereby qualify for the destructive criticism of a *reductio*.

There are several points which must be made here. In the first place, although the actual examples we have given are meant to illustrate our discussion of intra-categorial violations of meaning, it may well be that some or even all of them illustrate inter-categorial violations; or even both kinds of type violation. To determine which of these actually obtains requires a rather careful textual analysis which we cannot do here. But at least some of the *statements* in which the authors of the above-mentioned views have expressed these views are non-absurd, though they do involve misuse of ordinary language.

In the second place, we must draw the reader's attention to the fact that a *reductio* may result from an incorrect *interpretation* or incorrect *analysis* of the ordinary meaning of a given expression. Interpretation in the present sense consists in a translation of the expression into another allegedly synonymous expression (a word or a phrase). If it is the interpretation of a word or a phrase in a given sentence, the interpretation may consist in providing one or more sentences which are regarded as synonymous with that sentence. Hence *an* interpretation will consist in an analysis (in the product-sense) of the word or phrase, or of the sentence in which the word or phrase occurs, in Moore's sense of 'analysis.' It may also be, and in difficult cases usually is, the outcome of exhibition analysis (in the process sense). In any case, where interpretation and/or analysis results in a *reductio*, the latter may be regarded as the final stage of the analysis. Thirdly, it is essential clearly to distinguish between (a) sentences in which intra-type violations of meaning occur and are, as a result, self-contradictory, and (b) sentences in which intra-type violations of meaning occur and as a result are false but *not* self-contradictory. And these two should be distinguished from (c) false sentences which do not involve (whose falsity is therefore not a result of) any type violation of either kind. Among the fore-mentioned classes of sentences, sentences in class (a) are the only ones that we have so far discussed. They are sentences, it will be recalled, which involve a change in the ordinary meaning of a sentence-factor that leads to contradictions by conflicting with the ordinary meaning of that factor. In order to lead to contradictions, hence in order to be distinct from sentences falling in class (b), the sentences involved must be declarative sentences of a particular kind. They can be sentences in which the grammatical predicate is a categorial term of wide generality – the kind of categorial term which we might call "metaphysical" or "ontological," or more generally, "philosophical." They can also be quite specific or restricted in scope. But they cannot be singular sentences; i.e., sentences in which the grammatical subject is a proper noun, a definite description, and the like. In every case the essential thing is that they must involve intra-type violations of meaning. This obtains if they contain some expression which, as occurring in that sentence, contains two or more incompatible features *of the same kind* in its connotation. In respect to expressions whose usual connotation is perfectly consistent, this would obtain if their connotation is *extended* to include features that are incompatible with features forming part of their original connotation. The danger of intra-type violation, as well as of inter-type violation, is therefore always present whenever the connotation of an expression, hence its meaning, is extended.

I should add here that there are certain extremely general statements, the assertions *par excellence* of traditional metaphysics, which, because of their great generality, inevitably entail assertions about objects of discourse that fall under different logical types (e.g., physical objects on the one hand and psychic occurrences on the other hand). They therefore give rise to *inter-* as well as (perhaps) intra-type violations. Examples are "The World is Will or Idea," "Reality is mental," "To be is to be perceived," "Everything is in constant change" – to mention a few classical assertions picked at random. It is also possible that some sentences, which patently involve intra-type violations, have some logical implications that give rise to inter-type violations. It is clear that if sentences of either of these kinds exist, it would be very difficult to trace the resulting contradictions to the particular kind of type violation which is responsible for them.

Finally, there are sentences of different degrees of generality which constitute borderline cases; which, due to a certain fluidity in ordinary usage, cannot be unambiguously classed with sentences belonging to class (a) or categorically excluded from their company. To this intermediate class appear to belong such sentences as "I saw a ghost the other night and I touched its arm"; or the more general "Ghosts are tangible." For there are some people who actually believe that "ghosts" can be touched; i.e., who do not regard intangibility as part of the connotation of 'ghost'; whereas others do so regard it, hence regard the foregoing sentences as self-contradictory.

We now pass to sentences belonging to class (b). Here the rôle of the *reductio* in uncovering and exhibiting misuses of language is, in practice, more restricted than in the case of sentences belonging to class (a). For the *reductio* arises only where a conclusion of the type $p \supset (p\bar{q})$ is possible; which is most often the case where *p* is not only false but is necessarily so. Whereas, *ex hypothesi*, the sentences under present consideration are only contingently false. However, one class of sentences of the latter type which can yield a contradiction (with the help of other sentences used as further premises) are singular sentences. And here I include sentences whose grammatical subjects are definite descriptions; as well as ones whose subjects are proper nouns or pronouns. In respect to a singular sentence, an intra-type violation obtains if one mistakenly attributes a property *x* to something A which, *qua* A, possesses some quality *y* that is incompatible with *x*; and if 'x' and 'y' are expressions of the same logical type. Thus let us suppose that I point to the figure of a triangle drawn on a piece of paper and mistakenly declare: "This figure is round." My statement would be empirical and, as such, only factually false; i.e., it would not be self-contradictory. A contradiction can however be easily shown to arise from it with the help of the true empirical statement that the figure I am referring to is a triangle. Thus:

This figure X is round;
X is a triangle;
∴ At least one triangle is round.

This conclusion is a palpable self-contradiction, given the relevant customary meaning of 'triangle' and 'round.' (For another, somewhat different sort of example, see page 191; in relation to my discussion of the Indirect Argument).

What we have said so far about the uses of the *reductio ad absurdum* argument can be further illustrated by means of a type of argument which is verbally different from the reductio argument but is logically equivalent to it. The argument I am referring to is what Max Black [1] calls the Indirect Argument. In an indirect argument one argues, chain-wise, from: $p \supset q . q \supset r . r \supset \bar{p}$ to $p \supset \bar{p}$; and hence to $\bar{p}$; since $p \supset \bar{p}$ implies $\bar{p}$. Now we saw earlier that the general form of the *reductio* argument is $p \supset q\bar{q}$, therefore $\bar{p}$. But $p \supset q\bar{q}$ is equivalent to $p \supset q . p \supset \bar{q}$. By contraposition the second element in this

[1] *Critical Thinking:* An Introduction to Logic and Scientific Method (New York, (c) 1950), pp. 88ff.

conjunction becomes $q \supset \bar{p}$. Hence the conjunction corresponding to the entire premise of the *reductio* argument becomes $p \supset q \cdot q \supset \bar{p}$. But this is precisely the form of the indirect argument; and from $p \supset q \cdot q \supset \bar{p}$ it can be inferred that $p \supset \bar{p}$ and hence that $\bar{p}$.[2] This being the case, the examples which we earlier gave of the use of the *reductio* argument in relation to exhibition analysis also serve as examples of the use of the Indirect Argument in the same capacity. We shall now give some explicit examples of Indirect Argument to illustrate its use in relation to exhibition analysis. These arguments can of course all be converted into *reductio* arguments, thereby further illustrating our earlier discussion of that form of argument.

(I) INTER-TYPE VIOLATION OF MEANING

An example of the use of the Indirect Argument as a means of detecting or demonstrating inter-type violations of meaning is provided by the "view" that time is the duration of things in the ordinary process-sense of 'duration.' This view entails that time itself is a process which endures. But if time endures, it must endure in (another) time; and so on *ad infinitum.* Hence either time is *not* duration, or (some) time endures in something other than time. That is, if time is duration, then it endures in something which is not time. But if time endures in something which is not time, it cannot be duration; since duration, *by the very meaning of the term 'duration'* (in the process-sense) is duration in time. Consequently if time is the duration of things, in the relevant sense of 'duration,' it cannot be the duration of things, in the same sense of this term. This means that time cannot be and hence is not the duration of things.

It is not very difficult to show that the identification of time with duration in the above sense involves an *inter*-type rather than an intra-type violation of the ordinary meaning of 'time'; i.e., that 'time' does not merely mean something other than 'duration,' but also belongs to a different logical category than the one to which 'duration' belongs. A little reflection on the preceding illustration should make it clear that, as a matter of fact, the conclusion that time is not duration was arrived at by showing, in effect, that 'time' is an expression of a different logical type than 'duration': that we cannot, without contradiction,

[2] I wish to thank the referee of the University of North Carolina Press for drawing my attention to the logical equivalence of the *reductio* argument and the Indirect Argument, and for supplying me with the above demonstration of this fact.

speak of the former in the same way as we can properly speak of the latter.

Another example, of the same kind is provided by Leibniz's argument in his "First Truths," which allegedly shows that there is no vacuum:

There is no vacuum. For the different parts of empty space would be perfectly similar and congruous with one another, nor would they be distinguished from one another, and so they would differ only in number, which is absurd. In the same way as space, time is also proven not to be a thing.[1]

The gist of this argument can be put in the following Indirect Argument:

> If empty space has (numerically) different parts [which, for Leibniz, follows from the assumption that there is empty space or a vacuum], then these parts would be qualitatively identical;
>
> But if these parts are qualitatively identical, they must also be numerically identical [by the principle of identity of indiscernibles, which Leibniz assumes];

> Therefore, if empty space has numerically different parts, it would have no numerically different parts;
>
> Therefore, space has no numerically different parts; i.e., there is no empty space or vacuum.

A little reflection will show that this argument, in order to be logically valid, must assume (and Leibniz does assume) that if there is a vacuum, space must be an extended, physical thing; a thing with numerical parts. In reality, therefore, what the argument shows – if we assume that the principle of identity of indiscernibles is true – is that in assuming or implying that the concept of a vacuum implies or involves the concept of space as a thing, as possessing extended parts, Leibniz is misconstruing the concepts of vacuum and of space. It shows that if 'vacuum' and 'space' are employed in the way indicated, their meaning will be violated. And this violation, it seems to me, is an inter-type violation; because it construes 'space' and 'vacuum' as belonging to a different category than the one to which they belong: the category to which physical, extended things belong.

[1] T. V. Smith et. al., editors, *Descartes To Locke*, pp. 304–305.

The identification or confusion of relations with qualities or properties provides us with a clear example of inter-type violation of the meaning of 'relation.' F. H. Bradley's well-known *reductio* argument, in which he attempts to show that Reality or the Absolute is supra-relational by demonstrating a self-contradiction in the notion that relations can relate absolutely (rather than in some degree or other), rests on this error. His argument can be easily transformed into an Indirect Argument.

Similarly the "view" or assumption that existence is an atrribute, in St. Anselm's celebrated Ontological Argument, provides us – in the Ontological Argument itself – with a further example of the use of the *reductio* or Indirect Argument in detecting inter-type violations of meaning.

(2) INTRA-TYPE VIOLATION OF MEANING

We shall first illustrate the use of the Indirect Argument in relation to (a) statements in which intra-type violations of meaning occur and which, as a result, are self-contradictory; then pass to (b) statements in which intra-type violations of meaning occur and which, as a result, are false but not self-contradictory.

(a) I shall construct an example from Russell's view that there is nothing self-contradictory in the hypothesis that the world came into existence five minutes ago, the way it then was, together with our memories and our records of (what we call) the past.[1]

Russell's view implies, among other things, the thesis that people can remember something unreal, something that has never happened. But this thesis is not only false – it is self-contradictory on the basis of the ordinary meaning of 'remember.' It involves, and the contradiction arises from, the use of 'remember' in a different way from the ordinary one.[2] At the same time, no inter-type violation of the meaning of 'remember' appears to be present (though it is clear from our earlier discussion that one cannot be absolutely certain) in the statement "People can remember something that has never happened, something unreal." The contradictory character of this statement can be quite easily demonstrated by an Indirect Argument: If we remember something unreal, we will not be remembering at all (on the basis of the ordinary meaning of 'remember'). But if we do not remember, we

[1] *The Analysis of Mind* (London, 1949), pp. 159–160.
[2] See Ronald J. Butler, "Other Dates," *Mind*, vol. LXVIII, No. 269 (January, 1959), p. 17.

will not remember anything unreal. Hence if we remember something unreal, we will not be remembering anything unreal. *Ergo*, we will not be remembering anything unreal; which means that "People can remember something unreal" is necessarily false.

The view just considered is, clearly, too palpably self-contradictory to require formal refutation by an explicit argument; particularly by means of the present circuitous and rather clumsy Indirect Argument. But the latter illustrates the point to be made.

The following example illustrates the use of the Indirect Argument in relation to sentences belonging to class (b). It must be noted, however, that one or more direct arguments must supplement any Indirect Argument that is used if the falsity (or the truth) of a statement formed by a sentence of the present type is to be established. The reason for this will become clear from our example. For our present purposes, let us take the example I used earlier in connection with my discussion of the use of the *reductio* in respect to sentences belonging to class (b). In other words, suppose I point to a drawing of what is really a triangle, X, and mistakenly declare that X is round. The falsity of the statement "X is round" can now be shown by means of the following argument:

If X is a triangle and is round, it has sides but no angles;

If it has sides but no angles, it is not a triangle (because it has no angles) and is not round (because it has sides);

Hence if X is a triangle and is round, it is not a triangle and is not round.

∴ It is false that X is a triangle and is round; i.e., Either X is not a triangle or it is not round, or both.

This conclusion, together with the true empirical statement that X is a triangle gives us, by direct argument, the desired valid conclusion that X is not round.

Finally, I shall borrow a simple example from Max Black's *Critical Thinking* to illustrate the use of the Indirect Argument in relation to statements which, though false, do not involve any misuse of language, any inter- or intra-type violation of meaning. The example, in other words, illustrates the use of this form of argument in relation to sentences belonging to class (c):

The time is 3 P.M., the place any office. Miss Smith, a stenographer, is trying to decide whether she can leave a little earlier than her usual time of 5 P.M. She reasons in the following way: "If I am to leave early, I must get all these letters typed first." But an inspection of the letters convinces her she has two hours' work ahead of her; she continues, sadly, "If I am to get these letters typed, I must work two hours more." A look at the clock convinces her that "If I am to work two hours more I cannot leave early." [1]

The logical chain here gives us "If I am to leave early, I cannot leave early"; from which the final conclusion, "I cannot leave early" validly follows.

It is a significant commentary on the nature of philosophical argument that it is extremely difficult to come by actual philosophical examples of this sort of Indirect Argument in the literature. At any rate, it is easier to construct examples of it from everyday life, as in the foregoing illustration.

Finally, is there any way of discovering, in any instance of the use of the reductio or Indirect Argument, whether a misuse of language is involved and, if so, whether it consists in an inter-type or in an intra-type violation? The answer appears to me to be the following: If the premises of the argument are all analytic propositions, and if these propositions lead to an absurdity, an inter-type – or both an inter-type and an intra-type – violation of meaning in one or more of the premises is indicated. If they lead to a contradiction but no absurdity, an intra-type violation alone is indicated.

On the other hand, if *all* the premises of a *reductio* or Indirect Argument are synthetic, no inter-type or intra-type violations of meaning can be present in any of the premises. The argument then would show that (and only that) at least one of the premises is factually false.

A difficulty arises when some of the premises in such an argument are analytic and the rest are synthetic propositions, and a contradiction but no absurdity arises from them. For then two alternatives are possible: either (1) an intra-type violation of meaning occurs in one or more of the premises; or (2) no violation of meaning, of any sort, occurs in any of the premises. In order to find out, in any given instance, which of the possible alternatives is the case, we must appeal to exhibition analysis of the ordinary or the technical meanings of the relevant expressions, as the case may be.

[1] *Op. cit.*, p. 80. Reprinted by permission of Prentice-Hall, Inc., Englewood Cliffs, New Jersey, U. S. A.

CHAPTER NINE

LANGUAGE AND TRUTH

In earlier chapters we spoke about some of the major ways in which a close study and analysis of ordinary language can be philosophically fruitful. There is one major philosophical use of ordinary language, however, which we left out of our discussion; though what we said there is related to it and to some extent implies it. I am referring to what seems to me to be the fact that ordinary language provides us with a criterion of truth: that it enables us to discover the truth or falsity of certain classes of statements that are, or may be, philosophically important. The discussion and analysis of this use of ordinary language – in particular the discovery of the kinds of statements whose truth or falsity it enables us to know, and the exact manner in which it can do so – constitutes the subject-matter of the present chapter.

(I) In launching on the present inquiry, an important though perhaps rather obvious distinction needs to be made. We have already seen how the observation and analysis of correct ordinary usage enables us to arrive at the ordinary meanings and other kinds of uses of ordinary expressions, or at the content of ordinary concepts. Here our attention is centered on *how* people ordinarily speak or write; how they use given ordinary expressions in ordinary sentences. If you like, our attention is focussed on the *form* of the statements they make. We can also observe the statements people ordinarily make from another angle. We can focus our attention on *what* people assert or deny, what information they purport to convey in correct ordinary sentences. Here our attention will be focussed on the content of the sentences uttered, not (or not specifically) on their form. The latter way of observing what people ordinarily affirm or deny about things or situations that are or may possibly be encountered in actual life supplies us with information as to the *beliefs* or *opinions* ordinary people actually have about various matters. (Some of these are so-called "common sense" beliefs or opinions). It is thus different from getting information about the ordinary uses of ordinary expressions. The beliefs or opinions ordinarily expressed are of various sorts. Many of them are beliefs or opinions about ourselves, other men and the world around us. Their truth or falsity depends on what they themselves are and the nature of what they affirm or deny. In each case they are empirical in nature; and their truth or falsity cannot be decided merely by appeal to ordinary language.

The situation is not materially different where the statements expressing a belief or opinion report the speaker's or writer's personal experiences; including what he finds (or thinks he finds) by introspection. We may be inclined to accept what he reports as true; but it is clear that this has nothing to do with the fact of his reporting his experiences in correct language. A sentence must be a correct sentence in order that it may express a true *or* a false empirical statement.

(II) The situation is different in an important respect, in some cases where a statement is about ordinary language as a whole, or about some particular feature of or expression in it. The statement will still be empirical; but it will be an empirical statement about language, not about extra-linguistic matters. Here the correct observation and analysis of ordinary language – or of the particular feature of expression which the statement is about – *does* enable us, without appeal to extra-linguistic facts, to discover the particular statement's truth or falsity. Statements of the present type are second (or higher) order statements about linguistic facts; and their truth or falsity is determined, hence is discoverable by, the observation or analysis of these facts.[1] The importance of this is appreciated if we recall that the statements expressing the results of semantic analysis are of this type. Thus it includes the presentation of the results of exhibition analysis as well as the formulation, or the attempted formulation, of nominal and (one form [2] of) real definitions of ordinary expressions: in general, the replacement of a sentence containing the expression whose meaning is to be analysed by another sentence not containing that expression. Of this type, therefore, are statements of the form:

(1) 'X' means "Y" or

(2) "All X's are Y's";

[1] I do not wish to claim, however, that we can always tell with assurance whether a given statement purportedly about language is really analytic; hence that its truth or falsity can be discovered solely on linguistic grounds. It is a common fact that a completely satisfactory criterion of analyticity has yet to be found.

[2] The reason for this qualification will be seen in the next chapter.

(3) "'X' is correctly used in such and such an ordinary language (say English) to mean "Y." Also, specific applications of the foregoing, such as:

(4) "The word 'X' is correctly (or incorrectly) used in sentence A (a given sentence in a given ordinary language)";

Also, statements that rightly or wrongly attribute a given general feature to a given ordinary language or to a number of ordinary languages. For example, such statements as:

(5) "Some (many, a few, the majority of) ordinary expressions involve marginal indeterminacy" (Black),

(6) "Some (many, a few) things called by a given general name possess only certain criss-crossing 'family resemblances'" (Wittgenstein).

(III) It is clear that what is true of the kinds of statements in (II) above is not true of statements that purport to *explain* the nature of ordinary language or a given part of it with the help of extra-linguistic empirical facts. For instance, statements which express a philosopher's belief that a given feature of some ordinary expressions – say marginal indeterminacy – can be explained by the nature of language as a tool invented by man for the realization of certain human ends. Another example is the present author's belief that human purposiveness explains why the notion of capacity-to-serve-a-given-end is implicitly involved in the ordinary uses of names of man-made artifacts.[1]

The truth or falsity of these and of similar statements or beliefs cannot be determined solely by observation or correct analysis of ordinary language as a whole or of any particular part or aspect of it. In order to do so, it is necessary to find out, in addition to the analysis of ordinary language, whether the alleged facts adduced as an explanation are really facts; and if so, whether they really explain what they are intended to explain.

(IV) What we have said so far is rather obvious if not quite commonplace. We now come to something which, if not more interesting, is at least more controversial.

We have seen – or I have attempted to show – how we can discover the ordinary uses of ordinary expressions by appeal to correct usage. In the case of any expression 'X' that functions as a general name, this means that appeal to correct usage enables us to discover the "defining features" of the things called by that name; i.e., the features that a thing must have so that it may be properly called an "X." It follows

[1] See, for instance, my "Common Names & 'Family Resemblances,'" *passim.*

trivially that if we know that a given thing is properly called 'X' in ordinary discourse, it must, *qua* "X," possess certain characteristics – the defining features of "X." Such a knowledge is clearly present in respect to general names that are ostensively defined; hence in respect to names whose correct uses are or may be taught by one's pointing to parts of their denotata. For instance, if certain patches of color are ordinarily used in daily life to define or to teach the meaning of the word 'red,' we know that these patches *are* red – indeed, that they are red if anything is red. We know that these patches do possess the "defining features" of things properly called "red."

The upshot is that statements of the form "Object (quality, event, etc.) *a* is a Y (or is Y)" will be *true* if *a* is ordinarily used to define or to teach the meaning of 'Y.' And their truth can be discovered by observing how 'Y' is actually used in ordinary discourse (which is a straightforward empirical matter and does not merely consist in a knowledge or an analysis of the meaning of 'Y').

Now suppose that the observation of how 'Y' is actually defined by a group of people reveals that a given thing *b* is not actually used by them to define 'Y' or to teach its meaning. Can we conclude that *b* is not a "Y" – that a statement of the form "*b* is a Y" is false? Clearly not. For perhaps *b can* be properly used to define 'Y' or to teach its meaning, although it is never actually used in that way. In order to discover whether or not this is the case, i.e., whether or not *b* is a member of the class Y, we need to compare its characteristics with unquestionable examples of Y. In the present type of situation, we need to compare them with objects that are taken as Standard Examples or Paradigm Cases of Y; viz., with objects actually used in defining 'Y' or in teaching its ordinary meaning. And this comparison is (once again) an extra-linguistic empirical matter. In the case of sensible qualities, or even sensible objects, the comparison is often relatively easy to make. The difficulty in practice arises chiefly where 'X' is the name of a complex activity or of something intangible. Consider for instance the difficulty of deciding, in some cases, whether a given action that looks like theft *is* an instance of theft – assuming that there are Paradigm Cases of theft with which it can be compared.

The preceding may be summed up in the following way: the analysis of the ordinary usage of an expression 'X' shows that for anything to be an X, it must normally possess such and such (defining) features. Where the expression 'X' functions as a general name, we can discover whether or not a given object *a* is an X by noting whether *a* is actually used to define or to teach the meaning of 'X.' If yes, the matter is settled – *a is* an X. If no, we have to note whether *a* is identical with, or highly resembles, things that are unquestionably "X's," in respect to the features the latter possess *qua* "X's." To determine the nature of these defining features we need, once more, to observe and analyse the correct ordinary usage of 'X.'

A new factor arises in the case of names of artifacts, man-devised activities or processes, and the names of certain natural things (such as 'composer,' 'swimmer,' 'teacher'). Thus suppose 'X' is a general name of the present type, e.g. 'X' stands for 'pen,' 'pencil' or 'car,' or for 'swimmer,' 'writer' or 'teacher.' The word 'X' is then properly applicable to certain things if they possess the "defining features" implicitly involved in the ordinary meaning of 'X,' under what I have elsewhere called Normal or Standard (environmental) Conditions.[1] Paradigm Cases of "X," if and where they arise here, determine or define *both* the defining features" of "Xs" and the Standard Conditions relative to 'X.'

The following alternatives are then possible in relation to a given thing *c* of the kind under discussion, which, at the same time, is not actually used to define 'X' or to teach its meaning:

(i) If *c* possesses the requisite defining features, it will be an X whether the prevailing environmental conditions are Standard or non-Standard Conditions.

(ii) If *c* does not possess the requisite defining features, the following alternatives are open:

(a) The prevailing conditions *are* Standard Conditions; in which case *c* is *not* an X [2]; or

(b) The prevailing conditions are non-Standard Conditions; in which case the question whether *c* is an X cannot be, or cannot be conclusively, answered. To answer it, *c* has to be observed under Standard Conditions – if necessary, by deliberately creating these conditions.

The notion of Standard Conditions is by no means confined to names

[1] For the notion of Standard Conditions see *Ibid., passim,* and chapter six, pp. 98ff. and 114 of this book.

[2] Provided that it is what we would call intact, complete or unbroken. If it is incomplete, broken or otherwise not intact, we frequently do not judge it to be a not–X, if it lacks *some* of the requisite defining features. Quite frequently, we say that *c* is simply an incomplete, unfinished or broken X, as the case may be, rather than a not–X. Actually, the situation is rather complicated; since a good deal depends on *what* particular features *c* lacks, and *how many* of them, relative to the ordinary meaning or uses (or the technical meaning or uses) of 'X,' as well as on whether all or only some of the requisite Standard Conditions are present. Where only some of the latter conditions are present, further complications arise; and so on. I should add that in actual practice the situation with respect to (ii) above, as a whole, is considerably more complicated than we have stated in the text. The same applies to (i).

of the sort mentioned above. Different types of Standard Conditions are involved in the ordinary uses of different classes of ordinary expressions. For instance, one special type of Standard Condition arises in respect to the ordinary applications of names of sensible qualities and objects in general. Take the name 'red.' An object which appears (is perceived as) red is considered to be red (is called "red") provided the conditions under which it is perceived are regarded as standard or normal conditions of perception; e.g. if it is perceived in sunlight or under a white electric light, etc. It follows that no patch of color can be properly regarded as a paradigm case of red unless it is perceived as red under the appropriate Standard Conditions of perception.

Before I proceed further let me state that "defining features," as I use the expression in connection with the uses of ordinary expressions, are not necessarily confined to determinate or relatively determinate characteristics and/or certain criss-crossing "family resemblances." "Defining features" may be of many types, and the types of features I just mentioned are only two of these. Let us also recall that in the case of vague expressions no fixed "defining features" obtain; while in the case of expressions that involve marginal indeterminacy the applicability of a given expression without qualification, on the basis of the "defining features" involved, is not always determinate.

Finally, let us note that although some examples actually used by people to define or to teach the meaning of a given ostensively definable expression 'Y' may be incorrect examples, this cannot be true of *all* the actual examples used by all or most people who define or teach 'Y's' meaning. What actual examples are correct examples and what are not can be determined, in any given case, by noting how the majority employ the given expression.

We now come to the question as to whether the *existence* or non-existence of an object of discourse X can ever be determined by appeal to correct usage in general, or any one form of it in particular. Stated otherwise, we are concerned to discover whether the question Does X exist? or the question Are there any X's? can *ever* be answered by appeal to correct ordinary usage. If the answer is Yes, it would clearly mean that correct usage can supply us with a criterion of the truth or falsity of at least some statements of the form: "X exists," "Y does not exist"; and "There are X's," "There aren 't any X's."

Contemporary philosophical opinion is divided on this point: some philosophers answer the above question affirmatively, while others answer it in the negative. The controversy has centered chiefly round the merits of one form of the so-called Paradigm Case Argument, or PCA as we shall henceforth refer to it (which itself is a special case of appeal to ordinary usage). Our task now is to examine the merits of this argument.

In one form of the argument, it is claimed that "X exists, or that there are X's, if in the standard cases of the use of "X" it is used to refer to something *a*." [1] A different formulation of this argument is given by J. O. Urmson. Urmson states (actually claims) that by this argument –

> The philosophical doubt whether something is really an X is exposed as being in some way improper or absurd by means of a demonstration that the thing in question is a standard case by reference to which the expression 'X' has to be understood, or a doubt whether anything is X is exposed by showing that certain things are standard cases of what the term in question is designed to describe.[2]

A similar formulation is given by R. J. Hirst. He maintains that it cannot be validly argued, and it would be improper and absurd to hold that there are no "X's" if the meaning of the word 'X' is or can be taught by reference to paradigm cases. The same applies to the view that any of the paradigm cases by reference to which the meaning of 'X' is taught, is not an "X." [3]

We shall begin with the first, positive formulation of the argument, then pass to the second and third, critical formulations of it.

In its first, positive formulation the argument seems to me to be perfectly sound, and even a truism; provided that by the phrase" 'X' is used to refer to something *a*" is meant "'X' is used to refer to some *existent* thing *a*," in any one of the ordinary uses or senses of 'exist.' (The proviso is necessary since the word 'something' can be properly used to refer to fictitious things as well). For instance, if *a* is an actual sensible object or quality, an actual event or occurrence, a sensation, a feeling or emotion.[4] Stated in other words, the argument would be correctly applicable whenever we can truly affirm that there is an *a* or there are *a*'s (in a certain place, at a given time, and so on, as the nature of *a* may require); in a sense of 'there is' or 'there are' in which it has the meaning of 'exists' in any one of *its* ordinary uses.[5] (The last

[1] Panayot Butchvarov, "The Paradigm-Case Argument," *The Journal Of Philosophy*, vol. LV, No. 21 (October 9, 1958), p. 886.

[2] "Some Questions Concerning Validity," *Essays in Conceptual Analysis* (London, 1956), p. 120.

[3] *The Problems of Perception* (London, 1959), p. 121.

[4] See my "On Existence," *Methodos*, 1957, *passim*.

[5] Note that in English it would be improper to use 'exists' in lieu of 'there is' (or 'are'), even where the latter refers to something existent. Thus it would be incorrect to say, e.g., "Elephants existi n the Antwerp Zoo" instead of "There are elephants in the Antwerp Zoo."

qualification is essential, since it is perfectly correct to say "There are centaurs in books on Greek mythology," even though centaurs do not exist). Some examples are: "There are elephants at the Antwerp Zoo," "I have a toothache," "Something, I don't know what exactly, worries me," "Our yard is full of ants."

Our proviso, and hence the present argument, can be stated in terms of the broader concept of "reality" without detriment to its soundness; i.e., we can interpret "'X' is used to refer to something *a*" in the PCA as meaning "'X' is used to refer to some real thing *a* (or "to something *a* that is real," or "something *a* that has reality")." The reason I say that the notion of reality is broader than that of existence is that the expression 'is real' can be used in contexts where the word 'exists' cannot be used; or that 'exists' cannot be substituted for 'is real' in all the occurrences of the latter word.[1] The following are examples: "Numbers are not unreal." This way of speaking seems to me to be perfectly proper, and may be occasioned, say, by someone's asserting that numbers are fictions; or that there are no such things as 7, 8, 5, etc. Similarly, sentences of the form 'There *is* such a thing as–1,' 'There *are* such things as numbers,' are perfectly proper, it seems to me. A use of the first sentence is illustrated when someone says: "You can't subtract 5 from 4, since 5 is larger than 4." One proper retort is, "Yes you can: there is such a thing as–1."

Now if the PCA in its broader formulation is perfectly cogent, it would seem that it can provide us with a valuable *test* of the truth or falsity of certain statements asserting or implying the reality (or the unreality) of something or other. To ascertain whether this is really so, we must discover whether it is possible to determine (and if yes, how) (i) That a given application of 'X' is or is not a paradigm case of its employment; and if and when a given application constitutes a paradigm case, (ii) whether in that application it refers to something real.

A general way in which we can discover whether a given application (or type of application) of 'X' is or is not a paradigm case of its employment is by observing, and sometimes analysing, the way in which people apply 'X' in ordinary discourse. Take, for example, the word 'calculate.' A paradigm case of the employment of this word consists in its application to the process of estimating the product of two or more numbers. This fact is easily discovered (if we do not know it already) if we observe that people unhesitatingly say, for instance:

[1] By contrast, and for obvious logical reasons, we can truly (hence correctly) speak of something as *non*-existent if and when we can truly (hence correctly) speak of it as *un*real.

"My eight-year old son correctly calculated the product of 750 and 1956"; or "He doesn't know how to make the simplest calculations: he cannot correctly multiply (say) 7 and 8."

I need not add that, in many cases, a much faster way of discovering whether a given application of a particular word is a paradigm case would be to look up the word's meaning in a standard dictionary.

The answer to the first part of the query, (i), will also be in the affirmative if 'X' can be defined or its meaning can be taught (or learned) ostensively. 'X's' application to particular things *a*, *b*, *c*, etc. that are pointed to in defining 'X' or teaching its meaning, clearly provide us with paradigm cases of 'X's' employment. And by the very fact that *a*, *b*, *c* are things that can be pointed to, the answer to the second part of our question, (ii), will also be in the affirmative. Stated in general terms, where (a) 'X' can be defined or its meaning taught (or learned) by reference to a thing, *a*, and (b) *a* is a sensible thing or a kinaesthetic sensation, we know by (a) and (b) together that 'X' refers to something real. But (and this is important) the criterion of (b)'s truth, of *a*'s being a sensible thing or a kinaesthetic sensation, is always somebody's actual *sense*-perception or his "inner" sensations respectively; while the criterion of (a)'s truth is the way 'X' is ordinarily defined or how its meaning can be taught. This means that "appeal to usage" does enable us to determine the truth or falsity of certain statements of the form "X is real" and "X is unreal" (or "There are X's," "There are no X's"); but only because "appeal to correct usage," by the nature of the case, here includes or involves the apprehension of some sensible thing or the having of some sensation. In every case, therefore, it includes or involves an appeal to something extra-linguistic. The appeal to something sensible as partly determining paradigm cases of the use of an expression 'X' thus constitutes a special kind of case: a type of case where knowledge of 'X's' meaning necessarily involves or includes the knowledge that 'X' refers to something real.

I said above that observation of the way in which certain words are defined or their meaning is taught enables us to determine the truth or falsity of certain types of statements discussed above. A more correct way of putting this is that statements of the form "X is real" can be known to be *true*, and their negations can be known to be *false*, wherever 'X' can be defined or its use can be taught by our pointing to something sensible, *a*. We have not so far said what would be the case if 'X' *cannot* be defined, or its meaning cannot be taught, by pointing to something sensible. Can we legitimately infer from that that 'X' does *not* refer to anything real, that there are no X's in reality?

The answer is Yes and No.

(1) If 'X' names something that, if it is real, would be a sensible thing or a sensation, the answer is Yes. Consider the word 'centaur.' In the light of the correct ordinary usage of the word 'centaur,' we know that centaurs, if they did exist, would be sensible objects. We also know, from an observation of how 'centaur' is correctly used, that this word is never actually ostensively defined.[1] But this, of course, is not enough; it does not tell us whether the meaning of 'centaur' can or cannot be ostensively defined. For, unlike names of sensible qualities, the names of real sensible objects can be taught *without* our ever pointing to any sensible *object*. The only way in which we can discover that the meaning of 'centaur' cannot be defined (the world being what it is) by pointing to any sensible object, is by noting the empirical fact that centaurs have never been encountered on this earth.

It is worth noting here that if the expression 'X' is the name of an alleged sensible quality, and it is *never actually* defined or taught by one's pointing to anything sensible, we can infer that it names nothing real.

(2) By contrast with (1), the answer to the above question is No where 'X' does not name the sort of entity that would be something sensible if it exists or were to exist. For the existence of "X's" is logically possible, even though they would not be sensible things or sensations. For example, democracy and communism, nationalism, numbers and the Common Law are real things. It would be queer to say that when we talk about democracy or communism, about the Common Law or about numbers, we are not speaking about anything real. Yet all these and a host of other things are not sensible things at all. How then do we know that these are real, that they are not fictions?

As far as numbers are concerned, the answer seems to me to be this: we know that numbers are real because we *employ* them in daily life, in science and in pure mathematics; i.e., in computation. (The *kind* of reality they enjoy is also determined by the multifarious ways in which we do and can employ them.) Also, we know that numbers are real because of the manner in which we speak about numbers; i.e., the ways in which we employ such words as 'number' and the symbols of particular numbers. For the paradigm cases of the use of an expression 'X' on

[1] We can point to a drawing of a centaur (say) in defining (or teaching) the word; but this and similar devices are not what I have in mind in speaking of ostensive definition.

which the PCA rests, are nothing but some or all of the correct (ordinary and/or technical) uses of 'X.'

The question now is whether appeal to correct usage cannot be used in respect to our other expressions. For instance, can we not discover whether or not there is such a thing as democracy in the world at present (say) by finding out whether, in any standard (correct) case of the use of 'democracy,' the word is applied to something real? Is it not enough, for example, to observe that people correctly use the word 'democracy' in referring to the contemporary U.S.A. as a democratic country? The trouble is that we can equally correctly (though I believe falsely) *deny* that the contemporary U.S.A. is at present a democracy in any degree.

The statement "Blood is not red," made in ordinary, lay contexts (not in a philosophical or a scientific context) is not merely false but improper, confused, odd: the word 'red' in it is actually misused. Whereas there is nothing confused, odd or improper in the (false) statement that the contemporary U.S.A. is not a democracy in any degree. And the essential difference lies in the fact that whereas pointing to a pool of blood can perfectly well serve to define 'red,' we cannot say quite the same about the U.S.A. or England in relation to the use of 'democracy.' It is perfectly possible to define 'democracy' as the political, economic and social, state of affairs obtaining at present in the U.S.A. (and/or in England). But it would not be quite legitimate to do so – at least its legitimacy would be open to controversy – in the light of the ordinary, admittedly rather vague, uses of the word 'democracy.' The ordinary meaning of 'democracy' would be *restricted* if we did so (unlike the ostensive definition of 'red' by pointing to blood); and, apart from the vagueness of the ordinary meaning of 'democracy,' people disagree for factual reasons as to whether the U.S.A. or England is a democracy. This means that the present U.S.A.'s or England's being a paradigm case of the use of 'democracy' is contested (e.g., by Communists).

The political life in Pericles' Athens is *the* paradigm case of *one form* of democracy, one use of 'democracy.' We know that this form of democracy did exist, since 'democracy' in one sense is defined in terms of the political and social conditions in Athens at that time. The question whether or not the U.S.A. or England is a paradigm case of *another* use of 'democracy' remains, however.

We can now sum up the chief points we have arrived at in this section. The PCA in its positive form is logically sound. But in order that we may be in a position to infer that something X is real or is not real, we must already know whether or not 'X' does or does not refer to anything real in standard cases of its use. This knowledge can only be reached by the observation of extra- or non-linguistic facts; which itself does not and cannot constitute a part of the PCA.

Our conclusion is put, somewhat overemphatically, by Panayot Buchvarov in the following way:

> As a proof of the *existence* of X the argument is useless insofar as it does not provide us with a criterion for distinguishing between expressions which in their standard cases of use are used to refer to something and expressions which in their standard cases are not used to refer to anything. For if it is obvious that "X" belongs to the former class, then we do not need the PCA to show that the expression denotes an existent. And if this is not obvious, the argument merely proves the trivial truth that there are cases in which "X" is used, and not that there are X-things.[1]

The foregoing applies equally, *mutatis mutandis*, to Quine's well-known test of "existential generalization." [2] From the true statement (1) "Leeds is a city," we can indeed infer that

(1a) Something is a *real* city,

(1b) There is something real which is a city. Or even that

(1c) There is an X such that X is a real city.[3]

But these inferences can be validly drawn only because we assume as a premise besides (1) the actual existence (hence reality), somewhere in the world, of some city called Leeds. For though 'Leeds' does actually name a real city, it could very well have been merely the name of some imaginary city in a novel by Jane Austen or Aldous Huxley. And in the latter case we could still properly say, *in the context of the novel,* that Leeds is a city. True, we actually make the statement "Leeds is a city" in real-life contexts and not, or not only, in the context of works of fiction. But we do so precisely because we know that Leeds is a real city; whereas someone who does not already know that Leeds is a real city and wishes to find out for himself, can discover that the statement "Leeds is a city" is a true statement about some part of the world only by appealing to geographical and other non-linguistic facts about the cities that actually exist in the world at present.

One final point before we pass to the critical expositions of the PCA. It can be readily seen that the foregoing discussion applies to pairs of

[1] *Op. cit.*, p. 887.

[2] "Designation and Existence," *The Journal of Philosophy*, vol. XXXVI, No. 26 (December, 1939), pp. 701–709, *passim.*

[3] These examples, with some modification, are taken from G. J. Warnock, "Metaphysics In Logic," *Essays In Conceptual Analysis*, p. 79. This essay contains trenchant criticism of "existential generalization" and of Quine's second test, called "application."

ordinary adjectives or adverbs having the form 'X' and 'not-X' or 'X' and 'Y,' where 'Y' is the negative of 'X.' The fact that 'X' and 'not-X' are constantly used in ordinary discourse does not in itself imply that either of them refers to anything real. From the existence of such distinctions in ordinary language we can only infer that either or both of the terms of *some* of these distinctions – which ones we cannot say – refer to real things. But even this inference is partly based on the extra-linguistic fact that language has evolved and continues to function as an instrument of communication: of which the communication of actual facts is a very important part. It would thus be unreasonable, if not downright self-contradictory, if none of the distinctions obtaining in actual language distinguishes real things. But this is about all. To find out whether a given adjective or adverb applies to anything real, we must appeal both to its correct usage and to some extra-linguistic facts. For instance, in order to discover whether we ever act freely in some ordinary sense or senses of 'act freely' (i.e., whether "I am doing X freely" is ever true in respect to any human being) we must observe whether we can and do correctly apply the expressions 'free' and 'freely' to any actual human actions; hence whether any statements which affirm that some human actions are free, are ever *true*. Thus we know that we sometimes act freely because we note (say) that it is correct to speak of a prisoner who has just been let out of prison as "now free to go anywhere he wants, to do things he was not free to do in prison"; and that as a matter of fact there are prisoners who are let out of prison practically every day.

It is instructive to point out here some of the logical relations between a pair of expressions 'X' and 'not-X.' If 'X' does not refer to anything real, 'not-X' may or may not refer to anything real. It will not refer to anything real if the distinction drawn with the help of 'X' and 'not-X' is an imaginary distinction; a distinction drawn, say, within some imaginary or hypothetical world. It is also clear that if 'X' does not refer to anything real, 'not-X' (or 'non-X') *may* nonetheless refer to something real; and vice versa. Thus though 'centaur' does not refer to anything real, 'not centaur' can be used to refer to all real creatures or animals. For none of these real things possesses, *in toto*, the characteristics connoted by 'centaur.'

Further, if 'X' refers to something logically possible, it is often though not necessarily the case that 'not-X' refers to something logically possible. 'Not a square circle' can be used to refer to all logically possible geometrical figures; though 'square circle' does not refer to anything logically possible. In the case of pairs of expressions 'X' and 'Y,' where 'Y' is the *opposite* of 'X' in meaning and not merely its logical negative, the logical possibility of there being some Xs implies the logical possibility of there being some Ys. Thus if 'good' refers to anything possible (possibly real), 'bad' *ipso facto* refers to something possible; similarly with, say, 'changing' and 'unchanging.' Another way of saying this is that there can be no goodness without the logical possibility of there being some badness; no change without the logical possibility of there being something unchanging. This does not imply, nor is it the same as the *false* view that badness must exist in the universe at large if there is any goodness in it at all; or that if change is a real feature of the world, changelessness must likewise be real. I mention these two examples because the first view presents one traditional attempt to resolve the so-called Problem of Evil; and the second is an assumption underlying practically the entire history of philosophy until recent times.[1] All this does not logically preclude the existence, *as a matter of fact*, of badness as well as goodness, changelessness as well as change in the world. And indeed, the actual existence or non-existence of unchanging things – – and I here mean "unchanging" in the ordinary sense – may be debated; but who does not know that badness as well as goodness exists in this world?

The situation is somewhat different in the case of polar words, such as 'south' and 'north,' 'east' and 'west,' 'husband' and 'wife.' Two polar words 'X' and 'Y' either both refer to something real, or neither refers to anything real; if one of them, say 'X,' does not refer to anything real, the same would be true of the other, 'Y.'

We now pass to the critical formulations of PCA, and for our purposes we shall take Urmson's and Hirst's formulations of it as in intent the same. Our discussion will be brief, since the previous section partly foreshadows our conclusions.

To come straight to the point, what I have so far said shows, it seems to me, that Urmson and Hirst are right in maintaining that the PCA argument, *in the form they formulate it*, does show that certain questions of the form "Is X really an *a*?" or "Is *b* really an X?" are improper questions. Thus it is improper to ask (to borrow the example from Hirst) whether blood is really red; or to speak of a plank of wood, as *really* not solid.

[1] Though – and this makes the traditional philosopher's claim even more dubious – what is traditionally intended by 'something unchanging' (or 'permanent') is "something *absolutely, perfectly* unchanging," not what we ordinarily mean by 'unchanging' (or 'permanent'). The former includes, but is not exhausted by, the latter notion.

The two utterances are improper however only if they are understood to mean a certain definite thing. They may be, as I shall try to show, perfectly proper and meaningful if understood to mean something else.

Let us take the following two questions:

(1) Is this (coupled with the speaker's pointing to what looks like a pool of blood) really blood? and

(2) Is blood really red?

(1) is an ordinary perfectly proper question that may arise in daily life. It may be meaningfully asked by someone who is perceiving the "blood" under unusual, non-standard perceptual conditions. The "blood" could really be something else. It could be, for example, of quite a different color than red, and appear red only because, say, the light under which it is being perceived is red. The question may also be properly asked under standard perceptual conditions, when one is not sure whether the red mass he perceives possesses the other properties of blood – physical, biochemical, and so on. It would be plainly improper, however, to ask whether a given patch, perceived as red under standard conditions, is really red (as a perceived patch).

Now take the second question. This question may be regarded as a philosophical question, as expressing a philosophical doubt. Its legitimacy or illegitimacy depends on what it is intended to inquire about.

(a) The question would undoubtedly strike one as strange if asked by an adult – not to speak of a philosopher. But it would be quite proper and not at all strange if asked by someone who intends to inquire whether what we call blood, *as a perceived thing*, is red under normal perceptual conditions. The answer to the question is of course an emphatic Yes on the basis of the PCA.

(b) The question may also properly arise in a philosophical context; say in a passage on theory of perception. And this time the philosopher raising the question may be interested not in blood as perceived, but in blood as it would be if and when nobody were perceiving it. For instance, he may be thinking of a given pool of blood on a floor, and wondering whether it would be red if the lighting conditions were normal but there were nobody in the room to perceive it. In other words, the general question he could be interested in may be whether or not color is a property of things themselves or whether it is a property "they" have only when perceived (under certain conditions:) and he may wish to ask the question in the more specific form of blood Is *really* red? (Is grass really green? Is snow really white? etc.). Understood in this sense, the role of 'really' in the question becomes clear. Clearly, it is employed to indicate that something other than "Is blood, as *perceived* under normal conditions, red?" is intended. And whether or not the philosophical question can be definitely answered, it seems to me to be a perfectly proper question (see also chapter ten); but to *this* question the PCA does not apply, and provides no answer to it. For it is blood as perceived and perceivable, not blood as unperceived by anyone, that can provide us with a paradigm case of the use of 'red'; though in the actual contexts in which we employ ordinary language, we – philosophers and laymen alike – think of blood as red whether it is perceived or not.

(3) The question would clearly be improper, even senseless, if asked by an adult who knows what the words 'blood' and 'red' refer to, and intends to mean by it: "Does the word 'red' properly apply to blood as perceived under normal conditions?" The impropriety of this question can then be easily shown by appealing to the PCA. On the other hand, the question would be perfectly proper if asked by someone who knows the meaning of 'red' but not of 'blood'; or vice versa. In that case, too, the PCA can be of use, and would show that the answer to the question is a definite Yes.

So far we have concerned ourselves with a discussion of ordinary language – in particular, with its use in relation to the paradigm case argument – as providing us with a useful test of the truth or falsity of certain classes of statements. Our discussion of the paradigm case argument in particular and of language in general has a further value, in relation to the processes of exhibition analysis.

Now it is clear, to my mind, that exhibition analysis need not ever concern itself with how words are taught or learned. In our discussion and analysis of semantic analysis in chapter six, no reference was made to this latter matter; and that was not at all an oversight. The exhibition of the uses of (say) an ordinary expression requires the analysis of the way in which people ordinarily apply that expression in correct sentences in actual and possible situations. One fairly common way in which we apply an expression is in teaching those who do not know its meaning or its other (kinds of) uses, how that word is correctly applied; and in the case of some expressions this includes, or may include, their ostensive definition. But, as we pointed out earlier in this chapter, there are some, perhaps many words which cannot be ostensively defined; and even in the case of many expressions that can be so defined, their meaning or other uses can be taught or learned without appeal to ostensive definition.

On the other hand, as we also pointed out earlier, some words – e.g. color words – must be ostensively defined if their meaning is to be learned. What is more, language cannot be applicable to the world, we cannot say anything about actually existing things, unless some words are referring expressions. It may be thought, therefore, that the exhibition analysis of this type of word at least must concern itself, among other things, with the way in which these words are taught; and hence with the fact that they are ostensively defined. But this is not true. The uses of such words can be perfectly well exhibited without any reference to the way in which these words are actually taught. Take, for instance, the word 'blue.' This word is defined or taught by our pointing to blue objects, with the appropriate explanations to make the reference clear to the learner. But we can discover the ordinary uses of this word – e.g. the relation of the concept *blue* to the concept *spatial* or *extended*, its relations to the concepts *quality, relation, object, color, sense-perception*, etc. – without assuming that 'blue' is taught ostensively, and without appealing either to the fact that, or to the way in which, this is done. For example, the logical relation between the concepts *blue* and *extended* is discoverable by noting that it is self-contradictory to say: "X is blue but unextended," but that it is self-consistent to say: "X is extended but not blue (it has some other color; or it is colorless)." Similarly with the relation of *blue* to other concepts to which it is related. Of course, one can learn something about the ordinary uses of 'blue' – e.g. the elementary fact that 'blue' is the name of a visual (hence sensible) quality – by noting that we teach its meaning by pointing to blue objects. But this information can be easily got otherwise. One, a child for instance, can discover this by noting that we employ such statements as: "Look at that blue bird!" We can also get the information that 'blue' names a sensible quality by noting, as in our earlier example, that it is self-contradictory to say: "X is blue but is unextended"; while the odd: "X is blue but nobody can see its blueness under any circumstances," indicates that it names a visual quality.

What then is the relevance of the fact that we teach (or learn) the uses of certain expressions ostensively, and of the role which this fact plays in the PCA? The answer is quite simple. Although exhibition analysis need never appeal to this fact, and certainly does not need to assume that some words are (must be) ostensively defined, the appeal to the way in which a word is taught or learned – whether ostensively or otherwise – is one useful strategem which we can employ to discover or uncover some aspects of the uses of that word. It can thus be regarded as an adjunct to exhibition analysis, or even as one of the possible "moves" of exhibition analysis itself.

CHAPTER TEN

EXTRA-LINGUISTIC ANALYSIS

In chapters five, six and nine we have discussed, it will be remembered, three major forms of semantic analysis. In the present chapter we pass to the second type of philosophical analysis we distinguished in chapter one: to what I have called "extra-linguistic analysis." This type of analysis, it will perhaps be recalled, consists in the philosopher's conceptual analysis of (1) certain actual objects, occurrences or states of affairs, and/or (2) certain empirical facts – hence true propositions – about actual objects, occurrences or states of affairs arrived at through scientific investigation. In both cases – and this is absolutely essential in our present conception of *philosophical* extra-linguistic analysis – the philosopher's appeal to the nature of, or actual facts about, various existing things is, or must be, designed to help answer some philosophical question, or to throw light on some philosophical concept. In the latter case, the empirical facts which are utilized and interpreted may sometimes show the usefulness or desirability of reconstructing the concept in question, in view of the philosophical purpose or purposes it is intended to serve. In the light of our description of this method, it is seen that 'empirical analysis' would have been a better name for it than the one I have actually used, except for the following two reasons: First, that *semantic* analysis too is empirical in one sense – in being an analysis of actual languages or parts of actual languages; and second, that our present type of analysis, like semantic analysis, is conceptual in nature; as opposed to the kind of analysis which the chemist (say) practises in his laboratory.

The term 'object-analysis' is more appropriate in some respects; but it tends to give the impression that extra-linguistic analysis in my sense is limited, or is intended to be limited, to (1) above. That would indeed be a very serious limitation of the present type of method. The method would then be limited to what is by far the less important, useful or significant part or aspect of it. As a matter of fact, I should make it perfectly clear at the outset that I am strongly against the philosopher's venturing into factual observation or fact-gathering except in relation to certain relatively circumscribed areas of empirical facts, or in relation to certain limited kinds of philosophical questions.

More precisely and explicitly, the philosopher's indulgence in this aspect or part of extra-linguistic analysis must be confined to those empirical areas of inquiry into which empirical science has not yet moved; or in which it has not yet made substantial advances. At the present time, this is only true of the empirical study of man, in its manifold aspects; and so in relation to philosophical questions chiefly if not wholly limited to man's moral, religious, aesthetic, social and political activities. (Not that this unduly limits the philosopher's scope of activity in the present connection! The vastness and immense complexity of these areas of inquiry is evident). The essential point, however, is that the philosopher's "period of grace" lasts only as long as the scientist has not provided the necessary empirical facts or laws for the philosopher to make use of, if and when the need arises. Further, the philosopher's indulgence in "object-analysis" (by which I shall henceforth refer to the present possible aspect or part of extra-linguistic analysis), does not exempt him from the demand that his observations be made as carefully as possible. That is, he should avoid sweeping generalizations and should take into careful consideration possible disconfirmatory instances. He must therefore rely, as carefully as possible, on genuinely random sampling, and must pay close attention to the multiplicity and complexity of the possibly relevant factors in a given case – in general, he should attempt to employ, whenever the facts at his disposal make this possible, the reasoning involved in Mill's canons of induction (more sophisticated forms of these canons are not possible for the philosophers not trained in exact experimental observation. In any case, such exact observation is not and has never been a part of philosophy proper).

I mention these obvious things because a vast amount of the traditional philosopher's factual pronouncements – or, at least, pronouncements that purport to be factual – are reached in disregard of these and other elementary rules of inductive reasoning. Many examples can be cited, but a few will suffice. One obvious example is the view of the Expression Theory of Art that the artist, whenever he creates a work of art (at least, whenever he creates a good work) labors under a strong feeling or emotion which he attempts to "express" in, and by creating, the work. Similarly the related view, held by some advocates of this aesthetic theory, that the artist is an exceptionally emotional person. Other examples, chosen at random, are Clive Bell's statement that "All sensitive people agree that there is a peculiar emotion provoked by works of art," [1] and that "as a rule, most people feel a very different kind of emotion for birds and flowers and the wings of butterflies from that which they feel for pictures, pots, temples, and statues." [2] Examples of this kind, in contemporary as well as in traditional aesthetics, can be multiplied almost indefinitely. In Ethics, the theory known as psychological egoism (likewise, psychological hedonism, which is one special form of the theory) provides us with a good example. In the philosophy of man, we can cite the pronouncements of many traditional philosophers on the nature of man or other, related matters. It is only necessary to recall some of the factual pronouncements of such thinkers as Plato, Aristotle, Hobbes, Spinoza, Hume, Schopenhauer, Nietzsche, and the modern (atheistic or religious) Existentialists to see the truth of what we are saying. Finally, it is incumbent on the philosopher to make it clear – to be fully aware of the fact to begin with – that the factual results he claims he has reached are extremely tentative. He must think of his results more as a possible hypothesis, "hunch" or worthwhile guess than a full-fledged and already-verified theory, not to say "the truth."

Stressing the matter from another angle, I want to make it clear at this early point in our discussion that, by far, the greater part of the possible merit or usefulness of philosophical extra-linguistic analysis (if any) must lie in its second part or aspect, (2), outlined above. Our discussion in the rest of this chapter should make this point amply clear, if not provide concrete support for it.

Our discussion in the rest of what follows will be divided into two main parts. In the first part, I shall speak about the possible use of extra-linguistic analysis in relation to (a) reductive concept-analysis of the Moorean form, which we discussed in chapter five; and (b) non-reductive concept analysis: actually, of concept analysis in general, whether reductive or non-reductive. In the second, longer and more important part, I shall deal with extra-linguistic analysis in relation to three major related types of questions, inquiries or concerns with which philosophy deals (though it is not exhausted by them). This will include

[1] "Significant Form," in *A Modern Book of Esthetics*, Revised Edition (New York, Holt, Rinehart and Winston, Inc., 1952), edited by Melvin Rader, p. 317.

[2] *Ibid.*, p. 320.

the important question as to whether it is useful for the philosopher to reconstruct any ordinary concepts partly or wholly in the light of new empirical discoveries.

A. EXTRA-LINGUISTIC ANALYSIS IN RELATION TO REDUCTIVE CONCEPT-ANALYSIS

We saw in chapter five that Moore's reductive concept-analysis presupposes or logically rests upon a corresponding form of reductive object-analysis. We also saw, though not very explicitly or clearly, that the different sorts of reduction or analysis to which (for Moore) a given concept *X* is amenable correspond to and result from the different sorts of reduction or analysis to which *things* called "X's" themselves are amenable. Thus the concept of a physical object (say that of a table) is analysable reductively in one or more ways, by virtue of the fact that physical objects (say tables) are analysable in a certain way or certain ways. On the other hand, the concept of a "complex quality" (assuming that such things exist) is, or may be, analysable in a different way from the foregoing; by virtue of its being the concept of a complex *quality* rather than an object. And so on. For example, the concept *horse*, we saw, is conceived by Moore as analysable in terms of the concepts *head*, *trunk*, *liver*, *legs*, etc. in certain logical relations to one another, because horses are themselves composed of a head, a trunk, legs, a liver, and other qualitatively differentiated parts, in a straightforward sense of 'part.' At the same time, the concept *horse* is partly analysable in terms of the concepts of certain sense-data, because (according to Moore) we directly perceive certain sense-data whenever, as we ordinarily say, we perceive a horse. On the other hand, Moore regards the concept of "good" as unanalysable because it is the concept of a simple quality or property; i.e., of something which cannot be analysed into simpler qualities or properties.[1]

[1] In the light of this we can see that any attempted analysis of the concept *good* partly or wholly in terms of other *ethical* concepts, cannot be successful unless it is first shown that 'good' does not name any simple quality or property (or even a simple relation). Thus, to my mind, A. C. Ewing's (say) attempted analysis of good (in "A Suggested Non-Naturalistic Analysis of Good," *Readings in Ethical Theory*, pp. 231–249) in terms of the concept of moral obligation and the concept of choice fails as a suggested analysis. And one main reason – it is not the only one – is that Ewing fails to show first that 'good' does not name any simple quality or property. For that reason at least the suggested analysis cannot be regarded as really an analysis of the meaning of 'good' but rather of 'a good thing (experience or action).' It might be replied that this, or a similar analysis *itself* succeeds in showing that 'good' does *not* name any simple quality or property – or any quality or property at all – since it successfully gives us the ordinary *meaning* of 'good' in terms of 'ought,' etc. (This, or something like it, is stated by P. F. Strawson in his "Ethical Intuitionism," *Ibid.*, p. 257). However, the

From this it follows that if reductive concept-analysis does really rest on or logically presuppose the analysis of objects, occurrences or states of affairs (as Moore's utterances and practice implicitly assume it does), this connection between the two would provide us with one possible use of extra-linguistic analysis. That is, extra-linguistic analysis would have to be practised whenever a philosopher desires to practise reductive concept-analysis. We shall now attempt to find out whether the alleged relation really obtains. But before we do so, let us point out that if it does obtain, our earlier criticism or reductive concept-analysis in chapter five would make extra-linguistic analysis, at best, of very limited usefulness in its present capacity.

The question now is whether we need to analyse any objects or other existing things at all in order to be able to analyse a "complex" concept into "simpler" concepts; in order to analyse certain concepts in terms of "more fundamental," "more ultimate" concepts. The answer, to my mind, is a definite Yes. For unless we have been wildly mistaken in outlining the nature of Moore's conception of reductive concept-analysis, the notions of conceptual reduction or division, of simplicity and complexity, of analysability or unanalysability of concepts all rest on, or make sense in terms of, the (alleged) complexity or simplicity, analysability or unanalysability of the things falling under the concepts to be analysed-if-possible. This also means that our earlier thesis (in chapters five and six) that *exhibition analysis* offers a much sounder and more general method of arriving at the definitions which Moore's concept-analysis is interested in reaching, whenever such definitions are possible or useful to begin with, is really tantamount to an abandonment or rejection of reductive concept-analysis. For even if we claim, in any given case, that exhibition analysis reveals that a given concept A is analysable in terms of two or more related concepts B and C, etc., but not vice versa, this will not be due to any belief or assumption that B and C, etc. are "simpler," more fundamental, more ultimate than A. The reason may simply be that the verbal expression stating the analysans (the expression which refers to B and C, etc. in a certain

whole question is precisely whether the alleged translation, or any other proposed translation, does give us the meaning, in the sense of provide a *definition*, of 'good.' For Moore himself holds that we can *explain* the meaning of, but not define, 'good' in terms of *ought* and other concepts. Unless it is shown that the proposed translation does give us the ordinary meaning of 'good,' and that the concepts in terms of which this is done do not themselves logically *presuppose* the concept *good*, such attempts will not have proved their point. But to do this itself requires the *exhibition analysis* of the concepts *good, ought* and other, related ethical concepts: which well illustrates the more fundamental character of this form of analysis, at least in this particular instance, relatively to reductive concept- *cum*-object-analysis itself.

logical relation, and which is synonymous with the verbal expression referring to concept *A*) is *syntactically more complicated than the expression expressing the analysandum.* The following passage from P. F. Strawson's "Ethical Intuitionism" will illustrate what I mean:

> *"Right"-sentences, "good"-sentences are shorthand for "ought"-sentences.* And this is enough in itself to explode the myth of unanalysable characteristics designated by the indefinable predicates, "right" and "good." For "ought" is a *relational* word; whereas "right" and "good" are *predicative. The simplest sentences containing "ought" are syntactically more complicated than the simplest sentences containing "right" or "good." And hence, since the equivalences of meaning hold, the various ethical usages of "right" and "good" are all definable: variously definable in* terms of "ought."[1]

The reason which earlier made us regard exhibition analysis as a much sounder and much more widely applicable method of analysis is also the reason why the usefulness of extra-linguistic analysis as a logical basis of semantic analysis (here reductive analysis) is severely limited whenever the analysandum in question is an *ordinary* concept. This limitation is imposed by the fact that ordinary concepts are delimited or "defined" in and by actual everyday usage. The observation and analysis of actual matters of fact, whether by the philosopher himself (to the extent that he can or may profitably do so) or by the scientist, are simply irrelevant for the *analysis* of such concepts; though they are very important in other ways which we shall later outline. The following example will illustrate this. Modern Chemistry has shown that water is chemically analysable into two parts of hydrogen and one part of oxygen, combined in a certain way. This fact is, or may be, part of the chemist's concept of water; but this concept is certainly not the same as the ordinary concept of water: to say that water is a compound of hydrogen and oxygen in certain proportions, etc. is not to give the ordinary meaning of 'water' (what we ordinarily mean, or intend to mean by it); hence it does not provide us with an analysis of that concept. Other, much more important illustrations will readily come to mind; for example, in relation to our modern physical knowledge of space and time, motion, matter, change, causality; or our modern psychological knowledge of feeling, emotion, sense-perception, volition, imagination, conception, learning, desire.

Appeal to scientific or other empirical facts are also irrelevant, to my mind (though I am not absolutely definite about this) to the *analysis*

[1] *Readings in Ethical Theory* (New York, Appleton-Century-Grofts, Inc., (c) 1952), edited by Wilfrid Sellars and John Hospers, p. 257. I have italicized the relevant sentences. Other italics in original.

of *scientific* concepts in which the philosopher may be interested. But the reasons are different from those which make scientific and other empirical facts irrelevant to the analysis of ordinary concepts. The philosopher who sets out to analyse some of the key concepts of modern psychology – e.g. those of psycho-analysis – or of some other social science, can discover the logical content of these concepts by finding out how psychologists, sociologists, etc., as the case may be, explicitly define in their writings the expressions which convey them. Or if the concepts in question are not explicitly "defined" but occur as "undefined" concepts (i.e., only defined in use) in some hypothesis or theory, or a number of hypotheses or theories, he can discover what they involve by an analysis of their role in the particular hypothesis or hypotheses, theory or theories. This is also, I think, required for an understanding of the contents of the technical concepts of the physical scientist. Where a concept is operationally "defined," its content can be discerned from the scientist's descriptions of the defining operations. In general, in the same way as the content of a given ordinary concept is discoverable by one's noting and analysing the way or ways in which this concept is employed in everyday contexts, the content of a scientific concept is discoverable by one's noting and analysing how scientists, in the particular discipline, actually employ it.

Now it is an important feature of Moore's form of reduction concept-analysis, which we noted in chapter five, that it aims at reaching "real definitions" and not any "verbal definitions," including "proper verbal definitions" (to use Moore's own words). But from what Moore says, and from the examples he gives in chapter one of *Principia Ethica*, referred to in chapter five – e.g. the analysis of the concept *horse* or the concept *the good* – it is clear that "real definition" in Moore's use of this expression may or may not coincide in particular cases with "connotative definition." Take "the good." Moore wishes to discover its "nature" or "essence" in the sense of pin-pointing the quality (or qualities) which is (or are) necessary and sufficient for a thing to be a part or the whole of "the good." He does not (necessarily) seek to discover the *ordinary* "defining features" of good things *qua* called good. The "essential features" of "the good" and its ordinary "defining features" may coincide; but if they do, this coincidence will be a purely empirical, contingent matter: it will not be due to any necessary connection between them. This being the case, we can easily see how and why Moore believes, in effect, that to discover the nature of "the good," one must examine or analyse different intrinsically good things (experiences, states of affairs, etc.). I need not add that Moore appeals to the ordinary meaning of '(intrinsically) good thing' in order that he may be able to identify (what he believes are) the different intrinsic goods – things we ordinarily *call* "(intrinsically) good." But the discovery of the essential features of intrinsically good things is not reached by an analysis of the meaning of 'the good' or 'a good.' It is a matter of extra-linguistic analysis of the things named by 'a good' or those named by 'the good.'

Notwithstanding Moore's failure to draw a distinction – or, at least, a clear distinction – between the discovery of the ordinary defining features of a class of things and the discovery of their "essential" features in Moore's understanding of the latter, his *synonymity* condition (which is obviously necessary if, as he wishes, an analysis is to ensue in a correct *definition*) makes extra-linguistic analysis of doubtful utility. Trying to satisfy the latter condition while aiming at discovering the "essential" features of a class of things is precisely like running with the hare and hunting with the hounds. For the latter will sometimes, perhaps quite often, determine a more or less *different* concept from the *ordinary concept* which is, ostensibly, our analysandum. This will be the case whenever – quite likely, very often – the "essential features" which empirical investigation discloses are partly or wholly distinct from the ordinary defining features. This is very likely to be *always* true if the empirical data utilized for the analysis are experimental scientific facts, not the superficial observations of the philosopher (I am assuming that the philosopher here is not also a trained scientist). The new concept *N* delimited in terms of empirical facts may have the same logical extension – may delimit the same class of objects – as the ordinary concept which is our ostensible analysandum *C*. Hence the statements in which *N* occurs may be *logically equivalent* to the statements resulting from the substitution of *C* for it; and vice versa. But logical equivalence is not the same as synonymity; though it is a necessary condition of the synonymity of two or more statements. (An expression necessarily synonymous with the expression 'C' can only be reached by analysis (if and when it is reached by analysis), through the examination of what 'C' actually means, is used to mean). Our earlier example about water illustrates this. The ordinary and the scientific concepts of water are not the same; yet they have, I think, the same logical extension; and though "A compound of hydrogen and oxygen combined in certain proportions by a certain kind of bond, etc" (all these are assumed to be specified in the statement) does not mean what we ordinarily mean by 'water,' [1] it is logically equivalent, I believe, to any correct definition of the word 'water' in its ordinary meaning. The word 'fish,' on the other hand, is an example of an ordinary expression whose extension (or comprehension, in C. I. Lewis' sense) as well as meaning has somewhat changed on the basis of the scientific discovery of certain common features in many objects ordinarily called fishes. For in the light of biological investigations, the class of whales is excluded from the extension of 'fish' in its biological use; while it is (still) included in the extension of the word in its ordinary use. Here and in like cases, even logical equivalence between the expression conveying the analysans of the *scientific concept* (e.g. *fish*) arrived at by empirical observation, and the expression conveying the analysandum of the *ordinary concept* (e.g. *fish*) does not obtain.

Connected with these is the fact that it is impossible to determine, on the basis of extra-linguistic empirical observation alone, whether a given proposition "A Y is a WX" itself arrived at by empirical observation, is a correct analysans of a proposition that we set out to analyse, "This is a Y"; or whether it is merely logically equivalent to it. In other words, it is impossible to determine, apart from semantic analysis, whether the statement "A Y is a WX" is a correct definition of the expression 'Y' (and therefore is analytically true); or whether it is a true universal synthetic statement about all Y's. The following example will illustrate a type of case where it is particularly easy to confuse the two, or to mistake the latter for the former. Empirical observation may perhaps reveal that all (observed) morally right acts are at the same time conducive to the production of the greatest good that is possible in the circumstances; and so the statement "All right actions are conducive to the production of the greatest good . . ." may express a true universal proposition.[2] But whether this is only a true universal synthetic statement or whether it is analytically true about actions ordinarily called right actions, can only be determined by semantic analysis of 'right action.' If now this reveals that 'right action' does not ordinarily mean "Conducive to the production of the greatest good. . .,"

[1] Thus "'water' means so-and-so" entails "'water' is ordinarily, customarily intended to mean so-and-so," or "'water' customarily purports to mean so-and-so." And what a word purports, or is intended to mean, is what the majority of its users purport to mean by it when it is first coined or otherwise comes into circulation. It is also what later users of the language – whether a majority or a minority of the users of that language – purport to mean by it as long as, or whenever, they employ it (as we say) in the same meaning or sense to which we are referring.

[2] I have borrowed this example from W. D. Ross, "The Meaning of 'Right,'" *op. cit.*, pp. 169–170.

though this statement is universally true, it may be thought desirable to (re) define 'right action' in terms of this empirically-discovered alleged common feature of all right actions. If this is done, what we will have is a partly different meaning of 'right action' and a correspondingly different concept of right action from the ordinary meaning and concept respectively. So what is only a true universal synthetic statement relative to the latter, now becomes analytically true relative to the modified meaning or modified concept. The essential point is that it will not be analytically true of the old meaning or the old concept, and cannot provide us with an analysis of this meaning or this concept.

B. EXTRA-LINGUISTIC ANALYSIS IN RELATION TO NON-REDUCTIVE CONCEPT-ANALYSIS

Extra-linguistic analysis is irrelevant – hence cannot be of any possible utility in relation – to the *analysis* of concepts, whether ordinary or scientific, that is non-reductive in character. Thus it does not arise in relation to exhibition analysis or Russell's form of "replacement analysis," insofar as these aim at the analysis of particular concepts (the former), or the "translation" of certain kinds of statements into other statements that are logically equivalent to them. This should be perfectly clear from what we have said about the nature of these forms of analysis in chapters six and seven respectively.

The ever-expanding body of empirical scientific knowledge is, nevertheless, relevant to *exhibition analysis*, the most valuable and generally applicable form of semantic analysis we have discussed, in another way or respect. I mean, in relation to the question of the possible *reconstruction* of ordinary concepts in the light of advancing scientific knowledge; whenever such reconstruction is useful or otherwise desirable. The precise way in which this is so, and the manner in which exhibition analysis and the appeal to empirical facts collaborate here, will be outlined at the end of this chapter; though we shall meet a number of illustrations of it before that. But there are still other ways in which the appeal to empirical facts (hence extra-linguistic analysis) can be useful in philosophical inquiry. There are (at least) two kinds of *questions*, one wholly empirical, the other partly semantic and partly empirical, which cannot be satisfactorily answered without it. In the latter kind of question, the reaching of a satisfactory answer requires the appeal to *both* semantic (exhibition) analysis and extra-linguistic empirical facts.

(I) The first kind of question I have in mind is empirical in a straightforward sense of this word; it is purely extra-linguistic or extra-semantic.[1] Because of their purely empirical character, scientists and many contemporary philosophers would regard them as *bona fide* scientific rather than philosophical questions. There are a number of important reasons, however, why I think they should be placed on our present list, and discussed in relation to philosophy in general and philosophical analysis in particular. These reasons are, first, that the discovery of correct answers to these questions is necessary for our reaching correct answers to certain questions which are unquestionably philosophical in nature. The second reason is that, so far, scientists themselves have not dealt with some or all of these questions; though science is perfectly equipped to reach correct answers to them. Since it is fundamentally the scientist's prerogative rather than the philosopher's to deal with them, it is my belief that the philosopher is only provisionally or tentatively entitled to try to provide answers to them – and then only in the light of the most reliable empirical data he can draw upon. In the case of some of these questions, there is a third reason why I believe the philosopher should try to fill the gap until scientists themselves provide us with reliable experimental answers to them. I mean the fact that, due to the continuing "openness" of the concept of philosophy (despite the attempts of logical positivism, Wittgenstein and the Oxford school to establish a sharp demarcation-line between philosophy and science), some of these questions are, or may be, neither clearly scientific nor yet clearly philosophical in character. They are questions which arise in, or in relation to, the still hazy, ill-defined – in some directions perhaps still undefined – borders between science and philosophy. These questions I shall label "marginal questions" relative to science and to philosophy.

Perhaps we can make our position clearer on this matter – though I think that what I have already said makes it quite clear – in this way. Granting the advantages which would accrue to both science and philosophy if the philosopher never attempted to do what the scientist

[1] This does not mean, and is not intended to mean, that knowledge of and about the meanings or other kinds of uses of words is irrelevant to the determination of the *truth* or *falsity* of any proposed answers to these questions. The point is, however, that unlike (purely) semantic questions, they cannot be given a true answer merely on the basis of our knowledge – including our analytical knowledge – of the particular language in which they happen to be expressed.

is far better equipped to do (and if the scientist, likewise did not attempt to do any part of the philosopher's job), it is an undeniable fact that at the moment I am writing, such a sharp and complete division of labor would actually leave philosophy (if not also science) definitely the poorer. There are certain important questions which simply must be answered; and if the scientist does not at present provide answers to them, the philosopher must draw the scientist's attention to them and urge him to try to answer them. At the same time, as a stop-gap, the philosopher can attempt to provide provisional answers to them; in the light of his direct personal experience where this is relevant, and, in any event, in the light of available scientific facts. The main point is that responsible attempts be made to provide correct answers to them: the question whether they are to be called scientific or philosophical questions is, for the present purpose, quite secondary. (The question of what constitutes a philosophical as opposed to a scientific question is, nevertheless, very important in its own right).

(2) The second class of questions is, by all accounts, a class of *bona fide* – and peculiarly – philosophical questions. Unlike questions falling under (1) above, they are what I shall label semantic (categorial) *cum* empirical questions. This label is only used for convenience, and should not be taken too literally. (Obviously, a question cannot be 'partly' one thing and partly another thing, in a literal sense of 'partly.') As I stated earlier, they are questions which can only be answered by the cooperative utilization of both empirical facts and semantic analysis.

What these questions precisely are like will be seen when we discuss them in some detail. Let me merely point out here that an important relation exists between the provision of correct answers to these questions, and the possible reconstruction of ordinary concepts in the light of empirical facts. I mean that the empirical facts which are adduced to help provide a correct answer to these questions may at the same time make it desirable to modify the concepts involved in them.

(1) I shall begin with a discussion of some questions which I consider to be genuinely philosophical in character, despite their wholly empirical character. These, as with all other examples I shall give in the rest of this chapter, are designed to clarify and illustrate the use of extra-linguistic analysis in philosophy.

(a) First of all, there is a cluster of philosophical questions that we mentioned in chapter six, in relation to the first major use of exhibition analysis. The philosopher's appeal to empirical facts in that connection arises with respect to his attempt to arrive at empirical *explanations* of various uniformities that exhibition analysis, for instance, reveals in particular ordinary languages. In order to reach such explanations, it is necessary to discover the exact relationship of the various ordinary languages to man – to human life – and to the world in which he lives and of which he is a part. For instance, as philosophers we are or may be interested in discovering why the names of artifacts and man-devised activities do, and why the names of many natural objects do not, involve the notions of function, use or purpose in their ordinary applications [1]; or why many ordinary concepts are "open textured." Some or all of the empirical facts about man and the world which are relevant here are supplied by the sciences; particularly the social sciences. But it is the philosopher and not any scientist who is most competent to select from the mass of possibly relevant scientific data those which are actually relevant to the questions under consideration, and to trace their bearing upon the latter. For both purposes, the careful conceptual analysis of the empirical data (extra-linguistic analysis) is necessary.

Theoretically speaking, nothing prevents a social scientist (e.g. a social anthropologist) from raising these specific questions and discovering the answers to them in the way we described; even though, as far a I know, this has not actually been done. But, at the present point in the development of the social sciences, the philosopher must direct the scientist's attention to these questions. For the latter, unless he is also a linguistic philosopher or has an adequate knowledge of the nature of ordinary language, will normally not be aware of these specific inter-disciplinary questions; or he may simply not be interested in them *qua* social scientist. The inter-disciplinary collaboration of philosophers and social scientists here is but one of the many instances in which philosophy and science can work together, to the enrichment of the one or the other or both. Examples can be multiplied by considering questions about other general features of ordinary language which exhibition analysis may reveal.

(b) The utilization of empirical data, again derived from experimental scientific work wherever possible, is also necessary in the philosopher's closely related attempt to gain a full understanding of *how* various philosophically–important expressions (or the concepts they convey) are actually employed in concrete contexts; and, in particular,

[1] This is particularly important with regard to art-names, hence in relation to aesthetics; since these names do involve in their ordinary applications the notion of purpose or aim. See my "Art-Names and Aesthetic Judgments," *Philosophy*, vol. XXXVI, No. 136 (January, 1961), pp. 30–48.

why they are used in the way they are. I have already mentioned one important class of such words, namely art-names, in connections with (a) above (in footnote 1). The same applies to key expressions (or concepts) that are important in other branches of philosophy, such as ethics, epistemology, metaphysics and political and social philosophy. Thus a full understanding of the nature and roles of ethical expressions, such as 'right' and 'wrong,' 'good' and 'bad,' requires an analysis of the actual-life situations in which these expressions are employed; including the analysis of the purposes and choices of moral agents, and the kinds of consequences that generally result from right and wrong moral actions. I therefore agree with P. H. Nowell-Smith when he says:

> Psychology is not as irrelevant to ethics as some philosophers insist; for ... we cannot understand what the terms used in moral judgments mean unless we examine them in the contexts of their use .... The various ways in which 'good' is used is unintelligible unless they are directly or indirectly connected with choice ....[1]

And again:

> They [the great philosophers] do not seem to have been mistaken in their basic assumption that the language of obligation is intelligible only in connection with the language of purpose and choice, that men choose to do what they do because they are what they are, and that moral theories which attempt to exclude all consideration of human nature as it is do not even begin to be moral theories.[2]

In the foregoing passages, it is clear, Nowell-Smith is (i) emphasizing, and rightly, the importance of a consideration of the *language* of purpose and choice; or as we might put it, the uses of the ordinary expressions which refer, or are otherwise relevant, to human purposes and choices, He is also, it appears, (ii) emphasizing the importance of the moral philosopher's utilization of the empirical findings of the *science* of psychology which he thinks are relevant to ethics.[3] That he means (ii) as well as (i); that he is calling for the sort of thing we have been recommending is not perfectly clear; though he says "*Psychology* is not ... irrelevant to Ethics," etc. which certainly gives the impression that he is thinking about scientific psychology and not (or not merely)

[1] *Ethics* ([N.P.], 1954), p. 182.

[2] *Ibid.*

[3] The findings of psychology, sociology and history concerning human motivation – e.g. whether men are completely and thoroughly egoistic, or whether there is such a thing as genuine altruism or benevolence – provide us with an obvious example of the utility of extra-linguistic facts relevant to age-old controversies in the history of ethics. Important consequences follow, among other things, regarding various theories of ethics – for psychological egoism on the one hand, and non-egoistic theories on the other hand – in the light of the relevant empirical findings of these sciences.

"philosophical psychology." [1] For whereas the subject-matter of the former is men's actual feelings, emotions, volitions, choices, purposes, etc. the subject-matter of the latter is the body of mental expressions that occur in *ordinary* language; such *ordinary* words as 'feel,' 'feeling,' 'emotion,' 'perceive,' 'perception,' 'conceive,' 'think,' 'imagine,' 'desire,' 'imagination,' 'thinking,' and so on.

The moral philosopher can also profitably consider whatever knowledge men have acquired through the centuries – both scientists and non-scientists, philosophers and non-philosophers – about man's psychological and moral nature, through their actual experiences as human beings. Thus the moral philosopher can benefit from a consideration, including the analysis, of *what* people say about their behavior and the behavior of others, as well as *how* they say these things: the language employed to convey these beliefs. In the same way, the philosopher of *science* – in this case the philosopher of psychology – is interested in the language of scientific psychology; apart from or in addition to the interest he may have in the *true* statements the psychologist makes, *qua* true statements about human behavior. But the former does not concern the moral philosopher himself.

To sum up, what I am affirming is that a consideration of the actual facts of human life or behavior, as described by psychology, sociology, history and the other human sciences, as well as an analytical knowledge of the nature or functioning of our ordinary moral and psychological language, is necessary for the elaboration of an adequate and complete moral philosophy. But further, in view of the rather undeveloped state of the social sciences; and until these sciences pass from the partly or wholly descriptive stage in which they now are to the law-making stage, it is useful for the moral philosopher provisionally to utilize this and other people's personal knowledge of human thinking, feeling and behavior. This knowledge, or presumed knowledge, may enable him to formulate tentative hypotheses which the relevant social science may subsequently verify. The same remarks apply equally, *mutatis mutandis*, to aesthetics.

But further, one of the things that cannot fail to strike the serious student of the history of ethics is the great lack of adequate studies of social ethics. The numerous cogitations and treatises on ethics written since the beginnings of philosophy, and those that continue to be written, are mostly devoted to "personal ethics": to the discovery of

[1] A good example of a treatise in philosophical psychology is Gilbert Ryle's *The Concept of Mind.*

the nature of right and wrong, good and bad conduct in the individual's relations to other individuals. A consideration of the nature of the moral relations (if any) between the individual and the State, and between him and various social organizations, has often been ignored in technical moral philosophy. It has been left to literary writers and to popular or semi-professional philosophers to supply the deficiency. Similarly the equally if not more important moral relations that obtain, or which ought to obtain, between whole countries or even groups of countries have been barely touched upon by moral philosophers.

However, even the individual's moral relations to other individuals, on which so much attention has been bestowed, are often discussed and analysed in a virtual social vacuum. Little or insufficient attention is paid to the varied and variable social, political, economic and other conditions obtaining in the particular country or society in which the moral standards studied, or the set of *prima facie* duties set out or advocated, are actually found. This in in good measure responsible for that air of artificiality, unreality or triviality which hangs about much of the ethical discussions of technical philosophers.

The point which I wish to make is that the remedying of this situation requires the close collaboration of moral philosophers with social scientists. The latter can and will supply the former with the relevant empirical data they will need in the above inquiries. In those cases where the data are not available because the social scientist has not hitherto had the opportunity or the interest to work in that area, the philosopher himself can provide him with the factual question he wants answered.

Our foregoing remarks about the desirability of cooperation or collaboration between science and philosophy for the latter's benefit [1] apply equally to aesthetics, social and political philosophy, and philosophical anthropology.[2]

[1] Although this does not concern us in the present work, it should be mentioned that the collaboration of philosophy and science can also be of considerable value to the latter in ways other than those usually involved in Philosophy of Science. For two quite different examples of this, the interested reader is referred to Charles Morris, "Philosophy, Psychiatry, Mental Illness and Health," *Philosophy and Phenomenological Research*, vol. XX, No. 1 (September, 1959), pp. 47–52; and H. Bondi, "Some Philosophical Problems in Cosmology," in *British Philosophy in the Mid-Century* (London, 1957), pp. 195–201.

[2] An exhaustive discussion of the role of philosophical analysis in respect to the possible relations of philosophy to psychology would outline the philosopher's possible analysis of the findings of that new branch of psychology known as para-psychology. For example, the philosopher can profitably analyse the experimental findings respecting extra-sensory perception and telekinesis; to mention only two major kinds of parapsychological phenomena. The possible implications of these (like the possible implications of cybernetics) for philosophy

(c) Let us now turn to epistemology and consider some important questions that arise in relation to perception, as our final major example in the present discussion.

One of the central questions facing a philosophical theory of perception has traditionally been the "ontological status" of preceived objects. I mean the question whether perceived objects exist independently of any – and in the case of man, of human – perception, and whether some or all of their sensible qualities continue to exist when unperceived. A cluster of other questions, both ontological and epistemological then arise, depending on the answer to the preceding question; in particular if it is held that perceived objects do *not* exist independently of human perception. For instance, it can be asked in the latter case whether perceived objects are cerebral processes or objects, hence are material; or whether they are psychic entities, existing "in" the perceiver's mind. It can also be (and has repeatedly been) asked whether there are any entities existing independently of human perception (a so-called independently existing External World).

Similarly, a host of questions arise regarding the differences in ontological status between "veridical" and "wild" data: the ontological difference between perceived tables, chairs and mountains on the one hand and, on the other hand, hallucinations and other perceptions occasioning "perceptual error."

The essential point for us here is that in the attempt to answer all these and like questions, the philosopher must discover the precise nature of perceived phenomena; how and under what conditions an act of perception takes place. And this presupposes or involves a careful

of mind are still largely unexplored, but may well be very fruitful. I have also said nothing about the philosophical analysis of the findings of psychoanalysis. That discipline, however, is now drawing the increasing attention of philosophers; though, as far as I know, the philosophical analysis undertaken to date has so far been chiefly methodological and logical in the strict or narrow sense of these terms. Little use has hitherto been made of the actual content of psychoanalytic discoveries for the purpose of answering or helping to answer philosophical questions proper.

In relation to aesthetics, the interested reader is referred to Thomas Munro, "The Psychology of Art: Past, Present, Future" (*Journal of Aesthetics*, Spring 1963, pp. 263–282) for a very timely discussion of many issues relevant to, or actually illustrative of, what we have been saying. For one thing, Munro lists and discusses a large number of fundamental empirical questions, all falling in principle within the Psychology of Art (i.e., within the science of Psychology) which have not yet been dealt with at all, or which have only been inadequately dealt with by psychologists. Adequate answers to these questions, Munro makes clear, are necessary for the elaboration of a systematic and scientific aesthetics. Cf. also R. Arnheim, "Agenda for the Psychology of Art," *Journal of Aesthetics*, vol. X, (June, 1952), pp. 310–314; and D. W. Gotshalk, "A Next Step For Aesthetics," *ibid.*, vol. XVIII (September, 1959), pp. 46–54.

consideration of the physics, physiology and psychology of perception, with all that these entail. Indeed, according to Dr. Russell Brain, "the philosopher who would do justice to perception to-day must have in addition to his philosophical training an advanced knowledge of neurophysiology, electronics, neurology, psychology and psychiatry, and preferably should himself have taken a hallucinogenic drug." [1]

Whether this is not going too far we need not here inquire. My view however is that *some* knowledge of scientific data connected with the phenomenon of perception is useful, and even perhaps necessary, for the arrival at a satisfactory answer to our aforementioned questions. At the same time, I do not think that any amount of scientific or ordinary empirical facts would, by themselves, provide us with the proper answers. For instance, I believe that empirical analysis and other methods of utilizing empirical data about perception have to work hand in hand with and must follow a thorough analysis of the ordinary language of perception. How great an appeal to empirical facts about perception and appeal to what particular empirical facts is necessary or useful, cannot be determined except through actual attempts to construct an adequate philosophical theory of perception.

This brings us to another point. Apart from what I have just said, and even if all what I have said is false, the necessity of appealing to, analysing and interpreting *some* actual perceptual data in relation to our questions would still remain. For at the very least we need to become acquainted, directly or indirectly, with the bewildering variety of perceptual objects, and with both their common and distinctive features. We must become acquainted, in other words, with the empirical facts – with so-called veridical data as much as with bent sticks, mirages, pink elephants and the dream-world of opium or mescaline – that we are setting out to explain, account for, understand. (And let me say here that logically speaking the discovery of the ontological status of "veridical" data is as imperative as the discovery of the ontological status of "wild" data). It will be recalled, for instance, that the relativity of perceived qualities and the empirical fact (or alleged fact) of apparent multiple inherence pose a major and formidable problem for the theory of perception. Numerous theories of perception have been advanced to account for these (and other) observed facts – and they still remain the rock on which theories of perception are shattered.

[1] Quoted from Everett W. Hall, "The Adequacy of a Neurological Theory of Perception," *Philosophy and Phenomenological Research*, vol. XX, No. 1 (September, 1959), p. 75.

The need for empirical analysis here is, I think, obvious. By means of such analysis we discover the general fact of relativity of perceived qualities; and with the fact that this relativity embraces some or all "primary" as well as "secondary" qualities. With its help we discover that such things as distance and perspective, intervening media and light, physical, physiological and psychological conditions play essential roles; and with its help we discover the particular roles which these (and other) empirical factors play.[1]

The existence of empirical facts of perception that require explanation will not be denied by those who would confine philosophy to the task of discovering, in Gilbert Ryle's phrase, "how certain words work" – to semantic analysis as a whole. What they will deny, however, is that these themselves could possibly give rise to *philosophical* questions; or that there can be any philosophical questions which these facts can possibly help answer; or, finally, that any attempts on the part of philosophers to "account for" these facts can be regarded as anything but mis-guided and futile amateurish dabbling in science. Thus Stephen Toulmin says –

When one says 'account for' the phenomenon [of the stick which looks bent when its end is dipped into water], this does not mean coming down on one side or the other in the vacuous dispute as to whether 'in ultimate reality' the stick is bent or not: it means that, given the angle of viewing of the stick and the refractive index of water, one can actually *construct*, in a diagram . . . the 'apparent position' of the stick, and so confirm that it is to be expected, light travelling as it does, that the stick will appear as it is in fact found to appear.[2]

In other words, the contention of thinkers such as Toulmin is or would be that accounting for the phenomena of perception that we have referred to a little earlier is the scientist's job; and that the way in which the scientist accounts for them is the only proper way of doing so.

A great deal can be said in reply to the foregoing view, and we shall ourselves say something about it later on. What concerns us at the moment is to recognize that there is at least one characteristically philo-

[1] *A propos* of the entire preceding section, cf. R. J. Hirst, *The Problems of Perception* (London, 1959), Chapter V, in which the author attempts to show, among other things, that the problems of perception have not been and cannot be adequately resolved by purely linguistic methods. Although I am in agreement with this thesis, my agreement should not be taken as implying that I necessarily agree with everything the author holds there. (Nor should this last statement be taken as implying that I do *not* agree with everything he says there!) Cf. also Richard H. Schlagel, "Language and Perception," *Philosophy and Phenomenological Research*, vol. XXIII, No. 2 (December, 1962), pp. 192–204.

[2] *The Philosophy of Science*, (London, 1958), Fourth Impression, p. 61. Italics in original.

sophical problem of perception which is not, and by the nature of science itself cannot be, answered solely and wholly by appeal to scientific laws and theories. I have no quarrel at all with Toulmin's – with the scientist's – way of accounting for bent sticks, elliptical coins, pink elephants, and so on. That is certainly one legitimate and important way of accounting for the facts of perception. But one central *philosophical* question of perception is whether bent sticks – indeed, any perceived objects – exist independently of percipient organisms, when unperceived; and if so, whether they continue to have all or some of the qualities they are perceived to have. If, on the other hand, they exist only when and as perceived by some percipient organism, the following philosophical questions, among others, arise: (i) whether the existence and character of perceived objects depend in part on the presence of an act of *consciousness*, or only (as far as the percipient organism is concerned) on the presence of intact and functioning sense organs, a nervous system and a brain; and (ii) whether there are some other objects or other kinds of entities that do exist independently of any percipient organism and which are, causally, partly responsible for the existence and character of perceived objects. That is, whether perceived objects are effects arising in, or in relation to, a percipient organism; resulting from the causal action of certain entities existing independently of him. These and other questions I mentioned earlier cannot be answered merely by appeal to scientific laws or theories; such as the laws of refraction in the case of the bent stick. I must add that the "vacuous dispute as to whether 'in ultimate reality' the stick is bent or not" is not one into which a philosopher would be drawn if he really understands the philosophical problems of perception. As phrased by Toulmin, the "issue" is just plain confused and a result of confusion. Its vacuousness – or its senselessness as it stands – does not in any way reflect on the meaningfulness of the questions I have given as philosophical questions about perception.

Now it may be true that no philosopher has yet succeeded in giving perfectly adequate answers to the philosophical questions I mentioned. As a matter of fact, though I am not here concerned to demonstrate it, I do think that that is indeed so. It may even be that no empirical facts we have or will ever have, and no amount of argument based on them, will ever enable us to discover the answers to some or all of these questions. That is, it may be that the only tenable stand to take in regard to them is a cautious agnosticism. But I do not see that this necessarily means, as it is taken to mean by many contemporary philosophers, that these are pseudo-questions [1] (whether or not they are also expressions of certain attitudes or feelings, or imply something about the psychological make-up of the philosophers who ask them).

It is possible that the belief in the objective existence of some perceived things can be verified by means of certain observations; for example, by going back and looking at an object that was unperceived by anyone for some time. It would not do, however, to identify a description of these or any similar observations with the statement that the objects under consideration continue to exist when unperceived. Finally, it is interesting to note that such an astute champion of the "division of labor" between philosophy and science in the manner of the later Wittgenstein and the Oxford School as Everett W. Hall (I think he would not regard me as misrepresenting his general philosophic outlook if I call him a member of the Oxford School itself) has recently proposed a "neurological theory" of perception.[2] The interesting point here is the fact that the neurological theory which the author proposes is, at least in part, an empirical theory of perception – a theory which includes certain empirical propositions – in the usual, straightforward meaning of 'empirical.' [3] It is significant that Hall found it necessary to do so, despite his general philosophical outlook.

Now I agree with Hall that the "philosophical problems here ... are ... not resolvable by observational procedure *alone* ..." [4] I would also add that they are partly categorial, and require for their solution or resolution the (exhibition) analysis of the ordinary language of perception. Thus I would regard the questions or the problems discussed above as illustrating *one* important way in which semantic (exhibition) analysis and the utilization (including the conceptual analysis) of empirical facts can fruitfully cooperate in philosophical inquiry. The

[1] To vindicate this we should need to go into the merits or demerits of the verifiability theory of meaning. This is not possible in the present work. I can only mention (though this would not blunt the edge of the dogmatism with which I am stating my contention) that the many criticisms levelled against this theory have shown it to be quite vulnerable, if not downright erroneous. For instance, it can be strongly argued that this theory involves an appreciable, perhaps even a drastic and unjustifiable, *change* in the most common ordinary meaning of 'meaning' (our first sense. See chapter three). Apart from all this, and even if the verifiability theory is sound, we cannot discover whether our questions have empirical answers, hence whether or not they are proper questions, except (among other things) by careful observation and analysis of the empirical facts of perception and of our scientific knowledge about them. In any case, therefore, extra-linguistic analysis is necessary.

[2] *Op. cit.*, pp. 75–84. The entire paper is revealing from the standpoint of our discussion as a whole.

[3] If I understand it correctly, the theory proposed is, in effect, a form of epistemological realism; which Hall attempts to vindicate, at least partly, on straightforward empirical grounds.

[4] *Ibid.*, pp. 75–76. Italics mine.

same is perhaps true, in part, of some or all of the other questions which we discussed earlier in this section (II); and which, I claimed, necessitated an appeal to empirical data in the philosopher's attempt to provide adequate and complete answers to them.

On the other hand, I do not accept Hall's view that the questions of perception – and the same applies to the other questions we discussed in this section – are therefore *wholly* "not empirical ... but logical, conceptual, systematic, or ... categorial." [1] If they were purely logical or conceptual, no extra-linguistic empirical facts at all would be relevant to their solution. This is seen more clearly as Hall himself decides, in his own words, "to put caution aside, that is, to leave the mild therapeutics of analysis and treat our case with a dangerous dosage of speculation...." [2] And this leads him to an "interrogation of our own experience," and to analyses of the observable features of these experiences.[3] At the same time, I do not call these questions categorial *cum* empirical questions because I have reserved that label to questions of type III which, as we shall presently see, are different from though related to the present type of question. These latter questions, and perhaps also those discussed under (IIa) above, *are* "categorial" questions; though I have contended that they are not merely so, in the first and possibly also the second of the following two senses:

(i) They necessitate for their solution the (prior) exhibition analysis of the ordinary language of perception, the language of ethics, aesthetics, etc., as the case may be: or, if you like, the categorial scheme or structure of ordinary language or of the particular part of it in question; and

(ii) They may necessitate, and I think that at least the foregoing questions about perception do necessitate, the making of *decisions* concerning the *schematization* of some or all of the fundamental concepts involved. This includes the making of decisions as to whether it is desirable to *modify* or *reconstruct* the relevant ordinary concepts, in the light of the empirical facts considered. For example, in the case of perception, it would include the making of a decision as to whether it is desirable, in the light of the relevant physical, physiological and psychological facts considered, to broaden, restrict or completely change – even to abandon – (say) our ordinary concept of a physical or material object. Thus, for instance, if empirical facts show that sensible

[1] *Ibid.*

[2] *Ibid.*, p. 77.

[3] For instance on pp. 81 and 83.

objects do not, as we perceive them, exist independently of the percipient's psychological make-up by showing that the content of what is perceived varies with various changes in it, [1] it *may* become desirable for the philosopher to stop using the words 'matter' and 'material' in relation to perceived objects, and to adopt some other term or terms instead. In any event, the acceptance of Epistemological Dualism of this kind, or of subjective Idealism, may entail the broadening of the ordinary concept of 'mental'; since in ordinary language all non-hallucinatory objects sensibly perceived in our waking hours are referred to as non-mental (they are called physical or material) things.[2]

The foregoing brief discussion of the possible impact of scientific discoveries on ordinary language in the way just described leads us immediately to the second type of philosophical question listed earlier – to what I have labelled categorial *cum* empirical questions. It also leads to the final section of this chapter, III; to a more detailed and general logical discussion of the deliberate reconstruction of ordinary concepts by philosophers, in the light of new scientific discoveries.

(II) It is not difficult to find a considerable number of questions of the type I have called categorial *cum* empirical questions, in contemporary philosophy. A few concrete examples, discussed in some detail, should however suffice for our present purposes. The main features of such questions are (1) That in order to arrive at a proper answer to them it is necessary, first, to indulge in semantic (exhibition) analysis of the uses of the relevant verbal expression(s), or of the contents of the relevant concept(s). What distinguishes them from purely semantic questions (such as those discussed in chapter six) however, is that this semantic analysis, though necessary, is not sufficient to provide correct answers to them. For that – and this constitutes the logically second step or stage in their consideration – we must (2) consider certain empirical facts that are relevant to them. The "answer" to these questions would then consist in making a decision, in the light of both (1) and (2), whether or not to modify the ordinary use or uses of (or the concept or concepts conveyed by) the expression(s) in question. Thus (3) these questions are not really questions in the usual sense of this expression: questions that call for an answer in the form of a statement or a set of statements that are (believed to be) true. This distinguishes them from the type of questions we discussed in section (I), as well as from the purely semantic questions which analytical philosophers raise

[1] Assuming that empirical facts can, in principle, show this (or the opposite) to be the case.
[2] But see Richard H. Schlagel, *op. cit.*

regarding the meaning, or the correct analysis, of particular expressions or classes of expressions. They are, by the same token, also different from the factual questions which scientists ask and attempt to answer; and from the factual questions which we constantly ask in daily life.

There are two general forms of the present kind of question: Some questions concern the "marginal" or "borderline" cases of the application of a given ordinary expression 'X'; while others concern objects which are definitely *excluded* from the class of things ordinarily called by a given name 'Y.'

It is clear that both forms of "decision-questions" may arise in relation to one and the same expression (here 'X' or 'Y'). (a) It is evident that questions of the first form arise only in relation to expressions whose ordinary applications involve "marginal" cases; or, in terms of concepts, where the concepts in question are open-textured. Since many, perhaps most, ordinary concepts are open-textured, the present form of question can theoretically arise in relation to a vast number of ordinary concepts. The philosophically-significant concepts of this kind are much less numerous, however.

One cluster of philosophically-significant questions of this sort arises in Ethics; another, in Aesthetics. For instance, the questions: "Is killing an animal morally wrong or bad (or is it morally indifferent)?" "Is it wrong or bad to torture such animals as dogs, cats, horses, elephants?" "Is euthanasia wrong?" "Is killing the lover of one's unfaithful wife (or husband) wrong?" "Is refusing to kill an enemy in wartime because of moral or religious scruples wrong?" "Is it morally right to cooperate with the enemies of one's people or country in order to save one's life – or even to save the lives of others?" Or are some or all of these actions neither right nor wrong? Again: "Is animal 'painting' art?" "Is child 'painting' art?" "Is 'indeterminate music' really music?" "Is *art trouvé* art?"

Other interesting or even important questions that arise in relation to other branches of philosophy are: "Are viruses living things, or are they non-living things?" "Do electronic 'brains' (e.g. IBM computers) think?" ("Can they remember; learn; reason; invent; etc.?")

It will be noticed that many, perhaps all of these and like questions, have the appearance of being questions in the usual sense of 'question'; they appear to be of the same sort as: "What is the temperature at the centre of the earth?" or like "What are the major ordinary uses of 'reasonable'?" They have the appearance of being questions that call for a factual – semantic or empirical – answer; and this is, indeed, the way in which they have been usually regarded. In reality, they are "questions" which demand a decision as to whether or not to modify the concepts of good, bad, right, wrong, art, music, painting, life, etc. as the case may be; whether definitely to include in, or definitely to exclude (some or all) animals, euthanasia, persons who kill their unfaithful spouses or their (the latter's) lovers, "animal painting," "child painting," "indeterminate music," "viruses," etc., as the case may be, from the class determined by the relevant concept. (Or, alternatively, to let these things remain borderline cases; neither definitely included in nor definitely excluded from the particular class).

In order that a proper decision may be reached regarding each of these questions,[1] the ordinary concept(s) in question must be carefully analysed with the help of the method of exhibition analysis. One must next consider and analyse the observable features of the borderline objects, occurrence or states of affairs – viruses, electronic computers, child paintings, acts of euthanasia (including their actual or probable consequences) etc. – in order to discover what precise *similarities*, and what precise *differences* obtain between these borderline cases and the features of things which exhibition analysis shows are definitely included in the class determined by the particular concept. Now many ordinary concepts are delimited in terms of criss-crossing "family resemblances" rather than common determinate or relatively-determinate qualities or properties which are severally necessary and are jointly sufficient conditions for a thing's being subsumed under that concept.[1] One must therefore match the similarities and the dissimilarities in question with the whole "range" of things subsumed under the particular concept, '*C*,' beginning with the paradigm, most unquestioned and unquestionable or most typical instances at the "center" of the class of "C's," down to the most atypical or least representative instances, "near" – but nonetheless still "inside" – the "border." The correct decision would then depend on how great

[1] Similar questions can and, I think, do sometimes arise in science itself, in relation to various open-textured scientific concepts. But this does not concern us here.

[2] There is a close logical connection between the open texture of (some) ordinary concepts and the fact that some concepts are ordinarily delimited in terms of criss-crossing "family resemblances." But this does not concern us here. Let me merely state – what is germane to our discussion – that although I am here employing the notion of open-texture as elaborated by F. Waismann, or of "marginal cases" as discussed by Max Black, I am far from happy with these formulations of this notion. For one thing, and apart from important differences between the two formulations, both involve a pictorial, figurative way of speaking about concepts (which I myself have exploited in the above discussion) that is misleading if taken literally. However, it is not possible for us here to elaborate a more adequate reformulation of this concept, and we must be satisfied with the present proviso.

and, especially, how important are the similarities, and how great and important are the dissimilarities between the particular borderline (kind of) objects and the paradigm or even other, less representative instances of that class. Thus in order properly to decide whether or not to "sharpen" the present ordinary concept of life at its "periphery" by deciding definitely to include viruses in the class of living things, the philosopher must utilize the available virological and other observed facts about the properties of viruses. He must note such things as the fact that known viruses are composed of protein molecules (which in the rest of nature have only been found to-date in living things) and multiply in living tissue (similarities). On the other hand, he must consider the fact that viruses do not – or do not appear to – multiply outside living tissue and do not behave very differently in other ways from (other) organic compounds which scientists would unhesitatingly regard as inanimate. Similarly with our other examples.

It is worth noting here that "borderline cases" of the uses of an ordinary expression (whenever they do obtain) arise for one or both of two kinds of reasons: (i) Disagreement among the users of the expression concerning its meaning or its analysis; and/or (ii) disagreement on – or ignorance of – certain empirical facts about the objects, the "borderline cases" themselves. This is why both semantic analysis and an appeal to the relevant empirical facts is necessary to resolve the disagreement; or at least to enable one to arrive at a judicious decision regarding the matter. A good example illustrating the former, (i), and even the latter, (ii), (depending on the outcome of the semantic analysis) is euthanasia. The disagreement among people regarding the moral rightness or wrongness of euthanasia cannot be rationally resolved as long as agreement is not reached regarding the precise moral use or uses of 'right' and 'good,' and their opposites; or the precise analysis of the ordinary concepts of right and good, and their opposites. More precisely, the disagreement hinges on the question whether or not the rightness or wrongness, and the goodness or badness of moral actions is totally independent of the nature (the goodness or badness) of their actual or probable consequences; and/or the nature (the goodness or badness) of the motives behind them. If careful analysis reveals the correctness of a strictly deontological conception of *right* and *wrong*, the matter is settled: euthanasia would be morally wrong. If, on the other hand, analysis reveals that the *goodness* or *badness* of an action is determined by the goodness or badness of the motive underlying the action, euthanasia would be morally good.

In contrast to this, the question is not wholly settled on semantic grounds alone if analysis reveals the correctness of a teleological rather than a deontological account of rightness and wrongness. Whether or not acts of euthanasia are ever right now comes to depend on the goodness or badness of their (actual or probable) consequences. This is, partly, an empirical matter and requires the analysis of the observable consequences of many acts of euthanasia. But it is not a wholly empirical matter. For even when agreement is reached about the actual or probable consequences of acts of euthanasia, disagreement may still arise concerning the goodness or badness of these consequences themselves. This disagreement is, once again, partly or wholly semantic; it can only be resolved by an analysis of our ordinary uses of 'good' and 'bad' as they apply to states of affairs, including experiences.

(b) So far we have discussed some questions that involve the making of decisions about borderline cases. There are other questions, again involving the making of decisions, in the light both of semantic and empirical considerations, but concerning non-borderline objects. I am referring to objects that, given the ordinary uses of a particular expression 'X' at a time T under consideration, are definitely excluded from the class of "X's," but which some people (e.g. some philosophers, artists, critics, or scientists) wish to include in that class. The reason for this desire is, in every case, the belief that the objects in question bear marked and important similarities to things normally called "X's"; and their wish to see this recognized in the names or other expressions by which we refer to them. There are many examples of this state of affairs, and new ones keep coming up practically every day with new scientific discoveries and inventions. A simple example is provided by the question whether or not the ordinary concept of motive, which I think essentially includes the notion of deliberateness and hence consciousness, should be broadened to include certain unconscious (sub-conscious) urges, impulses, or other forces postulated by modern depth (e.g. Freudian) psychology. The fact, or what I think is the fact, that "X is a motive" ordinarily entails "X is deliberate and, hence, conscious" shows that "unconscious (sub-conscious) motives" do not and cannot constitute *borderline* cases of the present ordinary applications of 'motive.' For these urges, impulses etc. to be included in the (present) ordinary concept of motive, a much more drastic or fundamental modification of this concept is necessary than is involved in the subsumption of mere borderline cases under the relevant concept. This is clearly seen if we compare the question of the possible inclusion of "subconscious motives" in the ordinary class of motives, to the question of the possible inclusion of "children's paintings" or even "animal paintings" in the class of art. In both types of cases there is (in the latter cases, there *may* be) an absence of deliberateness. The child or the monkey that indulges in "painting" may be merely giving expression to a strong playful urge; normally (in the case of the monkey, in every case) it will not be aiming at creating what we call a work of art. Similarly there will (always) be an absence of deliberateness, due to the absence of consciousness, when a kleptomaniac, say, is "motivated" to steal something; or when a person, suffering from a phobia for dogs, runs away at the sight of a dog. Or if the impulses involved in the latter are not counted as the kind of subconscious impulsions to which the name 'subconscious motive' is to be attached, we can think of more "normal" actions or activities which the psychoanalyst would regard as impelled by subconscious urges. The important point is that deliberateness is *not* an essential part of the present ordinary concept of art. After all, Coleridge's "Kubla Khan" and Tartini's "Devil's Trill," to give only two examples, were composed quite undeliberately, independently of their authors' conscious mind or will; and yet they were unquestionably regarded as works of art by the artists' contemporaries. However, most works that people in the West have traditionally regarded as art; in particular, most if not all of those traditionally regarded as great art, *have* actually involved some – often, a great deal of – conscious, deliberate effort or work in their creation. Thus some or all of the *paradigm* cases of art in the West (which, for many people still, consist of pre-20th century works) do involve – or have, so far, involved – this element in their production. Thus while deliberateness or conscious effort is not an essential part even of the traditional ordinary concept of art, the fact just mentioned has been one important cause of the (borderline) dispute concerning the aesthetic quality of "children's paintings" and "animal paintings." (Other reasons for the dispute are the child – or animal – "painter's" lack of technical training; and/or the "painter's" lack of (human) experience, emotional maturity, etc. This is most clearly the case with "animal painting.")

The example I gave earlier about viruses provides us with an instance of a *borderline* case of an intermediate kind. It involves a definitely greater or more fundamental modification – literally a reconstruction – of an existing concept than in the above illustrations drawn from the field of art. But it nonetheless involves, I think, a somewhat lesser modification relative to the ordinary concept of life, than our example concerning "subconscious motives," relative to the ordinary concept of motive. In any case, and even if this last statement is false, the statement before it is I think definitely true. But enough has been said about these examples for our present purposes, I think, and I shall say no more about them.

Now although clear-cut cases of the two sorts we have discussed in the present section, (a) and (b), are perhaps not lacking, many instances can be recalled of a more uncertain character. That is, in some cases we are unsure as to whether a particular example really falls under (a), or whether it falls under (b). The reader may himself feel that some of the examples we cited under (a) really come under (b); though I do not think that anyone would regard the example we gave about the schematization of the ordinary concept of motive as possibly illustrative of (a). I shall now consider, as our second and last example under (b) a situation which I think is of the same type as the foregoing; and which I think would be so regarded by those who consider the matter carefully.

As is well-known, a controversy is raging at the time I am writing as to whether electronic computers can be said to think – to store information, to recall the information fed into them (hence, to have a "memory"); to learn from their past "experience," including their past errors; and so on – in a non-Pickwickian use of 'think.' The question may be raised, of course, on two different levels; the ordinary and the scientific. It may be asked whether computers think in the *ordinary* meaning of 'think'; or whether they think in the psychologist's meaning of this word (assuming that this latter is in any way different from its ordinary meaning). Our present concern is with the former question. The peculiarity of this kind of question in relation to computers lies in the fact that, due to their very recent invention, these complex machines have not had time, so to speak, to become borderline cases of "brains." Thus I do not think that, at the time I am writing, the question "Do electronic computers think"? can be regarded as a question about a borderline class of objects; though by and by it may well become so. Of course, some people already call these computers "electronic brains"; and therefore they have already made a decision – though they may be quite unaware that this is what they have done – to include them in the class of "thinking things," *viz.* brains (mostly, I think, in the psychologist's or some other scientific sense of 'thinking'). The fact that these people recognize that computers cannot, in their present stage of development, perform certain (the so-called "higher") mental operations such as "reasoning" and "imagining," means that they consider them as thinking things only with very important and extensive qualifications. It might be thought, therefore, that for these people, electronic computers are borderline cases of thinking things. But this is not so. The qualifications which they would make regarding the "thinking capacities" of these machines is based on the awareness that they only possess *some*, perhaps as yet only a few of the properties or capacities of things which constitute paradigm cases of thought-activity – i.e., human brains (or should we rather say "minds"?). On the other hand, those who disagree with them consider computers as fundamentally different from human brains and human minds and therefore definitely, and "far" outside the class of thinking things. For instance, they would regard them as even more definitely non-thinking things than the brains of cats or dogs or even, perhaps, mice or frogs or fleas; some or all of which themselves are perhaps borderline cases of organs of thought on the *ordinary* use(s) of 'thought.' They would probably be regarded as little capable of thought proper as an amoeba or a paramecium, if not even less so!

All this notwithstanding, the chances are that electronic computers will come to be regarded as borderline cases of "brains," if and when they are so improved as to be able to perform further "mental" activities; particularly "imagination" and "reasoning." Eventually, they may even come to be regarded as one sub-class of thinking things in the scientific, if not also the ordinary use(s) of 'thinking' and 'thought.' So far they appear to have demonstrated a limited capacity for "learning."[1] Now suppose we imagine the members of a class delimited by some ordinary concept as occupying different "distances" from the "center," which is occupied by the paradigm cases. Electronic computers would then, at the moment I am writing, occupy a position *near* the border, on the inside, for those who would, or actually do, include them in the class of "thinking things." As their "mental capacities" improve, they would

[1] The interested reader is referred to R. M. Friedberg *et al.*, "A Learning Machine," Parts I and II, in *IBM Journal of Research and Development* vol. 2, No. 1 (January, 1958), and vol. 3 No. 3 (July, 1959), respectively. Information provided by cybernetics about the workings of electronic computers is also important in relation to our discussion under (I) above. Detailed knowledge in this area is likely to suggest some fruitful hypotheses about the workings of the *human* mind. These hypotheses may help psychologists to discover hitherto – unknown facts about human thinking, as well as provide possible accounts of the nature of mental operations and explanations of already-known psychological facts. This may have an indirect value for the philosophy of mind; first insofar as the new facts may make it desirable to reconstruct ordinary mental concepts; and second, in providing these reconstructed concepts with actual empirical content: with actual instances of objects, processes or activities that logically fall under them.

move closer to the center. But their bare introduction into the class of thinking things would mean *some* modification of our ordinary concept of thinking; and a greater modification of it would be required for them to move further toward the center.

The examples I gave under (I) and (II) above illustrate the philosopher's actual or possible appeal to empirical facts, in connection with inquiries all involving philosophical analysis. The philosopher's appeal to these facts may be direct or indirect. That is, the philosopher may himself observe, conceptually analyse and interpret various phenomena which are normally accessible to him as a human being and as a man equipped with the logical and methodological tools of philosophical inquiry. He will then apply the results to the philosophical questions he has set out to answer, or the concepts he is concerned with. Or he may – which would be much more adequate and fruitful – draw upon the available fund of scientific knowledge in the form of presumed true empirical propositions, and analyse, interpret, relate and apply these to the questions or concepts in hand. Since the data utilized are, or can be, expressed in the form of true propositions, we can say that the philosopher, in his present capacity, studies and analyses the factual content of what is asserted by presumably true empirical propositions. And it is because what is analysed is the factual content of empirical propositions and its bearing on the particular philosophical question with which the philosopher is concerned, not the meaning of the words, or the concepts which convey this content, that the method of analysis involved is an extra-linguistic rather than a semantic method of analysis. As a matter of fact, *any* empirical proposition can be analysed semantically or extra-linguistically in the present manner depending on whether the analysandum strictly speaking is the semantic aspect of the proposition or its empirical content. Following a distinction made by Paul W. Taylor in a recent article,[1] I shall distinguish these two "modes" in which philosophical analysis may be carried out as the *utterance mode* and the *content* mode respectively.[2] We have in effect met this distinction on a number of occasions, as when we distinguished the beliefs (and the truth-value of the beliefs) that people hold, and the correctness or incorrectness of the sentences

[1] "Moral Rhetoric, Moral Philosophy and the Science of Morals," *The Journal of Philosophy*, vol. LVI, No. 17 (August 13, 1959), pp. 689–707.

[2] Taylor makes this distinction in relation to ethical theory (he also distinguishes a third "mode" which he calls the *functional mode*). But it is applicable to all branches of philosophy, to philosophy as a whole.

in which these beliefs are expressed. We also met it in our insistence on the difference between appealing to the ordinary meanings or other kinds of uses of expressions, including sentences, and appealing to the (alleged) truth of "common sense beliefs": or any beliefs for that matter whether "commonsensical" or not. The distinction was also involved in some of our criticisms of Russell's objections to the philosopher's appeal to ordinary language. Russell's objections referred to rest on a confusion between the "utterance mode" and the "content mode" in which philosophical inquiry may be carried out. The distinction between the two "modes" is of the utmost importance; since our distinction between semantic and extra-linguistic types of philosophical analysis, where it does arise (i.e., in relation to *synthetic propositions*),[1] logically rests upon it.

Awareness of this distinction is of particular importance in Ethics (in value theory as a whole) because, as Taylor points out, it is quite easy to forget or to overlook the distinction there; particularly as, I might add, the "utterance" aspect and the "content" aspect of moral judgments are so closely related – more closely related than in factual (or in purely factual) propositions. The questions stated by Taylor to illustrate the distinction show the difference between, but also the closeness of, these two aspects and the two "modes" of inquiry they involve. Thus to use Taylor's examples, we may ask such questions as the following concerning a person's moral utterances:

> What moral prescriptions and evaluations does the person pronounce in what sorts of circumstances? For what purposes and in what ways is moral discourse carried on by the person? How does the person use moral or non-moral expressions when giving an argument in support of a moral prescription or evaluation? These questions demand descriptions and explanations of a person's use of language ....[2]

The following questions, on the other hand, are questions in the content mode: "What are a person's moral beliefs? What standards does a person appeal to in morally evaluating actions or character? What rules of inference does a person use in his moral reasoning? What views of man's nature and the nature of the world underlie a person's moral beliefs and moral reasoning?" [3] I shall not dwell on the logical relation between our two "modes" of inquiry. Let me merely mention a few rather obvious aspects of it before we proceed. Thus it is clear that, in

[1] I am here including value judgments. If these do not express propositions, we have to add "and value judgments" to the phrase "synthetic propositions."

[2] *Ibid.*, pp. 689–690.

[3] *Ibid.*, p. 690.

respect to any area of philosophical inquiry, we can frequently discover what somebody believes by observing what he says; and that we have to know the meaning of the sentences (hence of the words) he utters in order to know what he is saying, hence what he believes. On the other hand, the meaning of an expression can be discovered by one's observing how it is actually employed: usually, as expressing some empirical content. In other words, one way in which we can discover the nature of the "utterance aspect" of statements is by observing the latter in action, as conveying some content (e.g. some belief).

The essential point is that analysis of empirical propositions, if and when it is analysis of their "content aspect," does not cease to be extra-linguistic analysis because it can be looked upon as one kind of analysis of propositions. It may be true that a given ordinary ethical language-game, say, has been and continues to be shaped by the beliefs and attitudes of the community employing that language-game. It may also be true that a given ordinary ethical language, once it comes to exist in some form or other, tends to perpetuate the beliefs and attitudes it has enshrined. (As a matter of fact I do think that both statements are true.) The same relation may perhaps be found to obtain in the case of any ordinary language taken as a whole. But it would not in any way obliterate the logical distinction between the "utterance aspect" and the "content aspect" of empirical propositions; or, correspondingly, the distinction between the utterance mode and the content mode in which philosophical analysis – philosophical inquiry as a whole – can be conducted.

(III) It will be remembered that in chapter seven we raised the question of the legitimacy and desirability of the philosopher's redefinition of ordinary concepts on purely logical grounds. The question of whether such redefinition by the philosopher is or may be permissible and desirable on empirical grounds, in the light of empirical facts, was not there dealt with. A discussion of the redefinition of ordinary concepts in philosophy (hence a discussion of so-called "replacement analysis") would not be complete, however, without the latter. We are also led naturally to this question by our discussion of philosophical extra-linguistic analysis in the present chapter. For the philosophical analysis of empirical data and the application of its results to certain philosophical concepts, questions or problems, leads us to the question as to whether the existence of these things or other empirical data may not sometimes make it useful or otherwise desirable to reconstruct ordinary concepts used by philosophers. It is clear at the outset, however, that the reconstruction of a concept purely in the light of empirical facts (if observed facts alone ever make it desirable to reconstruct an ordinary concept) cannot help to answer [1] any questions that are about, or in some way involve, that concept. Similarly with concepts that are reconstructed partly in the light of logical and partly in the light of empirical facts. For by definition, the questions would be about, or would involve, the-as-yet unreconstructed concept: modifying it would leave the original questions unanswered. If a concept is reconstructed partly or wholly on empirical grounds, the original question suffers a corresponding change; it will now become a different question. Where it is reconstructed wholly in the light of empirical facts, the question will not, moreover, become a logically better, more adequate question than it was. Whatever logical flaws the original question may have (if any) will be carried over into the new question; or if the latter is logically proper, so will the former be.

It follows from all this that the philosopher's reconstruction of ordinary concepts (partly or wholly) on factual grounds has to be discussed independently of his possible use of empirical facts to help answer or resolve philosophical questions or problems. It also follows that we cannot properly argue for or against the reconstruction of any ordinary concept on factual grounds by merely considering the possible impact of the reconstruction on questions or problems involving this concept.

Now it is almost a platitude that contemporary scientists constantly employ ordinary expressions in new ways – such expressions as 'space,' 'time,' 'probable,' 'motive,' 'wave,' 'ray,' 'acid,' 'salt,' 'fish' and a thousand other expressions – thereby effecting a reconstruction in the concepts conveyed by these expressions.[2] It is likewise almost a platitude that ordinary expressions undergo all sorts of changes over the years and centuries, partly as a result of the impact of current scientific usage, and partly as a result of the prevailing social, political, economic, moral and other ideas and practices. It is also noteworthy that the philosophical ideas and practice, and the general philosophical "climate of opinion" in different ages or places, have been and will

[1] In contrast to redefinition on purely logical grounds. For instance, the elimination of internal inconsistency or vagueness through redefinition helps us to reach satisfactory answers to questions about, or otherwise involving, an internally inconsistent or vague concept. For only by such a redefinition would we get a logically proper (re-) formulation of our question or problem – i.e., a question or problem that can be answered or resolved. This is one major positive use of redefinition of concepts on logical grounds, that would be absent in the case of any redefinition of concepts wholly or even partly on factual grounds

[2] Whether or not we can go as far as to hold with some philosophers of science that most if not all expressions that occur in science proper – as distinguished from what they call "natural history" – involve a "shift of meaning."

probably continue to be one important cause of the modification of the ordinary uses of expressions, including the concepts they may convey.

As far as I know, no philosopher or scientist has found anything wrong with all this. A philosopher or a scientist might be unhappy about the modification of the uses of particular expressions. But as far as I know no scientist or philosopher has objected *in principle* to the redefinition of expressions in the foregoing manner. An issue arises (one indeed, that has already generated considerable heat among philosophers) only as regards the *philosopher's* modification of the uses of ordinary expressions; in regard to the effecting of redefinitions for *philosophical purposes*. And, as far as our present discussion is concerned, the issue is restricted to the question whether the redefinition is permissible partly or wholly on the basis of new *empirical* discoveries or facts.

All this is still vague. There are, actually, at least two major types of cases that should be distinguished here: (1) the type of case where the philosopher appropriates a conceptual modification already effected by science in the light of empirical facts; and (2) the type of case where the philosopher himself introduces a conceptual modification into philosophy not (or not yet) effected in science, in the light of (a) scientific discoveries and/or (b) the philosopher's own empirical observations – for example, in connection with his employment of extra-linguistic analysis.

(1) Theoretically speaking, or speaking purely abstractly, I see no harm at all in the philosopher's appropriation of a reconstructed scientific concept for philosophical purposes; provided that the philosopher doing so is aware of what he is doing, and conveys to his hearers or readers the exact content of the concept as employed by him. Thus (to take two famous examples) I see no objection at all to a philosopher's using the word 'motive' in the sense in which it is used in psychoanalysis, or 'time' in the way in which it is used in Relativity Physics – so long as misunderstanding or confusion is sufficiently guarded against. As to whether it is useful, hence desirable, to appropriate a given reconstructed concept, that clearly depends on the particular concept, and on the philosophical uses to which it is to be put. Individual concepts must therefore be examined on their own merits, and cannot be properly accepted or dismissed on the basis of a set of abstract, general rules. Thus it may be useful – whether or not it is so requires a rather lengthy discussion into which we cannot enter – for philosophers to employ 'motive' in the psychoanalytic sense, in order to "bring in

the new significations of psychoanalysis and behavioral psychology." [1] Similarly it may be useful to employ in philosophy such *present-day* scientific concepts as those of atoms, waves, force, mass, instinct, evolution, etc., in one way or another. But it will *not* be useful to employ older (say 18th or 19th century) forms of these concepts – except, say, if one regards the latter as more adequate than the present-day concepts and wishes to incorporate them into his philosophy (e.g. in his metaphysics, if he has one).

(2) Passing to our second type of reconstruction, we may note that the majority, if not all of the significant modifications of ordinary (or even of present-day scientific) concepts will inevitably be effected in the light of scientific discoveries rather than of the personal empirical observations and analysis of philosophers. For as we have stated before, the philosopher's actual observations and analyses are, in general, quite limited in scope; and only the more obvious and rather superficial features of existing things can be revealed by them. The fundamental structure and the really important features of existing things can only be discovered through the use of the rigorous, experimental methods of modern science. At the same time an examination of our ordinary, everyday concepts themselves reveals, if I am not grossly mistaken, that some but by no means all of these concepts are framed in terms of rather superficial and obvious features and/or relations of things. (Consider for instance the ordinary concepts of water, salt, acid, alkali, fish, plant, animal, and so on almost indefinitely; then contrast them with the corresponding present-day scientific concepts.) Some of the concepts of which this is not true are those which, originally occurring only in science, gradually become incorporated into ordinary discourse; replacing the original ordinary concepts or peacefully co-existing with them. An example of the latter is afforded by the word 'unconscious,' which continues to be used in its old ordinary sense as well as, in the appropriate contexts, in the somewhat different sense of modern psychoanalysis. The word '*sub*conscious,' on the other hand, illustrates the introduction of a new scientific concept into ordinary language.

It must be confessed that, generally speaking, it is unlikely that philosophers will effect any changes in any ordinary concepts in the light of new scientific facts, *before* scientists themselves effect these same changes. One simple reason is that scientists discovering these facts will frame the appropriate concepts in terms of which the new

[1] Paul W. Kurtz, "Has Mr. Flew Abandoned 'The Logic of Ordinary Use?'" *Philosophical Studies*, vol. IX, Nos. 5–6 (October-December, 1958), p. 76.

discoveries can be expressed – thus effecting the necessary modifications – in the course of, if not actually *before* making the discoveries (though modifying these concepts as they go along, whenever necessary, in the light of theoretical and empirical considerations). But a philosopher may conceivably effect a different modification – e.g. a different extension or restriction – in a given ordinary concept than the one effected by the scientists; even, though not necessarily, in the light of the same scientific discoveries that give rise to the scientist's reconstruction of the concept he starts with. I do not definitely know whether this has ever actually happened. It is possible that the concepts of space and time (space-time) in Whitehead's philosophy come nearest to being actual instances of it. For Whitehead's conception differs from Einstein's conception of space and time (space-time) which dominates modern physics. It is also, partly at least, based on the physical facts that gave rise to Einstein's conception.

It may be felt that value concepts constitute an exception to what we said at the beginning of the preceding paragraph about the philosopher's reconstruction of ordinary concepts *vis-à-vis* the scientist. For instance, it may be felt that our quite extensive present-day scientific knowledge of man necessitates the reconstruction of our conventional moral concepts; that a genuinely "humanistic" morality, fashioned upon man's actual nature as we now know it, is eminently desirable. These or like reconstructions cannot be properly effected by the scientist *qua* scientist; at least so long as Ethics remains a branch of philosophy. They are, it may be felt, the proper concern of the philosopher himself. This view, despite its seeming plausibility, ignores, first, the important fact that according to one powerful tradition in present-day philosophy (which I happen to share as far as the present consideration is concerned; see chapter seven), the effecting of reconstructions in value concepts is not the philosopher's job either. Unless we return to the older, broader conception of philosophy we find in such philosophers as Socrates and Plato (which does not limit philosophy to knowledge or understanding), a philosopher can effect such reconstructions solely as a social or moral reformer, or the like, not as a philosopher. The view in hand ignores, second, the fact that the legitimacy and desirability of any such reconstructions of ethical concepts that may be proposed are partly determined by axiological considerations; by considerations respecting the moral and social desirability of the kinds of actions and states of affairs that the reconstructions are likely to lead to, as well as by matters of fact.

With respect to the permissibility of conceptual reconstructions in the type of case falling under (2), my answer is basically the same as in the case of conceptual reconstructions falling under (1) above. If anything, one should be even more careful here to avoid and prevent confusion or misunderstanding; since, *ex hypothesi*, the philosopher cannot refer us to any extant scientific usage in his attempt to explain the logical content of his new concept. Hence it is imperative that the philosopher, in Paul Kurtz's words, "establish a paradigm case of use"[1] for the verbal expression he proposes to use to convey his new concept.

It should be emphasized here (and what I shall say applies to both types of cases we distinguished) that, unlike logical facts, no empirical facts can, *by themselves*, necessitate a reconstruction of any ordinary concept in philosophy. Nor is the existence or the discovery of any empirical facts a sufficient basis for the effecting of any such conceptual reconstructions. The existence or the discovery of certain empirical facts will make the reconstruction of some ordinary concept *desirable* provided that this reconstruction serves a logical, methodological or some other, pragmatic end. Thus it may be perfectly desirable on one or more of the grounds I enumerated, to "assimilate" (say) viruses to living things: to modify the ordinary connotation of 'living thing' so as to include viruses in the latter's denotation – if it is found that viruses have greater similarities than dissimilarities to anything ordinarily called a "living thing." Another example which we discussed earlier and which we might mention again here is the possible inclusion of electronic computers in the class of thinking things through the appropriate restriction – and perhaps also the stretching – of the ordinary meaning of 'thinking thing.' Similarly it may be desirable to restrict the ordinary meaning of 'motive' in philosophical contexts by eliminating the elements of consciousness and voluntariness from the ordinary concept; thus arriving at the present psychoanalytic concept of motive, or something close to it. The reconstruction may be desirable for logical, methodological or other, pragmatic purposes *if*, let us say, it is discovered that many of our actions are actually of the kind psychoanalysts call "unconsciously" or "subconsciously" motivated.

The fact – or what seems to be the fact – that the existence of no empirical facts is by itself either absolutely necessary or sufficient (in a factual sense of these terms) to justify any reconstruction of ordinary concepts in philosophy, explains why the legitimacy of any such reconstruction as may be proposed or actually effected can always be logically

[1] *Op. cit.*, p. 76.

contested. This I think can be readily seen, and I shall not say anything about it here.

It will be remembered that in earlier chapters I emphasized, and attempted to show in some detail, that the utilization of the conceptual framework provided by any particular ordinary language at any given time is necessary for the pursuit of philosophical inquiry (analysis) and the expression of the results thereby arrived at. At the same time we saw (in chapter seven) that the ordinary conceptual framework a philosopher adopts is a growing, changing thing; and in the present chapter I mentioned that factual discoveries are, among other things, responsible for some of this growth or change. We also saw earlier that the philosopher may profitably modify limited parts of the particular conceptual framework he has adopted, in the light of certain purely semantic, logical or methodological considerations. In the present chapter, we further saw that some modifications in the utilized framework may be permissible and desirable in the light of new empirical facts, for logical, methodological or other, pragmatic reasons. Further, it was noted that any modifications effected in the light of purely logical facts (logically) necessitate corresponding modifications in other concepts and/or logical relations within the framework. The same can now be said about modifications introduced in the light of empirical discoveries. Insofar as the philosopher is concerned with semantic analysis, the ordinary conceptual framework he analyses will provide him, at the same time (with any modifications that may be necessary), with a framework in terms of which he can express his results. At this stage of inquiry the philosopher's main task is the full understanding of the particular framework dealt with. But as we have seen, this concern, together with the desire to comprehend the world of which that framework and its inventor, man, are parts, logically leads the philosopher beyond the framework, in the directions in which it points and which it broadly determines. That is, it leads him to the very limited and tentative observation and conceptual analysis of phenomena falling within the range of his experience; which may help answer some of his properly philosophical questions. This, together with the (much more important) immense and everswelling body of scientific knowledge may then, in turn, necessitate the effecting of further and further modifications in the framework. At the same time, the philosopher must do his best to remain abreast of the changes that keep occurring in his framework (or that part of it which still corresponds to the conceptual framework of some ordinary language) in the thick of actual life and action.

BIBLIOGRAPHY

Aldrich, V., "Pictorial Meaning, Picture-Thinking and Wittgenstein's Theory of Aspects," *Mind*, vol. LXVII, No. 265 (January, 1958).

Arnheim, R., "Agenda for the Psychology of Art," *Journal Of Aesthetics And Art Criticism*, vol. X (June, 1952).

Ayer, A. J., *Language, Truth And Logic*. London: Victor Gollancz Ltd., 1936.

Ayer, A. J. *et. al.*, *The Revolution In Philosophy*. London: Macmillan & Co. Ltd., 1957.

Bar-Hillel, Y., "Analyses of 'Correct Language,'" *Mind*, vol. LV, No. 220 (October, 1946).

— "Indexical Expressions," *Mind*, vol. LXIII, No. 251 (July, 1954).

Black, M., *Critical Thinking:* An Introduction to Logic and Scientific Method. New York: Prentice-Hall, Inc., 1950.

— *Language And Philosophy*. Ithaca: Cornell University Press, 1949.

— "The Paradox of Analysis," *Mind*, vol. LIII, No. 211 (July, 1944).

Black, M., ed. *Philosophical Analysis*. Ithaca: Cornell University Press, 1950.

Butler, R. J., "Other Dates," *Mind*, vol. LXVIII, No. 269 (January, 1959).

Elton, W., ed., *Aesthetics And Language*. Oxford: Basil Blackwell, 1954.

Flew, A., ed., *Essays In Conceptual Analysis*. London: Macmillan & Co. Ltd., 1956.

— *Logic And Language*. Second Series. Oxford: Basil Blackwell, 1955.

Friedberg, R. M. *et. al.*, "A Learning Machine," *IBM Journal of Research and Development*, vol. 2, No. 1 (January, 1958).

Gallie, W. B., "Art As An Essentially Contested Concept," *The Philosophical Quarterly*, vol. 6, No. 23 (April, 1956).

Goodman, N., "About," *Mind*, vol. LXX, No. 277 (January, 1961).

Gotshalk, D. W., "A Next Step For Aesthetics," *Journal Of Aesthetics And Art Criticism*, vol. XVIII (September, 1959).

Hall, E. W., "The Adequacy of a Neurological Theory of Perception," *Philosophy and Phenomenological Research*, vol. XX, No. 1 (September, 1959).

Henle, P., "Do We Discover Our Uses of Words?" *The Journal Of Philosophy*, vol. LIV, No. 32 (November, 1957).

Hirst, R. J., *The Problems of Perception*. London: George Allen & Unwin Ltd., 1959.

Holloway, J., Critical Notice of Antony Flew *Logic And Language*, First Series. *Mind*, vol. LXII, No. 245 (January, 1953).

Kant, I., *Critique of Pure Reason*. Trans. by J. M. D. Meiklejohn. London: G. Bell And Sons Ltd., 1930.

Khatchadourian, H., "Art-Names and Aesthetic Judgments," *Philosophy*, vol. XXXVI, No. 136 (January, 1961).

Khatchadourian, H., "Common Names and 'Family Resemblances,'" *Philosophy and Phenomenological Research*, vol. XVIII, No. 111 (March, 1958).
— "On Existence," *Methodos*, vol. 9, Nos. 33–34 (1957).
— *The Coherence Theory Of Truth:* A Critical Evaluation. Beirut. American University of Beirut, 1961.
— "Vagueness," *Philosophical Quarterly*, vol. 12, No. 47 (April, 1962).
— "What is rationality?" *Theoria*, vol. XXIV, 3; 1958.
— "Works of Art and Physical Reality," *Ratio*, vol. II, No. 2 (January, 1960).
Krzywicki, H., "The Analytic and the Synthetic," *Philosophy Of Sciences*, vol. 26, No. 2 (April, 1959).
Kurtz, P. W., "Has Mr. Flew Abandoned 'The Logic of Ordinary Use'?" *Philosophical Studies*, vol. IX, Nos. 5–6 (October-December, 1958).
Lewis, C. I., *An Analysis Of Knowledge And Valuation*. La Salle, Ill.: The Open Court Publishing Co., [1946].
Lewis, H. D., ed., *Contemporary British Philosophy*. Third Series. London: George Allen & Unwin Ltd., 1956.
Linsky, L., ed., *Semantics and the Philosophy of Language*. Urbana, Ill.: The University of Illinois Press, 1952.
Macdonald, M., ed., *Philosophy And Analysis*. Oxford: Basil Blackwell, 1954.
Mace, C. A., ed., *British Philosophy In the Mid-Century*. London: George Allen & Unwin Ltd., 1957.
Moore, G. E., *Philosophical Studies*. London: Routledge & Kegan Paul, 1948.
— *Principia Ethica*. New York: Cambridge University Press, 1903.
Morris, C., "Philosophy, Psychiatry, Mental Illness and Health," *Philosophy & Phenomenological Research*, vol. XX, No. 1 (September, 1959).
Muirhead, J. H., ed., *Contemporary British Philosophy*. First Series. London: George Allen & Unwin Ltd., 1924.
Munro, T., "The Psychology of Art: Past, Present, Future," *Journal Of Aesthetics And Art Criticism*, Spring 1963.
Nagel, E., Review of P. A. Schilpp (ed.) *The Philosophy of G. E. Moore, Mind*, vol. LIII, No. 209 (January, 1944).
Nowell-Smith, P., *Ethics*. Oxford: Basil Blackwell, 1954.
Ogden, C. K., *The Meaning of Meaning*. London: Kegan Paul Ltd., 1923.
Pap, A., *Semantics And Necessary Truth*. New Haven: Yale University Press, 1958.
Pole, D., The Later Philosophy of Ludwig Wittgenstein. London: University of London, The Athlone Press, 1958.
Proceedings Of the XII International Congress Of Philosophy, Venice, 1958, vols. I & V: Casa Editrice G. C. Sansoni, Florence, 1960.
Quine, W. V. O., "Designation and Existence," *The Journal Of Philosophy*, vol. XXXVI, No. 26 (December, 1939).
Rader, M., ed., *A Modern Book of Esthetics*. Revised Edition. New York: Holt, Rinehart and Winston, Inc., 1952.
Russell, B., *A History Of Western Philosophy*. Sixth Printing. New York: Simon & Schuster, [1965], [1945].
— *The Analysis Of Mind*. London: George Allen & Unwin Ltd., 1949.
— *Portraits from Memory and Other Essays*. London: George Allen & Unwin Ltd., [1956].
— "Vagueness," *Australasian Journal of Philosophy*, 1 (1923); 88.
Ryle, G., *Philosophical Arguments*. Oxford: The Clarendon Press, 1945.
— *The Concept of Mind*. New York: Barnes & Noble, Inc. [1949].
Schilpp, P. A., ed., *The Philosophy of G. E. Moore*. Evanston & Chicago: North-

western University Press, 1942. Now published by The Open Court Publishing Company.
Sellars, W. and Hospers, J., eds., *Readings In Ethical Theory*. New York: Appleton-Century-Crofts, Inc., 1952.
Schlagel, R. H., "Language and Perception," *Philosophy and Phenomenological Research*, vol. XXIII, No. 2 (December, 1962).
Shwayder, D. S., "=," *Mind*, vol. LXV, No. 257 (January, 1956).
Smith, T. V. and Grene, M., eds., Selections: *From Descartes To Locke*. Chicago: The University of Chicago Press, 1957.
Strawson, P. F., *Individuals:* An Essay In Descriptive Metaphysics. London: Methuen & Co. Ltd., 1959.
— *Introduction To Logical Theory*. London: Methuen & Co. Ltd., 1952.
Taylor, P. W., "Moral Rhetoric, Moral Philosophy and the Science of Morals," *The Journal Of Philosophy*, vol. LVI, No. 17 (August, 1959).
Toulmin, S., *The Philosophy Of Science*. Fourth Impression. London: Hutchinson Publishing Group Ltd., 1958.
Urmson, J. O., *Philosophical Analysis*. Oxford: Clarendon Press, [1958], [1956].
Warnock, G. J., *English Philosophy Since 1900*. London: Oxford University Press, 1958.
White, A. R., *G. E. Moore*. Oxford: Basil Blackwell, 1958.
Wittgenstein, L., *Philosophical Investigations*. Trans. by G. E. M. Anscombe. Oxford: Basil Blackwell, 1953.
— *Tractatus Logico-Philosophicus*. Trans. by C. K. Ogden and F. P. Ramsey. London: Routledge & Kegan Paul, 1922; trans. by D. F. Pears and B. F. McGuiness. London: Routledge & Kegan Paul, 1961.
Woozley, A. D., "Ordinary Language and Common Sense," *Mind*, vol. LXII, No. 247 (July, 1953).

INDEX